The Social Psychological Study
of Widespread Beliefs

The Social Psychological Study of Widespread Beliefs

Edited by
Colin Fraser and George Gaskell

CLARENDON PRESS · OXFORD
1990

Oxford University Press, Walton Street, Oxford OX2 6DP
Oxford New York Toronto
Delhi Bombay Calcutta Madras Karachi
Petaling Jaya Singapore Hong Kong Tokyo
Nairobi Dar es Salaam Cape Town
Melbourne Auckland
and associated companies in
Berlin Ibadan

Oxford is a trade mark of Oxford University Press

Published in the United States
by Oxford University Press, New York

© Contributors listed on pp. xv and xvi, 1990

British Library Cataloguing in Publication Data
The social psychological study of widespread beliefs.
1. Attitudes
I. Fraser, Colin   II. Gaskell, George, 1948–
303.38
ISBN 0–19–852134–0

Library of Congress Cataloging in Publication Data
The social psychological study of widespread beliefs / edited by Colin Fraser
and George Gaskell.
Includings bibliographical references and indexes.
1. Social values. 2. Belief and doubt. 3. Ideology. 4. Attitude
(Psychology) I. Fraser, Colin   II. Gaskell, George.
HM216.P76 1990   303.3'72—dc20   90–7621
ISBN 0–19–852134–0

Typeset by Downdell Limited, Oxford
Printed in Great Britain by
Bookcraft Ltd, Midsomer Norton, Avon.

To the memory of
Hilde Himmelweit
and
Jos Jaspars

Acknowledgements

The origins of this volume go back to at least 1985 when the Social Affairs Committee of the ESRC encouraged the editors to organize a small conference to consider the social psychological study of belief systems. The conference was held in the delightful atmosphere of Madingley Hall, just outside Cambridge. We are grateful to the ESRC for its encouragement and financial support in starting us on the trail that has led to the appearance of this book.

We are pleased to be able to thank Helen Gibson and the staff of the general office of the Department of Social and Political Sciences, University of Cambridge and Vanessa Cragoe and Pat Christopher of the London School of Economics.

Contents

Contributors

Douglas Bethlehem
Department of Psychology, University of Leeds

Michael Billig
Department of Social Sciences, Loughborough University

Glynis M. Breakwell
Department of Psychology, University of Surrey

Raymond Cochrane
School of Psychology, University of Birmingham

Willem Doise
Faculté de Psychologie, Université de Genève

Rob Farr
Department of Social Psychology, London School of Economics and Political Science

Colin Fraser
Department of Social and Political Sciences, University of Cambridge

George Gaskell
Department of Social Psychology, London School of Economics and Political Science

Miles Hewstone
Department of Psychology, University of Bristol

Hilde Himmelweit
Department of Social Psychology, London School of Economics and Political Science

Jos Jaspars
Department of Experimental Psychology, University of Oxford

Alan Lewis
Centre for Economic Psychology, University of Bath

Elinor Scarbrough
Department of Government, University of Essex

Patten Smith
Social and Community Planning Research, London

Dan Sperber
Centre National de la Recherche Scientifique et Centre de Recherche en Epistemologie Appliquée, Ecole Polytechnique, Paris

Part I

Introduction

1 The social psychological study of widespread beliefs

George Gaskell and Colin Fraser

The aim of the book

Our aim in this book is to explore both conceptual and substantive approaches to the following questions: to what extent and why do many people share similar views in socially significant domains such as politics, the economy, race, and the sexes? The questions raised by the book are, we believe, important ones for social psychologists as well as for other social scientists, but they have not been at the heart of social psychology's concerns in recent decades.

The phrase we are using to label the primary focus of the book, 'widespread beliefs', has not been a particularly common one in social psychological writings. We find 'widespread beliefs' a helpful phrase for our purposes because in itself it does not imply a particular theoretical or conceptual position on the substantive issues. Thus, the term widespread beliefs denotes a general domain and, in mapping out its contours with our contributors, we hope to stimulate research and theorizing in this neglected area.

The beliefs to be examined are widespread, not idiosyncratic or limited to particular interpersonal relationships. We might have used some alternative term in our title, as indeed many of our contributors have, such as 'common' or 'shared' or, perhaps most obviously, 'social'. Later in this chapter we refer to McGuire's (1986) description of six social psychological usages of the word 'social' and we suggest that widespread beliefs are indeed social in most, if not all, of these six senses. The primary emphasis in this book, however, is on 'social' as meaning 'widely shared by many people'.

We are using the term 'belief' to mean 'views of the world or of some socially significant aspect of the world', or just 'views' for short. We are not presupposing a particular specialist definition of 'belief', such as Fishbein and Ajzen's (1975) practice of using the term to refer to pure cognitions independent of evaluative associations. Instead of 'beliefs', we might conceivably have referred to 'attitudes' or 'representations' or 'opinions' or 'ideologies' or a number of other social scientific terms used to invoke what people think and feel about the world around them. Such terms, however, carry with them their own theoretical baggage. Efforts have, from time to time, been made to distinguish amongst such terms and also amongst alternative conceptions associated with single terms such as attitude (McGuire 1986) and ideology (Larrain 1979). Our position is that, provided they focus on similarities of views amongst people, proponents of attitude theory or of social representations or of the study of ideology are welcome, within these covers, to contribute. Indeed, presenting a diversity of conceptual starting points for examining widespread beliefs has been a deliberate intention on our part.

When social psychologists have studied beliefs or opinions or attitudes, they have often been concerned with differences between people rather than similarities amongst them. They have studied how attitudes and beliefs relate to personality differences (e.g., Adorno *et al.* 1950; Rokeach 1960) and how differences in the actions of different people can be predicted and explained by differences in attitudes and normative beliefs (e.g., Ajzen and Fishbein 1980). When they have studied hypothesized similarities, those have been supposedly universal similarities in underlying processes, indifferent to the particular content as, for example, in cognitive consistency (e.g., Festinger 1957; Abelson *et al.* 1968).

We are not arguing that such questions are of no interest. Clearly the study of individual differences and of individualistic psychological mechanisms are perfectly legitimate concerns of psychologists, although not necessarily of social psychologists. But we are insisting that other at least equally important issues, concerning similarities and at times near-consensus of content-laden socially significant views, have been largely ignored.

One of the most striking, and for some even frightening, features of living in Britain at the time of the Falklands crisis was the speed and scale of the emergence of nationalistic support for military action to recapture the islands. Reactions in Argentina to the capture of the Malvinas appear to have been very similar. In Britain, the widespread beliefs in favour of the government's policies and actions were not, of course, consensual. A contrary, albeit less widely held, set of views also developed. But it would be hard to understand adequately social and political life in Britain at that time and in certain respects, subsequently, without being able to explain how and why these two contrasting sets of views emerged. The Falklands may have been an extreme case, but other issues eliciting widespread shared beliefs, often fervently held, continually emerge. This was seen in connection with a national strike of coal-miners and, again, following the discovery of AIDS, and the acknowledgement of physical and sexual abuse of children and women. More routinely it can be observed in the variety of issues that come into and, sometimes, depart from the arena of public opinions.

In studying widespread beliefs we would, then, often be studying the novel, the dramatic, and the controversial aspects of popular thought. That, however, need not be the case. Even more frequently, such study would involve the analysis of views that usually seem much less dramatic though remarkably persistent. Indeed, if they appear sufficiently uncontentious and well established to a large enough segment of the population, we are likely to be dealing with aspects of the near consensual, taken for granted assumptions that underpin large numbers of major social and political practices and policies, such as parliamentary elections, the legitimacy of governments, the continuing existence of royalty, and the sacredness of private property. In fact, McGuire (1964) used such consensual beliefs or cultural truisms in his studies of inducing resistance to change via the metaphor of inoculation against attack from diseases. Cultural truisms were defined as widely shared within the social milieu and maintained in a monolithic ideological environment.

The variety of types of widespread beliefs is great and their causes and consequences may vary from the trivial to the catastrophic. Occasionally, social psychology has attempted to study them in particular domains, the most obvious being that of ethnic stereotyping and prejudice. We believe that a greater commitment to generating systematic theoretical and empirical studies of widespread beliefs would be a major step in the direction of creating a social psychology which is as social as it is psychological.

Attitudes and social representations: some recent developments

In so far as social psychology has broached the study of widespread beliefs, it has traditionally done so in the course of studying attitudes. It is conceivable that either a conceptual revitalization of the notion of attitude or a return to an older conception of attitude (see Jaspars and Fraser 1984) might eventually prove the most fruitful framework for further enquiry. It would certainly be premature, however, to take that for granted.

In recent years, the possibility of studying the widespread beliefs as social representations (Farr and Moscovici 1984) has attracted considerable attention amongst European, but not North American, social psychologists. Social representations could be argued to be the obvious framework to pursue. Again, however, that would be premature, for even in the unlikely and unfortunate event of enthusiasm for the study of social representations dissipating, the need to understand the emergence, maintenance, and disappearance of widespread beliefs would remain. A brief consideration of, first, the concept of attitude and then that of social representation does, however, make a sensible starting point for an introduction to the themes in this volume.

Attitudes have been asked to do a great deal of work in social psychology, perhaps rather too much. There have been at least three major questions facing the social sciences which social psychologists have tackled mainly in terms of attitudes. Historically, the first of these was asked by the person who initially made attitude a social psychological concept, W.I. Thomas. The question was, why do so many people have similar or shared views? (Thomas and Znaniecki 1918–20). Examination of that question persisted into the 1930s and occasionally reasserts itself in the context of racism and widespread prejudices. The second question was, what are the relations between the individuals' internal views of the world and their actions in the world? That question has been explored from LaPiere (1934) to Fishbein and beyond. The third question was, how are the views of the individual internally organized? That issue reached its zenith with the cognitive consistency theories of attitude organization. The historical ordering of these three questions hints at the gradual but persistent individualization of the attitude concept and of attitude research over the past 70 years.

Many of the most recent developments in the attitude field have related to the resurgence of interest in the second of the major issues, relations between attitudes and actions. While Wicker's (1969) analysis of empirical research on attitudes and behaviour created considerable doubts in the minds of some social psychologists about the validity of the attitude as an hypothetical construct, for others it was, in part, the catalyst for a revival of interest in theorizing about attitudes. The rather simplistic conception embodied in the three-component model of attitude as cognitive, affective, and conative, which well before Wicker's paper had been heavily criticized (cf. DeFleur and Westie (1963)), was developed in some new and interesting directions. Fishbein and Ajzen saw attitude as one of two antecedents of behavioural intention and consequent action; the second input being social normative beliefs related to the particular behaviour. In turn this model has been further elaborated by Bentler and Speckhart (1981) and by Ajzen (1988). The frequently discussed but rarely operationalized three-component model itself has turned out to be alive and in at least moderately good health (e.g. Breckler 1984).

Kelman (1974) argued that attitudes had been given too much explanatory potential and that the idea that attitudes are the mental triggers of action fails to recognize that attitudes and actions are linked in a continuing reciprocal process. Actions may be the result of attitudes but equally action is the ground upon which attitudes are developed and modified. Kelman also pointed to differences in the domains of thought and action, the former being relatively free from constraints, the latter being constrained not only by sequencing problems but also by the presence of social and physical objects.

Abelson (1976) linked attitudes to mainstream cognitive psychology and interpreted the apparent confusion over inconsistency in the light of scripts, that is, real or imagined sequences of events or actions. Of particular relevance is the distinction between participant and non-participant scripts. In the non-participant script there is no representation of the actor. Since the 'I' is absent, the sequence of events which are psychologically related in some way has no implications for the actions of the actor. Participant scripts have this extra motivational element. The 'I' is an integral part of the script and by implication is also a part of actions which may arise from the realization of that script.

Other theorists moved in different directions making no attempt to salvage the putative attitude–behaviour linkage. For Lalljee *et al.* (1984) attitudes are a part of a verbal repertoire of self-presentational utterances, while for Abelson (1986) the intriguing metaphor of possessions has been proposed to explain many findings in classical attitudinal research in which the assumptions of the rational-cognitive model are challenged.

In large measure these new conceptualizations of attitudes stayed closely within the scope of an individualistic social psychology. Empirically, that was equally true, in that studies of attitude–action relations were designed to predict inter-individual differences; variations in attitude and other measures were used to predict individual differences in actions. The focus was on the individual actor and on how more adequate theorizing about, or operationalizing of, cognitive states could contribute to the understanding of the individual's actions.

The rediscovery of the 'social' in social psychology has been led by Tajfel (1982) in relation to social categories and social identity theory and by Moscovici (1961) in the realm of social representations. For many European social psychologists whose work fell in the general area of attitudes, Moscovici's theory of social representations has had a profound impact. In a bold general thesis Moscovici goes beyond a reassessment of the conceptualization and role of attitudes in social life to advocate a change in the fundamental epistemology of social psychology and a new direction for the discipline.

To date, *Social representations* by Farr and Moscovici (1984) is the most definitive collection of essays on the subject. In brief, and at the cost of gross over-simplification, social representation theory embraces the epistemological perspective of constructivism rather than empiricism, sees social representations as theories in their own right which through a dynamic social process serve to anchor and objectify the innovations brought to a contemporary life by, amongst other things, science and politics, and in so doing serve to construct and to communicate realities. Social representations are representations with content, a content that must be acknowledged in their empirical investigation; a content that is collective, shared, or social as distinct from the individual representations of cognitive psychology.

Many readers will have encountered arguments for and against the concept about which, so it would appear, it is not easy to be neutral (cf. Jahoda 1988; Potter and Wetherell 1987). Here it is not our purpose either to review, or to attempt to weigh up the various debates. Indeed weighing up the debate is probably premature—bold conjectures such as social representations inevitably carry with them certain ambiguities and inconsistencies, a fact acknowledged by Moscovici (1984a). Assuming, for the sake of argument, that social representations are a paradigm shift, it will be only after what Kuhn (1970) characterized as a period of normal science that the social psychological community will be in a position to assess the various elements of the thesis for their conceptual and heuristic value.

Yet this book and the seminar which led to it were stimulated, at least in part, by our interest in social representations and in particular the new emphasis on the shared nature of such representations. Social psychology today is largely cognitive and individualistic in focus. Within the discipline there are very few currently used concepts which account for widely held beliefs. With individual attitudes, attributions, cognitive structures, and the like to the fore, the fact that people may hold similar views is largely seen as epiphenomenal in the pursuit of commonly held cognitive processes. Equally, with process as the focus the content of attitudes or attributions is largely irrelevant. Content is used merely as a vehicle for the presentation of stimulus vignettes to test models of process and if that content is largely trivial or meaningless then no matter.

But content is central to social representations—meanings which are shared are a *sine qua non* of a social representation. This emphasis on 'content' and the 'shared' struck a chord with our own work on economic beliefs, unemployment, energy conservation, and relative deprivation. Our research in these areas was in part stimulated by a desire to understand problematic issues in contemporary society, those which affected people either through innovation or politics or conflict. In the study of these issues we came to the view that social psychology has a major part to play in describing the actual beliefs of relevant actors in major social arenas and that widely held beliefs, those which are shared between members of social units, large and small, are of more than incidental interest. Shared attitudes and beliefs play an important role in defining groups and group behaviours, in the formation and maintenance of social identities and more broadly in collective realities. It was this feeling that led us to explore the 'social' in social representations, for here perhaps was the 'entrée' to the understanding of the functions and contents of collective beliefs systems. Before discussing how the 'social' is elucidated in social representations it is interesting to look at other conceptions of the 'social' in social psychology.

On the nature of the 'social'

While the greatest emphasis in the study of attitudes in recent decades has been on individual manifestations, that was not always the case (Jaspars and Fraser 1984). Furthermore, it is surprising to find that even a behaviourist such as Doob (1947) was at pains to incorporate a social criterion in his definition of attitude. For Doob, the distinction between attitude and other types of responses could not be made on a psychological but only on a social basis—its socially evaluated significance must be considered. A useful test Doob suggested was to discover whether a response is labelled desirable or undesirable by the individual's contemporaries—if it is, then it is an attitude. Along with much of the Hullian learning theory basis of his model, Doob's social criterion has long been forgotten. Similarly one finds a social orientation in the writing of Asch (1952), working in the Gestalt tradition. For Asch, attitudes are social sentiments. This means that not only are they cognitively deep-seated and emotionally crucial concerns of individuals which act as centres of reference for complex and extended actions, but also they are shared with others and refer to issues of general welfare. However, the idea that 'social' should be restricted to shared sentiments and attitudes has given way to a variety of other meanings of the term. McGuire (1986) reacting against the terminological confusion surrounding the prefix 'social', has adumbrated six different contemporary uses of the term. According to McGuire, 'social' has been variously used to mean:

1. attitudes or perceptions of social objects in contrast to non-social objects;
2. a shared representation in a Durkheimian sense in contrast to those which differentiate between people;
3. a representation arising via interaction with others, as exemplified by symbolic interactionism;
4. something that is interpersonally communicable;
5. a representation that serves to maintain a current social system or cultural form;
6. something that is almost transcendental, such as language structures which have an existence outside the heads of individuals.

This listing is not claimed to be exhaustive or mutually exclusive so, for example, the meanings implied in (2) and (5) seem similar, but rather it is a plea for greater conceptual precision in the usage of the term 'social'.

In the following paragraphs we outline a strong definition of widespread beliefs followed by some contrasts with social representations. This strong sense embraces the fifth of McGuire's meanings of the 'social' and in so doing it assumes (1), (3), and (4). Then we offer a weaker definition of shared beliefs, covering meanings (1), (3), and (4), and some pointers to research issues.

Let us take an example to help demarcate the definition of shared beliefs in the strong sense. Consider the Clapham omnibus on which a number of passengers are travelling for a variety of purposes. On this particular day the normally drab interior of the bus has been brightened by an advertisement for a round-the-world trip. Illustrating the enticing stopovers is a picture of the globe showing an aeroplane circumnavigating it. For the majority of the travellers this is of passing interest, but little more. In these days of mass transport the idea of a round the world voyage by air is quite unremarkable. The fact that all share a belief that the world is round is assumed by the copywriter whose efforts are directed at stimulating interest in this particular enterprise. A few of the passengers take an added interest in the fact that the flight is to be made on a far-eastern national airline and, in their ethnocentrism, they believe that it would not be safe, and probably not clean. Two passengers, however, are members of the Flat Earth Society and, curiously enough, they are travelling to an annual meeting. To them the advertisement is of concern—it challenges the rationale of their group. It is not our purpose to adjudicate on the rationality of their belief system but to juxtapose the views of different sets of people. For those who believe the world is round, sharing this particular belief is unremarkable, of little social consequence, and normally no cause for social cohesion. For the prejudiced critics of the airline, their particular beliefs have greater social significance. For the flat-earthers, however, belief in the flatness of the world carries with it a category definition. Holding that belief is a *sine qua non* of membership of their group and, without such a belief, it seems fair to assume the group would have no purpose or rationale. Thus while there are a variety of beliefs which, in statistical terms, are shared—greater or lesser numbers of any population will be found to have similar ideas and beliefs—such numbers are not a defining characteristic of widespread beliefs within the strong definition. Only when the holding of such a belief contributes in some important way to the social definition, as well as the life, of an aggregate—important not in the sense that not holding it would be thought of as idiosyncratic or eccentric but rather that it would positively exclude an individual from a category membership—can a shared belief be recognized as a social psychologically interesting shared or widespread belief. In the strong sense of the term widespread belief, it must carry implications for category membership, or what might be termed a 'social mechanism'.

To this extent establishing a widespread belief must go beyond the simple counting of heads. Many millions may believe that the moon is not made of cream cheese, but such a statistical consensus is largely irrelevant. A widespread belief could be held by a relatively limited number of persons providing that belief embodies the essential category definition. By holding that belief the people, however many, are united as a category and recognize the role of the belief in that unification.

This takes us back to McGuire's fifth image of the 'social', 'those representations that serve to maintain a current social system or cultural form'. This might be rewritten to specify the strong definition of widespread beliefs: 'those beliefs which define a social category and as such serve to maintain that social group or category'. Put in such terms, there are obvious links to Tajfel's social identity theory and to Turner's (1987) ideas on the cognitive definition of groups.

Such a conception is one part but certainly not all that is embraced in the definition of the social in social representations. Indeed it is with the nature of the 'social' part of representations that there is perhaps least conceptual clarification. One of the more illuminating perspectives on this issue comes from Harré (1984, 1985) in a review of Farr and Moscovici (1984). Harré argues that two conceptualizations of the social appear in the various essays in that book. One of these, which he does not warm to, refers to the distributive realization of a representation. In a distributive realization each member of a group has 'it' and 'it' is shared by every other individual. The second sense is more of a gestalt notion and refers to genuinely collective realizations. Each group member may have one part of 'it' but the totality is only realized when the group come together. Harré argues that this distinction is blurred in the writings on social representations and clearly believes that the latter definition is of more conceptual value. He, however, acknowledges that social representations might be both distributive and collective and that it is a matter for empirical enquiry to establish the links between the two.

However, Moscovici (1984a) is not willing to restrict social representations to the collective manifestations as defined by Harré. Moscovici sees these as more akin to the collective representations of Durkheim and as such not necessarily as active, dynamic, and transforming as the social representations of contemporary society. Equally Moscovici admits that his elaboration of the theory does not readily allow the concept to be defined by 'all the rules of the trade'. It is a 'fascinating' but 'obscure' concept that may or may not find its way into mainstream research. Our efforts to re-establish interest in widespread beliefs can therefore be seen as being not in opposition to the theory of social representations but rather as one part of the movement to rekindle interest in social aspects of social psychology, a movement in which Moscovici's writings are central.

Thus far we have presented a strong definition of a social psychologically relevant widespread belief. However, this as the sole formulation would be too restrictive. People may share similar views and beliefs without an explicit social category identification. Views on South Africa, national politics, economics, child-rearing, education, and crime are commonplace enough and we may agree or beg to differ with others we meet. In some cases these views are associated with a particular group membership such as those held by active members of anti-apartheid groups or political parties but for many a membership or reference group is not consciously registered. Some on our Clapham omnibus, while reading newspaper reports on recent events in China or current unemployment levels or East–West *détente*, register a personal view to the issues in question and approve or disapprove of developments without saying to themselves 'I am a member of a pro-democracy-in-China group', or whatever. Views on such matters are taken because they help to make sense of the world. Equally, holding and express-ing views on contemporary issues of moment is more or less a requirement of civilized social intercourse. Furthermore, such views may fulfil an expressive function giving the holder rights to some self-defining characteristics.

Lying behind such varieties of belief may be some overriding social representation of a general domain realized only via Harré's collective sense the term. Yet while these beliefs do not carry the explicit character of a social category as discussed in the strong sense of widespread belief, these are not neutral, merely factual beliefs, but carry a personal importance, some prescriptive connotations. Views on issues such as morality, child-rearing, and economics will, in different contexts, be of relevance to wider societal processes—to the family as an institution, the economic activities of citizens, or whatever—and they carry with them a value judgement, a view of what is right and wrong. By so doing they depart from the purely descriptive beliefs of the 'world is round' or 'ice is cold' variety.

The distinction here is not between 'facts' and personal values; both so-called 'facts' and values, as Kelvin (1969) argues, are embedded in the history of the community. Both are subject to change and over time some values may appear as simple matters of fact and some facts become values. The idea is, rather, that out of a plethora of taken-for-granted facts avail-able at any one time, some are singled out and invested with a special importance. For a variety of reasons they become the basis of judgements of value. This is part of the ordering of the social environment, an ordering which is reflected in culture and which determines, as Kelvin writes 'what members of a group or culture come to expect of one another, what they value and deem proper or improper'. For Kelvin, consensus or a presumed consensus is part of the process of validation and this may derive from agreements between people but also from other sources such as the mass media and from what might be called the 'social etcetera phenomenon', tradition based on largely tacit assumptions—'it's always been like this'.

Abelson (1986) offers a different perspective in his analysis of beliefs as possessions. Why, Abelson asks, do we hold distal beliefs when these are often only remotely experienced and not verifiable? In the tradition of rational man they seem almost useless. Abelson suggests that under certain circumstances such beliefs become equivalent to a possession. Circumstances inducing such feelings of possession include public commitment or the explaining, elaborating, or defending of the belief. Like possessions, beliefs vary in value and increased value may arise from, in different circumstances, the instrumental and expressive functions of the belief and from attributes such as sharedness, extremity, and centrality.

While it is likely that all widespread beliefs in the strong sense of the term have the characteristics of a possession, not all 'possessed' beliefs are associated with a category membership. Equally, as we have argued, there are categories of widespread beliefs which depart from the purely descriptive types, yet these do not necessarily carry an explicit association with a social grouping. It is those beliefs which are associated with a value or are thought of as personal possessions but which do not carry social category implications which comprise our weak definition of widespread beliefs.

On the whole, we think it premature to be over-specific in formulating criteria for the demarcation of widespread beliefs. At present it would seem useful to explore the area, looking at both content and process of widespread beliefs, guided by the strong and weak definitions. Such explorations would avoid the purely descriptive beliefs even if, through a counting of heads, they appear to be commonly held.

Methodological and conceptual pluralism

In our opinion it is quite inappropriate to offer a set of prescriptions for the study of widespread beliefs. To assume that one particular methodological approach will prove to be adequate to the task to the exclusion of others is simply misguided. In many respects social psychology is far more sophisticated and catholic methodologically than it is conceptually. Given a particular issue or hypothesis, there is a wide range of acceptable tools available, from which one, or more, should be drawn to suit the nature of the problem in question. There are qualitative techniques best suited to asking 'what is going on here?, what is in people's minds?, what is of real social significance?'. Depth interviews, participant observation, group discussion and content analysis all can offer insights into such key issues which are fundamental to a meaningful social psychological inquiry.

Quantitative techniques in general focus on 'how much' and on 'how much' in different sub-groupings. Here the range of inferential and data-reduction techniques of a multivariate nature are potentially all of value. Some argue for the superiority of qualitative over quantitative approaches, others for the opposite view. Indeed, within the qualitative and quantitative camps, there are advocates for particular approaches.

But, if we care to take widespread beliefs seriously, such enthusiasms must be set aside. It is likely that both qualitative and quantitative methods will be required in studies that are to elucidate both the distribution and content of widespread beliefs, the functions, and the process by which such beliefs change with different social groupings. If we were to point in one direction it would be to studies of a longitudinal nature. The sampling of widespread beliefs, over a period of time, may be one of the most fruitful approaches to the simultaneous investigation of content and process. The traditional cross-sectional design can only amount to a snap-shot in time, of interest indeed, but often posing more questions than it answers, questions often of an historical nature. Longitudinal studies using case studies or time series data from attitudinal surveys, or both approaches in combination, can add an historical and contextual dimension from which ideas about processes can be derived. If, as some argue, social change rather than external stability, conformity, and consensus is the dominating feature of contemporary society, it is difficult to see how social psychologists will be able to contribute to informed debate unless they have adopted a methodological approach in which process and change is an explicit focus. Thus, we prefer to advocate methodological pluralism as the most appropriate approach to the study of widespread beliefs rather than set our sights on one road to the elucidation of this important issue, and we would draw the reader's attention to the volume edited by Breakwell and Canter (in press).

Just as, currently, we wish to argue for a methodological pluralism, so, given the present state of knowledge and theory, we counsel openness to conceptual pluralism. Thus we would not wish to start from the assumption that conceptions of 'attitudes' and of 'social representations' are necessarily incompatible, although recent practices may well have encouraged such a view. As we have argued, it is not obligatory to study only inter-individual differences in attitudes. Many attitudes are widely shared (and many representations are individual representations rather than social ones, as Moscovici (1984b) recognizes). It is not necessary to study specific attitudes one at a time while avoiding the possibility that within a population specific attitudes can bear systematic relations to one another such that they do form structured systems of belief akin to what is implied by social representations. Attitudes, like social representations, should be construed as being more than purely cognitive constructs; they have affective, dynamic, and prescriptive functions too. Attitudes, as well as social representations, are always likely to be changing.

Indeed it is just conceivable that an enthusiastic proponent of attitude research might argue that the study of widespread, structured systems of attitudes using conventional attitude measurement techniques allied to multivariate statistics could replace the study of social representations. A less drastic possibility may be that of merging the two, as Fraser (1986) has proposed. The less ambitious, more realistic variant that we would settle for is the notion that attitudes and social representations need not be seen as incompatible concepts and that their exploration can continue partly side by side, partly together. A widespread attitude could be seen as more narrowly focused than a social representation. Social representations might be thought to be made up, at least in part, of widespread attitudes. All attitude studies, however, need not be on the arrays of related attitudes that would be found in a social representation, just as the study of a social representation need not wait until all its component attitudes have been fully elucidated.

If social representations are seen as organizing widespread attitudes, where, if at all, does the notion of public opinion fit? One extreme view of public opinion is that it is a near transcendental, all pervasive 'spirit of the time'; the opposite extreme, so heavily criticized by Moscovici (1963), is that it is the findings of public opinion polls (see Marsh and Fraser 1989). But Farr and Himmelweit (this volume, Chapters 3 and 5) rightly subscribe to an idea of public opinion as the currently shared views on socially significant issues of the public at large or of important sectors of the public. Particularly if public opinion is seen as implying currently 'on stage' issues with political implications (Marsh and Fraser 1989), then we can think of issues in public opinion as involving the most dramatic and immediately pressing social representations; such as the National Health Service or child abuse or AIDS. There are many other social representations which at any one time may not be dramatic issues for the national media, such as the human body, the city of Paris, or psychoanalysis. That is, the issues that make up public opinion can be thought of as a subset of social representations, a subset which in certain respects may conceivably show differences from the structure and operation of long-lasting, less newsworthy representations. Nevertheless, research into current public opinion might help provide empirical means of tackling questions of the appearance, change, and possible demise of social representations, and concepts taken from the study of social representations could offer needed theoretical input into public opinion research (Roiser 1987).

Potentially the trickiest concept to relate to the others is 'ideology' because it has been conceptually so contested and empirically so under-researched. But not only may shared attitude systems, social representations, and public opinion prove to be markedly overlapping concepts, they also share at least one obvious difference from ideology, namely their scope. Each of the three, in terms of content, seems to cover a circumscribed area, whether that consists of an ethnic group, a scientific theory or the future of the health service. None of those would be thought to be the entire focus of an ideology. When social psychologists have attempted to discuss the operation of ideology they have been inclined, as Scarbrough points out in Chapter 6, to think of an individual's ideology as the organized sum of all relevant attitudes. If we think of an institutionalized or intellectual ideology (Billig *et al.* 1988), such as Marxism or liberalism or Christianity, believed in by a committed ideologue, then such a view might just about be supportable. Such a sophisticated and elaborated ideology may well determine and specify the ideologue's attitudes or social representations or opinions on current issues. We assume, however, that such ideologues are the exceptions rather than the rule. What of the bulk of men and women in the street, the mass of the public? Do they have their views of the world organized as a coherent, overarching analysis? Some social scientists (e.g. Converse 1964) have claimed to have demonstrated empirically that they do not; the mass public does not engage in ideological thinking. Others have claimed to have empirically demonstrated ideological thinking in the public (e.g. Judd and Milburn 1980). Such arguments may hinge on the nature and number of measures of specific attitudes assessed and the presuppositions involved in the statistical analyses. Our view is that the majority of individuals do not subscribe to fully worked out institutionalized or sophisticated ideologies, but nevertheless they are likely to engage in ideological thinking. There is 'lived ideology' (Billig *et al.* 1988). We are inclined, following Scarbrough, to think of lay ideological thinking as involving a limited number of wide-ranging assumptions, the implications of which are not fully worked out for specific issues. Their ideological assumptions give some direction, supply a little of the content of their specific views; but many of the details of attitudes, opinions, or representations have to emerge from sources other than their ideological thinking.

Thus, our inclination is to see the four key concepts of this volume, and the theoretical frameworks constructed around them, as being potentially reconcilable. Prospects of substantially realizing the potential may, of course, lie in the rather distant future. The realistic hope, in the shorter term, is that the concrete possibilities for mutual assistance and even synthesis, will emerge gradually as alternative frameworks struggle, initially relatively independently, to produce social psychological analyses of widespread beliefs. Immediate efforts at synthesis might well prove unrealistic, even inhibiting and hence counterproductive.

To us, there currently seem to be two practicable, broad approaches well worth pursuing, one more quantitative and the other more qualitative. The former would make use of a revitalized, less individualistic attitude framework in conjunction with the comparably quantitative techniques and findings of public opinion research. This approach would have the strengths of apparent explicitness and well-established techniques for generating empirical evidence while having to improve on its legacies of gaps between concepts and measurement procedures, and overly simple, at times crass, operationalizations. The second approach would be via social representations. This would carry with it the strengths of freshness, flexibility, and a willingness to examine richer, often qualitative data, while having to convince critics that it was not inherently opaque or even self-contradictory.

There may, of course, be yet other approaches. One which, because of our biases, we may not have considered in sufficient detail has very recently emerged from the work of some British social psychologists, namely the analysis of discourse and rhetoric (e.g. Billig 1987; Potter and Wetherell 1987). Such an approach does appear in this volume in Chapter 9 (Cochrane and Billig), in which the authors emphasize the contradictions in commonly held political views of young people. But that chapter does not adopt the more radical stance of Potter and Wetherell who not only emphasize contradictions in discourse but also argue for the possibility of abandoning concepts of attitudes and social representations in favour of discourse analysis and alternative linguistic repertoires. Although we agree with a number of the specific criticisms they level against both of the traditions they criticize, their suggestions for abandoning them seem premature, to say the least, and possibly even regressive. Prematurity lies with the unavoidable fact that this social psychological brand of discourse analysis is still at a very early stage of development. Inevitably, sceptics will require much more evidence of systematic procedures, linguistic sophistication, and convincing applicability before they agree to abandon major areas of social psychology in its favour. The possibilities of positive regression seem at least threefold. An emphasis on situationally tied repertoires could produce a piecemeal situationism. A desire to eschew relatively stable dispositional concepts such as attitude could herald the return of an implicit behaviourism. An exclusive focus on discourse *per se* rather than on the events which and the persons who generate discourse would imply the fudging or trivializing of socially significant issues which, as Scarbrough comments, appears to be typical of discourse theories in the social sciences. Having raised our doubts, let us add that if the analysis of discourse does prove itself capable of illuminating widespread, socially significant views of the world, then we shall welcome it as yet another set of possibilities for tackling the real substantive issues of why, in many domains, so many people share similar views of the world and with what consequences. One test of the progress being made towards that end by proponents of discourse analysis or attitudes or social representations will be the success they have in helping us understand the contents of and processes in lay ideological thinking.

The structure and contents of the book

This introductory section is completed by a chapter from Dan Sperber who argues the case for an epidemiology of beliefs and, in a lucid style, both elaborates on and helps make concrete many of the less fully developed ideas of the editors. Among the questions his epidemiological approach would ask are, what causes families of representations 'to appear, to expand, to split, to merge with one another, to change over time, to die?' (p. 30). He assumes that the epidemiologies of different types of beliefs will differ; they will be more or less widely spread and will depend on different types of mechanisms for their destinations. Sperber, a cognitive anthropologist, bases his approach on a synthesis of largely speculative ideas about both cultural representations, where the ideas are mainly taken from social anthropology, and the cognitive organization of beliefs, where the ideas come from psychology. He regards the public representations as more basic than the mental ones.

The second Part of the book, *Conceptual perspectives*, consists of four chapters, each one concentrating on a different set of concepts, or framework, for the social psychological study of widespread beliefs. Though the chapters have different primary focuses, each includes numerous comparisons and points of connection with other frameworks. We choose to start with Rob Farr's Chapter on what is the most recent as well as currently the most favoured approach, that of social representations. First Farr outlines the development of the concept of social representations and contrasts them with the Durkheimian collective representations. He draws upon Jodelet (1988) for an adumbration of the concept. Social representations are concerned with common sense knowledge, how it is communicated, the functions it serves, and how it emerges. He then, helpfully, considers the links between social representations and the study of public opinion, attitudes, culture, and the sociology of knowledge. In each case, he emphasizes points of contact rather than incompatibilities. In each case an historical analysis drawing on key debates and figures from the past, so often neglected, shows the intellectual continuity and distinctiveness of the French tradition. As one would have expected, it is clear that Farr does regard the social representation approach as providing an appropriate— probably the appropriate—framework for the study of widespread beliefs.

Douglas Bethlehem then examines the most familiar set of concepts for social psychologists by asking 'whether the concept "attitude" provides a sufficient structure for the study of widespread beliefs' (p. 65). With regard to widespread beliefs, he first considers related concepts in the social sciences, namely myths, norms, social representations, and stereotypes, in the course of which he almost dismisses social representations on the grounds of their conceptual elusiveness and the lack of agreed operationalizations; he does propose that techniques used in stereotyping research might help in the empirical examination of social representations. Bethlehem's critical stance on social representations is not a prelude to an uncritical extolling of the virtues of notions of attitude. After a brief discussion of the history of the attitude concept from Thomas and Znaniecki (1918–20) onwards and an examination of how attitudes are acquired by individuals, he concludes that, although the continued study of attitudes could throw light on widespread beliefs, such studies will not provide the 'complete underpinning' for a full understanding of such beliefs.

Bethlehem's conclusion regarding attitudes is less optimistic than the views of the editors. With his feet firmly planted on well-worked soil, he focuses on the study of specific attitudes operationalized in conventional ways. With our heads in the clouds, we can envisage structured systems of attitudes being examined with, as yet, somewhat underspecified innovative techniques and multivariate analyses (Fraser 1986). Bethlehem's view, however, is probably more representative of attitude researchers and theorists than is ours.

With her detailed examination of the dynamics of public opinion, the late Hilde Himmelweit (Chapter 5) helps to rekindle interest in an approach to the study of widespread beliefs which in the 1930s was quite prominent in social psychology, as well as being closely related to the study of attitudes. But the development of public opinion research as primarily a commercial and descriptive enterprise relatively independent of academic social psychology impoverished both. The concept of 'public opinion' has had different meanings at different times (Marsh and Fraser 1989). For Himmelweit, 'public opinion is the expression by many individuals—it might be the public at large, particular segments of society, members of an institution or a crowd—of sentiments, evaluations, or beliefs about societal issues' (p. 79). The role of public opinion in the political process is discussed. There then follow analyses of three major issues: changes and measurement of changes in public opinion; factors which shape public opinion; factors which lead to differences in individual receptivity to changes in public opinion. Himmelweit concludes by discussing some theoretical and methodological implications of her analysis.

As frameworks for the study of widespread beliefs, public opinion, attitudes, and social representations reveal obvious contrasts. The study of social representations provides a conceptual framework for the analysis of widespread views, but is open to criticism on the clarity of its methods and perhaps, as a consequence, some of its findings. An attitude approach has concepts and techniques which still largely await direct application to an understanding of widespread beliefs. The study of public opinion has accumulated both techniques and findings but has, as yet, not developed clear theoretical frameworks for their interpretation. The study of public opinion could well attempt, not only to reinvigorate its links with academic work on attitudes, but also, as Farr urges in Chapter 3, to establish relations with the still relatively novel study of social representations (Roiser 1987).

Social psychology largely abandoned the notion of public opinion, persevered with that of attitudes, and recently accepted, with marked variations in enthusiasm, the idea of social representations. As for 'ideology', with few honourable exceptions, that has been systematically ignored. In keeping, however, with signs of some willingness at last to confront that particularly problematic concept (e.g. Billig 1982; Wexler 1983), we were pleased to prevail on Elinor Scarbrough, an empirically oriented political scientist, to offer an analysis of some of the possible relations between ideology and the social psychological literatures on social representations and attitudes. Scarbrough mainly tackles the twin issues of what the study of social representations might contribute to the empirical study of ideology and what the place of ideology might be in an understanding of social representations. But first she discusses attitudes and their relation to ideology. Scarbrough argues that, for an individual, an ideology is not a super-systematization of all her or his attitudes. Instead, ideologies function as underspecified 'maps'; they consist of 'general and abstract systems of beliefs, not specific answers to particular questions' (p. 105). A parallel view of relations between ideology and social representation is then offered. Social representations turn the abstract, which at least in part is ideologically given, into something almost concrete in its detail. Scarbrough's hope is that a detailed analysis or 'splitting' of social representations may provide an empirical route into the explication of common ideological beliefs. Clear implications of Scarbrough's chapter are that attitudes and social representations are intimately related not only to ideologies but also to each other.

Part II, then, examines four possible approaches, each organized around a different key concept, that social psychology might take in its endeavours to study widespread beliefs. Originally they were conceived of by the editors as competing approaches, but, in general, their exponents have emphasized links and overlaps rather than irreconcilable incompatibilities. It is surprising, for example, that more has not been made of the possibility that whereas 'traditional' analyses of attitudes and of public opinion presuppose an empiricist stance, the study of social representations is predicted on a constructivist one.

However, to reduce the risk of our consideration of widespread beliefs floating off into a conceptual stratosphere, we approach it from a second direction, a more empirically oriented one. In Part III we have invited a number of social psychologists to consider a particular substantive area or series of studies and indicate what the empirical work therein tells us about widespread beliefs. There are, in fact, several different types of contributions to Part III and the variety of approaches adopted illustrates at least some of the empirically-based possibilities available for the social psychological study of widespread beliefs. Glynis Breakwell and Alan Lewis mainly offer reviews of documented widespread beliefs in the areas of gender and economic life, respectively. Patten Smith and George Gaskell and Raymond Cochrane and Michael Billig discuss some of their own research on, respectively, relative deprivation and political socialization and its implications for the study of widespread beliefs. The first two chapters of this part (Chapters 7 and 8) might be thought of as transitions from the theoretical to the more empirical parts of the volume, for although both chapters do consider empirical evidence, they are also substantial contributions to theoretical thought.

Part III opens with an important chapter by the late Jos Jaspars and Miles Hewstone in which, as part of their programme to make attribution theory more social, collective beliefs are considered in relation to social categorization and causal attribution. They argue that in research on attribution making, information about the actor as an individual is usually implicitly confounded with information about her or his category membership(s). They demonstrate that social categorization of actors can and does affect causal attributions concerning their actions. Jaspars and Hewstone extend their analysis to intergroup attributions and the relevance of social categorization. Subsequently, they examine both the extent to which such attributions are based on social knowledge (i.e. widespread beliefs) and the variety of contributions that collective beliefs and social representations can make to explanations and causal attributions.

Willem Doise outlines and discusses a number of theoretical positions which can be used to study social beliefs relevant to intergroup relations. More specifically, he examines the contrasting ideas of four Parisian sociologists, Boudon, Crozier, Touraine, and Bourdieu. He then proceeds to demonstrate the relevance of ideas from each of these four theorists to experimental studies of widespread beliefs operating in intergroup relations. Doise's analysis is a development of his thesis on levels of explanation in social psychology (Doise 1978). For Doise psychological and sociological explanations complement one another as much in the analysis of widespread beliefs as in intergroup relations.

The next two chapters, both of which look at social beliefs of young people, are also mixtures of the empirical and the theoretical, with the balance pushed a little further towards the former. Raymond Cochrane and Michael Billig examine the political and social beliefs of adolescents, first by discussing some of the general features of the empirical literature on political socialization and then by describing their own work on the political views of fifth formers in the West Midlands. In both of these sections they identify moderately widespread political beliefs, but emphasize the willingness of young people to hold political beliefs which, logically, might not be expected to co-exist in one individual. In the final section of their chapter, they argue for a rhetorical analysis of political beliefs which highlights the contrary tendencies of everyday social beliefs (see Billig *et al.* 1988).

Patten Smith and George Gaskell consider some social and political attitudes of black and white school-leavers in London and attempt to interpret their findings within relative deprivation theory. They argue that, although the apparently more social notion of 'fraternalistic' (or categorical) comparisons provides a more fruitful approach than the individualistic concept of 'egoistic' comparisons, fraternalistic relative deprivation itself has been an insufficiently social concept. It has not systematically and explicitly addressed the problem as to whether fraternalistic comparisons made by individuals are themselves shared, widespread beliefs.

The last two chapters, though by no means eschewing theoretical issues, are primarily reviews of empirical findings in two major substantive domains where widespread beliefs might be expected to be encountered. Alan Lewis reviews evidence of social or shared economic beliefs. First, using survey data, he describes a variety of widespread economic beliefs relating to: costs, prices, profit, income, and wealth; the public sector; and inflation and unemployment. Then he describes some major national and sectional differences in economic beliefs. Finally, he discusses some explanations of some of the beliefs he has described, together with possible shortcomings in the methods used to demonstrate those beliefs.

In the last chapter of the book, Glynis Breakwell deals with social beliefs about gender differences and, in so doing, reintroduces interest in inter-group relations and in integrating different levels of analysis. She examines what is known about a number of widespread beliefs about differences between the sexes: psychological differences, including stereotypical differences; the role of the 'expert' in creating such beliefs; and sex roles. She then considers social beliefs and identity, or self-concept, in terms of androgyny and instrumental self-definition. Breakwell concludes that what is required is an integrative theory in which widespread beliefs would mediate between social structure and individual identity, a conclusion with which we the editors readily concur.

References

Abelson, R.P. (1976). Scripts processing in attitude formation and decision making. In *Cognition and social behaviour*, (ed. J.S. Carroll and J.W. Payne). Erlbaum, Hillsdale, New Jersey.

Abelson, R.P. (1986). Beliefs are like possessions. *Journal for the Theory of Social Behaviour*, **16**, 3, 223–50.

Abelson, R.P., Aronson, E., McGuire, W.J., Newcomb, T.M., Rosenberg, M.S., and Tannenbaum, P.H. (eds) (1968). *Theories of cognitive consistency: a source book*. Rand McNally, Chicago.

Adorno, T.W., Frenkel-Brunswik, E., Levinson, D.J., and Sanford, R.N. (1950). *The authoritarian personality*. Harper & Row, New York.

Ajzen, I. (1988). *Attitudes, personality and behaviour*. Open University Press, Milton Keynes.

Ajzen, I. and Fishbein, M. (1980). *Understanding attitudes and predicting social behaviour*. Prentice Hall, New York.

Asch, S.E. (1952). *Social psychology*. Prentice Hall, New York.

Bentler, P.M. and Speckhart, G. (1981). Attitudes 'cause' behaviours: a structural equation analysis. *Journal of Personality and Social Psychology*, 40, 226–38.

Billig, M. (1982). *Ideology and social psychology*. Blackwell, Oxford.

Billig, M. (1987). *Arguing and thinking: a rhetorical approach to social psychology*. Cambridge University Press.

Billig, M., Condor, S., Edwards, D., Gane, M., Middleton, D., and Radley, A. (1988). *Ideological dilemmas: a social psychology of everyday thinking*. Sage, London.

Breakwell, G.M. and Canter, D.V. (eds) (In press) *Empirical approaches to social representations*. Oxford University Press.

Breckler, S.J. (1984). Empirical validation of affect, behaviour and cognition as distinct components of attitudes. *Journal of Personality and Social Psychology*, 407, 1191–206.

Converse, P.E. (1964). The nature of belief systems in mass publics. In *Ideology and discontent* (ed. D.E. Apter). Free Press, New York.

DeFleur, M.L. and Westie, F.R. (1963). Attitude as a scientific concept. *Social Forces*, 42, 17–31.

Doise, W. (1978). *Groups and individuals: explanations in social psychology*. Cambridge University Press.

Doob, L.W. (1947). The behavior of attitudes. *Psychological Review*, 54, 135–56.

Farr, R.M. and Moscovici, S. (eds) (1984). *Social representations*. Cambridge University Press.

Festinger, L. (1957). *A theory of cognitive dissonance*. Stanford University Press.

Fishbein, M. and Ajzen, I. (1975). *Belief, attitude, intention and behaviour: an introduction to theory and research*. Addison-Wesley, Reading, MA.

Fraser, C. (1986). Attitudes, social representations and widespread beliefs. Paper presented at International Congress of Applied Psychology, Jerusalem.

Harré, R. (1984). Some reflections on the concept of social representation. *Social Research*, 51, 4, 927–38.

Harré, R. (1985). Review of R. Farr and S. Moscovici (1984). *Social Representations*, Cambridge University Press. *British Journal of Psychology*, 76, 1, 138–40.

Jahoda, G. (1988). Critical notes and reflections on 'social representations'. *European Journal of Social Psychology*, 18, 195–209.

Jaspars, J.M.F. and Fraser, C. (1984). Attitudes and social representations. In *Social representations* (ed. R.M. Farr and S. Moscovici). Cambridge University Press.

Jodelet, D. (1988). Représentations sociales: phénomènes, concept et théorie. In *Psychologie Sociale*, 2nd edition (ed. S. Moscovici). Presses Universitaires de France, Paris.

Judd, C.M. and Milburn, M.A. (1980). The structure of attitude systems in the general public. *American Sociological Review*, 45, 627–43.

Kelman, H. (1974). Attitudes are alive and well and gainfully employed. *American Psychologist*, 29, 310–24.

Kelvin, P. (1969). *The bases of social behaviour. An approach in terms of order and value*. Holt, Rinehart and Winston, London.

Kuhn, T. (1970). *The structure of scientific revolutions.* University of Chicago Press.

Lalljee, M., Brown, L.B., and Ginsburg, G.P. (1984). Attitudes: dispositions, behaviour or evaluation. *British Journal of Social Psychology*, 23, 233–44.

LaPiere, R.T. (1934). Attitudes versus actions. *Social Forces*, **13**, 230–37.

Larrain, J. (1979). *The concept of ideology*. Hutchinson, London.

McGuire, W.J. (1964). Inducing resistance to persuasion. In *Advances in experimental social psychology 1*, (ed. L. Berkowitz) pp. 192–231. Academic Press, New York.

McGuire, W.J. (1986). The vicissitudes of attitudes and similar representations in twentieth century psychology. *European Journal of Social Psychology*, **16**, 2, 89–130.

Marsh, C. and Fraser, C. (1989). Nuclear issues and the nature of public opinion. In *Public opinion and nuclear weapons* (ed. C. Marsh and C. Fraser). Macmillan, London.

Moscovici, S. (1961). *La psychoanalyse, son image et son public*. Presses Universitaires de France, Paris.

Moscovici, S. (1963). Attitudes and opinions. *Annual Review of Psychology*, **14**, 231–60.

Moscovici, S. (1984a). The myth of the lonely paradigm: A rejoinder. *Social Research*, **51**, 4, 939–67.

Moscovici, S. (1984b). The phenomenon of social representations. In *Social representations* (ed. R.M. Farr and S. Moscovici). Cambridge University Press.

Potter, J. and Wetherell, M. (1987). *Discourse and social psychology*. Sage, London.

Roiser, M. (1987). Commonsense, science and public opinion. *Journal for the Theory of Social Behaviour*, **17**, 71–91.

Rokeach, M. (1960). *The open and closed mind*. Basic Books, New York.

Tajfel, H. (ed.) (1982). *Social identity and intergroup relations*. Cambridge University Press.

Thomas, W.I. and Znaniecki, F. (1918–20). *The Polish peasant in Europe and America*. Gorham Press, Boston.

Turner, J. (1987). *Rediscovering the social group*. Blackwell, Oxford.

Wexler, P. (1983). *Critical social psychology*. Routledge & Kegan Paul, Boston.

Wicker, A.W. (1969). Attitudes v. actions: The relationship of verbal and overt responses to attitude objects. *Journal of Social Issues*, **25**, 41–78.

2 The epidemiology of beliefs

Dan Sperber

I would like to bring together two sets of speculations: anthropological speculations on cultural representations, and psychological speculations on the cognitive organization of beliefs, and to put forward, as a result, fragments of a possible answer to the question 'How do beliefs become cultural?' I will not apologize for the speculative character of the attempt. At this stage, either the question is answered in a vague, fragmentary, and tentative way, or it must be left alone: there just is not enough sound theorizing and well-regimented evidence in the domain to do otherwise.

Anthropological speculations

I use 'cultural representation' in a wide sense: anything that is both cultural and a representation will do. Thus, cultural representations can be descriptive ('witches ride broomsticks') or normative ('with fish, drink white wine'), simple as in the above examples, or complex as the common law or Marxist ideology, verbal as in the case of a myth, or non-verbal as in the case of a mask, or multi-media as in the case of a mass.

To begin with, two remarks about the notion of a representation. First, 'to represent' is not just a two-place predicate: something represents something; it is a three-place predicate: something represents something for someone. Second, we should distinguish two kinds of representations: internal or *mental representations* (e.g. memories, which are patterns in the brain and which represent something for the owner of the brain) and external or *public representations* (e.g. utterances, which are material phenomena in the environment of people and which represent something for people who perceive them).

Which are more basic, public or mental representations? Most cognitive psychologists (e.g. Fodor 1975) see mental representations as more basic: for public representations to be representations at all they must be mentally represented by their users; for instance, an utterance represents something only for someone who perceives, decodes, and comprehends it, that is, associates with it a multi-level mental representation. On the other hand, mental representations can exist without public counterparts, for instance many of our memories (and all or nearly all the memories of an elephant) are never communicated. Therefore, it is argued, mental representations are more basic than public ones.

Most social scientists and many philosophers, often inspired by Ludwig Wittgenstein (1953), do not agree: they see public representations as more basic than mental ones. Public representations are observable, both by their users and by scientists, whereas mental representations, if they exist at all, can only be surmised. More importantly, it is claimed, for instance by Vygotsky (1965), that mental representations result from the internalization of public representations and of underlying systems such as languages and ideologies, without which no representation is possible. If so, public representations must be more basic than mental ones, a view which denies representations to non-social animals, but holders of this view don't mind.

There is an obvious sense in which public representations do come before mental ones: a child is born in a world full of public representations and is bombarded with them from the first moments of life. The child does not discover the world unaided and then make public the privately developed representations of it; rather, a great many of her representations of the world are acquired vicariously, not through experience, but through communication, or through a combination of experience and communication; and the very ability to communicate efficiently is indeed contingent upon her acquiring the language and the other communication tools of the community. However, those who see mental representations as basic are not (or should not be) denying this point. What they are, or should be, denying is that public representations could be of use to the child if she did not have, to begin with, some system of mental representations with which to approach the public ones.

Conversely, those who see public representations as basic are not, or should not be, merely making the trivial point that each individual is born in a world full of public representations and crucially relies on them. They are, or should be, claiming that not only is the physical shape of public representations public, outside of each person's head and there for other people to perceive, but also the *meaning* of public representations is public, out there for people to grasp. On this view, meaning—the regular relationship between that which represents and that which is being represented—is social before being individually grasped; hence, in the relevant sense, public representations are more basic than mental ones. This leads anthropologists in particular to consider that 'culture is public because meaning is' (Geertz 1973: p. 12). Most anthropologists study culture as a system of public representations endowed with public meanings, without any reference to the corresponding mental representations.

I have a bias: I am a materialist (see Sperber 1987). Not in the sense this word too often takes in the social sciences, where a materialist is one who believes that the economic 'infra-structure' determines the ideological 'super-structure', but in the sense of philosophy and the natural sciences: all causes and all effects are material. I then wonder: what kind of material objects or properties could public meanings possibly be? I am not persuaded by Geertz when he dismisses the issue as follows.

'The thing to ask about a burlesqued wink or a mock sheep raid [two of Geertz's examples of public representations], is not what their ontological status is. It is the same as that of rocks on the one hand and dreams on the other—they are things of this world. The thing to ask is what their import is: what it is . . . that, in their occurrence and through their agency, is getting said' (Geertz 1973: p. 10).

I am not persuaded because the task of ontology is not so much to say which things are 'of this world' and which are not, as it is to say in which manner, or manners, things can be of this world; and regarding cultural things, the problem stands.

We understand reasonably well how material things may fit in the world; we don't know that there are immaterial things, and if there are we don't know how they fit. Hence, for any class of entities, rocks, memories, or cultural representations, a materialist account, if it is available at all, is preferable, on grounds of intelligibility and parsimony.

In the case of mental things such as memories, most psychologists nowadays accept at least the minimal materialism known as 'token-physicalism'. According to this view, token mental states and processes are identical to token neural states and processes, though mental types need not be identical to neural types (see Block 1980). Still, each mental type must be described in a way which indicates how tokens falling under the type might be materially instantiated. For example, cognitive psychologists try to describe mental representations as states which could be materially implemented on a computer. Thus, with the development of cognitive psychology, we begin to grasp what kind of material objects mental representations might be.

Now, when it comes to cultural representations allegedly endowed with public meanings, whether we pay lip service to materialism and declare them to be material too, or resign ourselves to ontological pluralism, the truth of the matter is that we have no idea in which manner they might be 'things of this world'.

The materialist alternative is to assume that both mental and public representations are strictly material objects and to take the implications of this assumption seriously. Cognitive systems such as brains construct internal representations of their environment partly on the basis of law-governed physical interactions with that environment. Because of these interactions, mental representations are, to some extent, regularly connected to what they represent, and, as a result, they have semantic properties or 'meaning' of their own (see Dretske 1981, Fodor 1987). Public representations, on the other hand, are connected to what they represent only through the meaning attributed to them by their producers or their users; they have no semantic properties of their own. In other terms, public representations have meaning only through being associated with mental representations.

Public representations are generally attributed similar meanings by their producers and by their users, or else they could never serve the purpose of communication. This similarity of attributed meaning is itself made possible by the fact that people have similar enough linguistic and encyclopaedic knowledge. Similarity across people makes it possible to abstract away from individual differences and to describe 'the language' or 'the culture' of a community, 'the meaning' of a public representation, or to talk of, say, 'the belief' that witches ride broomsticks as a single representation, independently of its public expressions or mental instantiations. What is then described is an abstraction. Such an abstraction may be useful in many ways: it may bring out the common properties of a family of related mental and public representations; it may serve to identify parsimoniously a topic of research. Mistake, however, this abstraction for an object 'of this world', and indeed you had better heed Geertz's advice: better ignore its ontological status.

From a materialist point of view, then, there are only mental representations, which are born, live, and die within individual skulls, and public representations which are plain material phenomena—sound waves, light patterns, etc.—in the environment of individuals. Take a particular representation—witches on broomsticks—at an abstract level: what it corresponds to at a concrete level is millions of mental representations and millions of public representations, the meanings of which (intrinsic meanings in the case of mental representations, attributed meanings in the case of public ones) are similar to that of the statement: 'witches ride broomsticks'. These millions of mental and public representations, being material objects, can and do enter into cause–effect relationships. They may therefore play a role both as *explanans* and as *explanandum* in causal explanations. The materialist wager is that no other causal explanation of cultural phenomena is needed.

Causal explanations should be carefully distinguished from interpretive explanations, i.e. paraphrases, summaries, or exegeses of cultural representations. I have argued elsewhere that, although both are important in anthropology, only causal explanations generalize into theoretical hypotheses. Since my interest here is theoretical rather than ethnographic or methodological, I do not discuss interpretive explanations at all (see Sperber 1985a, ch. 1, and Sperber 1989).

Consider a human group: it hosts a much wider population of representations. Some of these representations are constructed on the basis of idiosyncratic experiences, as, for instance, my memories of the day on which I stopped smoking; others are based on common experiences, as, for instance, our belief that coal is black; others still derive from communication rather than from direct experience, as, for instance, our belief that Shakespeare wrote *Macbeth*. Common experience and communication bring about a similarity of representations across individuals, or loosely speaking, they cause some representations to be shared by several individuals, sometimes by a whole human group. This loose talk is acceptable only if it is clear that when we say that a representation is 'shared' by several individuals, what we mean is that these individuals have mental representations similar enough to be considered as versions of one another. When this is so, we can produce a further version—a public one this time—to identify synthetically the contents of these individual representations.

When we talk of cultural representations—beliefs in witches, rules for the service of wines, the common law, or Marxist ideology—we refer to representations which are widely shared in a human group. To explain cultural representations, then, is to explain why some representations are widely shared. Since representations are more or less widely shared, there is no neat boundary between cultural and individual representations. An explanation of cultural representations, therefore, should come as part of a general explanation of the distribution of representations among humans, as part, that is, of an *epidemiology of representations* (see Sperber 1985b).

The idea of an epidemiological approach to culture is by no means new. It was suggested by Gabriel Tarde (1895, 1898). Contemporary biologists have developed it in various ways, e.g. Cavalli-Sforza and Feldman (1981); Dawkins (1976, 1982); Lumsden and Wilson (1981); see also Boyd and Richerson (1985). The value of an epidemiological approach lies in making our understanding of micro-processes of transmission and that of macro-processes of evolution mutually relevant. However, if the micro-processes are fundamentally misunderstood, as I believe they have been in previous epidemiological approaches, the overall picture is of limited value. Whatever their differences and their merits, past approaches share a crucial defect: they take the basic process of cultural transmission to be one of replication, and consider alterations in transmission as accidents.

The view of cultural transmission as a process of replication is grounded not only in a biological analogy—mutation is an accident, replication is the norm—but also in two dominant biases in the social sciences: first, as we have already seen, individual differences are idealized away and cultural representations are too often treated as identical across individuals throughout a human group or subgroup; second, the prevailing view of communication, as a coding process followed by a symmetrical decoding process, implies that replication of the communicator's thoughts in the mind of the audience is the normal outcome of communication.

In *Relevance: communication and cognition*, Deirdre Wilson and I have criticized the code model of human communication and developed an alternative model which gives pride of place to inferential processes (Sperber and Wilson 1986). One of the points we are making—a commonsensical point, really, which would hardly be worth making if it were not so often forgotten—is that what human communication achieves in general is merely some degree of resemblance between the communicator's and the audience's thoughts. Strict replication, if it exists at all, should be viewed just as a limiting case of maximal resemblance, rather than as the norm of communication. A process of communication is basically one of transformation. The degree of transformation may vary between two extremes: duplication and destruction. Only those representations which are repeatedly communicated *and* minimally transformed in the process will end up belonging to the culture.

The objects of an epidemiology of representations are neither abstract representations, nor individual concrete representations, but, we might say, strains of concrete representations related both by causal relationships and by similarity of content. Some of the questions we want to answer are: what causes such strains to appear, to expand, to split, to merge with one another, to change over time, to die? Just as standard epidemiology does not give a single general explanation for the distribution of all diseases, there is no reason to expect that these questions will be answered in the same way for every kind of representation. The diffusion of a folktale and that of a military skill, for instance, involve different cognitive abilities, different motivations, and different environmental factors. An epidemiological approach, therefore, should not hope for one grand unitary theory. It should, rather, try to provide interesting questions and useful conceptual tools, and to develop the different models needed to explain the existence and fate of the various families of cultural representations.

Although the factors which will contribute to the explanation of a particular strain of representations cannot be decided in advance, in every case some of the factors to be considered will be psychological and some will be environmental or ecological (taking the environment to begin at the individual organism's nerve endings and to include, for each organism, all the organisms it interacts with). Potentially pertinent psychological factors include the ease with which a particular representation can be memorized; the existence of background knowledge in relationship to which the representation is relevant; a motivation to communicate the content of the representation. Ecological factors include the recurrence of situations in which the representation gives rise to, or helps, appropriate action; the availability of external memory stores, writing in particular; the existence of institutions engaged in the transmission of the representation. For a discussion of the notion of an 'institution' from an epidemiological perspective, see Sperber (1987).

Unsurprisingly, psychological and ecological factors are themselves affected by the distribution of representations. Previously internalized cultural representations are a key factor in one's susceptibility to new representations. The human environment is, for a great part, man-made, and made on the basis of cultural representations. As a result, feedback loops are to be expected both within models explaining particular families and between such models. The resulting complexity is of the ecological rather than of the organic kind. Though 'organicism' has disappeared from the anthropological scene, the organicist view of a culture as a well-integrated whole still lingers. The epidemiological approach departs from such cultural holism; it depicts particular cultures as widely open rather than almost closed systems, and as approximating an ecological equilibrium among strains of representations, rather than as exhibiting an organic kind of integration. An interesting question is then to find out which strains of representations benefit one another, and which, on the contrary, compete.

The identification of epidemiological phenomena (in classical epidemiology) often arise out of the study of individual pathology, but the converse is also true: the identification of particular diseases is often helped by epidemiological considerations. Similarly, when types of mental representations have been identified at a psychological level, the question of their epidemiology arises, and, conversely, when particular strains of representations, or mutually supportive strains, have been epidemiologically identified, the question of their psychological character arises. More generally, like pathology and epidemiology of diseases, psychology and epidemiology of representations should prove mutually relevant.

Psychological speculations

Anthropologists and psychologists alike assume that humans are rational. Not perfectly rational, not rational all the time, but rational enough. What is meant by rationality may vary, or be left vague, but it always implies at least the following idea: humans beliefs are produced by cognitive processes which are on the whole epistemologically sound, i.e. humans approximately perceive what there is for them to perceive and approximately infer what their perceptions warrant. Of course, there are perceptual illusions and inferential failures, the resulting overall representation of the world is not totally consistent, but, as they are, the beliefs of humans allow them to form and pursue goals in a manner which often leads to the achievement of these goals.

I do not know why other anthropologists and psychologists assume that humans are rational, but I know why I assume it: it makes good biological sense. Why did vertebrates evolve so as to have more and more complex cognitive systems, culminating, it seems, in the human one, if not because this makes their interaction with the environment (e.g. feeding oneself, protecting oneself) more effective? Now, only an epistemologically sound cognitive system (i.e. one that delivers approximations of knowledge rather than pretty patterns or astounding enigmas) can serve that purpose, and, for that, it must be rational enough. That way of explaining why humans are rational implies that there is an objective reality, and that at least one function of human cognition is to represent in human brains aspects of that reality.

Fitting together reality and reason in this manner might seem common-sensical to psychologists, but many anthropologists—not so long ago, most of them—know better. People of different cultures have beliefs which are not only very different, but even mutually incompatible. Their beliefs from our point of view, ours from theirs, seem irrational. If we want to maintain, nevertheless, that they are, and that we are, rational, then an obvious escape from the looming paradox is to deny that there is an objective reality to begin with. Reality on that view is a social construct, and there are at least as many 'realities' or 'worlds' as there are societies. Different beliefs are rational in different socially constructed worlds. I have argued at length against this view (see Sperber 1974, 1985a). Here I will merely state my bias: I find a plurality of worlds even less attractive than a plurality of substances; if there is a way, I would rather do without that.

There is a way, but first we must do a bit of conceptual house-cleaning. The philosophical literature on beliefs is huge, see for instance Ryle (1949); Hintikka (1962); Armstrong (1973); Harman (1973); Dennett (1978); Dretske (1981); Stich (1983); Bogdan (1986); Brandt and Harnish (1986). However it pays little or no attention to those features of beliefs which social scientists have particularly been concerned with. Though 'belief' has always been a stock in trade term of anthropologists, Needham (1972), inspired by Wittgenstein, is the only thorough discussion of the concept from an anthropological point of view.

What are we referring to when we talk of 'beliefs'? Take an example: we tend to assume that Peter believes that it will rain, if he says so, or assents to somebody else saying so, or, in some cases, if he takes his umbrella on his way out. We do not mistake these behaviours for the belief itself; we take them, rather, as caused in part by Peter having the belief in question and, therefore, as evidence of the belief. We might be tempted to say then (as many philosophers have, e.g. Ryle (1949) that a belief is a disposition to express, assent to, or otherwise act in accordance with some proposition. As psychologists, however, we will want to go deeper: what kind of mental states might bring about such a disposition? Nowadays an often heard answer is that humans have a kind of 'data base' or 'belief box' (Steven Schiffer's phrase) where some conceptual representations are stored. All representations stored in that particular box are treated as descriptions of the actual world. When the occasion is right, this yields the usual behavioural evidence for belief: assertion and assent in particular.

The belief box story, however attractive, cannot be the *whole* story. Many of the propositions to which we are disposed to assent are not represented at all in our mind—a well-known point—and many of the propositions we are disposed not only to assent to, but also to express and, in some cases, to act in accordance with, are not, or not simply, stored in a database or belief box—a more controversial point.

You have long believed that there are more pink flamingoes on Earth than on the Moon, but no mental representation of yours had, until now, described that state of affairs. We may well have an infinity of such unrepresented beliefs, and a large proportion of these are widely shared, though of course they have never been communicated. It is reasonable, however, to assume that what makes these unrepresented beliefs beliefs (more specifically propositions to which we are disposed to assent) is that they are inferable from other beliefs which *are* mentally represented. What we need to add for this to the belief box is some inferential device which can recognize unrepresented beliefs on the basis of the actually represented ones. The inferences in question are not done consciously, so the inferential device paired to the belief box must be distinct from, and need not resemble, human conscious reasoning abilities (see Sperber and Wilson 1986, Chapter 2).

Beside accounting for unrepresented beliefs, complementing the belief box with an inferential device introduces a factor of rationality in the construction of beliefs. Suppose some of the representations in our belief box come from perception (broadly understood so as to include the 'perception' of one's own mental states) and all other beliefs are directly or indirectly inferred from the perceptually based ones. This will already ensure areas of consistency among our beliefs. Suppose furthermore that the inferential device recognizes an inconsistency when it meets one, and corrects it. This implies, by the way, that perceptually delivered beliefs may be inferentially invalidated, in other words, that perception may determine the content of a belief but is not enough, by itself, to make it a belief: inferential validation, or at least lack of invalidation, may also be necessary (see Fodor 1983). Then you get a tendency to enlarge areas of consistency (even though contradictory beliefs may still be held, provided they are never used as joint premises in an inference).

While perception plus unconscious inference might be the whole story for the beliefs of elephants, it could not be so for the beliefs of humans. There are two interconnected reasons for this: first, many, possibly most, human beliefs are grounded not in the perception of the things the beliefs are about, but in communication about these things. Second, humans have a meta-representational or *interpretive* ability. That is, they can construct not only *descriptions*, i.e. representations of states of affairs, but also *interpretations*, i.e. representations of representations. On this contrast between description and interpretation, see Sperber (1985*a*), Ch. 1, and Sperber and Wilson (1986), Ch. 4. Now, humans use this interpretive ability to understand what is communicated to them and, more generally, to represent meanings, intentions, beliefs, opinions, theories, etc., whether or not they share them. In particular, they can represent a belief and take a favourable attitude to it, and therefore express it, assent to it, and generally show all the behaviours symptomatic of belief, on a basis quite different from belief box inclusion.

For example, young Lisa is told by her teacher:

'There are male and female plants.'

She understands 'male' and 'female' more or less as an extension to animals of the distinction between men and women: females have children, males fight more easily, etc. She does not see in plants anything resembling this distinction and so she does not quite understand what her teacher is telling the class. On the other hand she understands it in part—she understands that in some species there are two types of plants, she guesses that this difference has to do with reproduction, etc. She trusts her teacher and if he says that there are male and female plants, then she is willing to say so herself, to say that she believes it, and to exhibit various behaviours symptomatic of belief.

Behind Lisa's belief behaviour, do we have a genuine belief? Not of the belief box kind anyhow, since such a half-understood idea could not have emerged from perception or from an inference from perception: it is a typical outcome, rather, of not totally successful communication. Remember too that we want the inferential device to operate freely on beliefs in the belief box so as to yield more mutually consistent beliefs; but then we should be wary of allowing half-understood ideas directly in the box, since their consistency with other representations and their implications are largely indeterminate.

But how, then, might Lisa's half-understood idea of there being male and female plants be represented in her mind? Well, she might have in her belief box the following representations:

What the teacher says is true.

The teacher says that there are male and female plants.

Lisa's partial understanding of 'there are male and female plants' is now embedded in a belief box belief about what her teacher said. This belief, together with the other belief that 'what the teacher says is true', provides a validating context for the embedded representation of the teacher's words.

This gives Lisa rational grounds to exhibit many of the behaviours symptomatic of belief—but grounds quite different from plain belief box inclusion.

What this example suggests is that the beliefs we attribute to people on the evidence provided by their behaviour do not belong to a single psychological kind; in other terms, quite different types of mental states can bring about identical belief behaviour.

I maintain that there are two fundamental kinds of beliefs represented in the mind: there are descriptions of states of affairs directly stored in the belief box; let us call this first kind *intuitive beliefs*. Intuitive beliefs are intuitive in the sense that they are typically the product of spontaneous and unconscious perceptual and inferential processes; in order to hold these intuitive beliefs, one need not be aware of the fact that one holds them, and even less of reasons to hold them. Then there are interpretations of representations embedded in the validating context of an intuitive belief, as in the above example; let us call this second kind *reflective beliefs*. Reflective beliefs are reflective in the sense that they are believed by virtue of second-order beliefs about them. In Sperber (1975*a*), Sperber (1985*a*), and Sperber (1985*b*) I used different terms for these two types of beliefs. These different terminologies were found to be misleading in some ways. I hope the present proposal will be more satisfactory.

Intuitive beliefs are derived, or derivable, from perception by means of the inferential device. The mental vocabulary of intuitive beliefs is probably limited to *basic concepts*, that is, concepts referring to perceptually identifiable phenomena, and innately preformed unanalysed abstract concepts (of, say, norm, cause, substance, species, function, number, or truth). Intuitive beliefs are on the whole concrete and reliable in ordinary circumstances. Together they paint a kind of common-sense picture of the world. Their limits are those of common sense: they are fairly superficial, more descriptive than explanatory, and rather rigidly held.

Unlike intuitive beliefs, reflective beliefs do not form a well-defined category. What they have in common is their mode of occurrence: they occur embedded in intuitive beliefs (or, since there can be multiple embeddings, in other reflective beliefs). They cause belief behaviours because, one way or another, the belief in which they occur embedded validates them. But then they may differ in many ways: a reflective belief may be half-understood but fully understandable, as in the above 'sex of plants' example, or, as I will shortly illustrate, it may remain half-understood forever, or, on the contrary, be fully understood. The validating context may be an identification of the source of the reflective belief as a reliable authority (e.g. the teacher), or an explicit reasoning. Given the variety of possible contextual validations for reflective beliefs, commitment to these beliefs can vary widely, from loosely held opinions to fundamental creeds, from mere hunches to carefully thought out convictions. Reflective beliefs play different roles in human cognition, as I will very briefly illustrate.

For Lisa, forming and storing the half-understood reflective belief that there are male and female plants may be a step towards a more adequate understanding of the male–female distinction. It provides her with an incomplete piece of information which further encounters with relevant evidence may help complete. After she achieves an adequate understanding of the matter, her reflective belief that there are male and female plants may well be transferred to, or duplicated in, her belief box as an intuitive belief. So, one role of reflective belief is to serve as 'hold' format for information that needs to be completed before it can constitute an intuitive belief.

Now, consider the following case. Young Bobby has in his belief box the two representations:

> What Mommy says is true.
>
> Mommy says that God is everywhere.

Bobby does not fully understand how somebody, albeit God, can be everywhere. However his mother's saying so gives him sufficient ground to exhibit all the behaviours symptomatic of belief: he will readily state himself that God is everywhere, he will assent to the same statement made by others, and he might even refrain from sinning in places where apparently nobody can see him. That God is everywhere is for Bobby a reflective belief. As he grows older, he may keep this belief and enrich it in many ways, but, if anything, its exact meaning will become even more mysterious than it was at first. Here is a belief which, like most religious beliefs, does not lend itself to a final, clear interpretation, and which therefore will never become an intuitive belief. Part of the interest of religious beliefs for those who hold them comes precisely from this element of mystery, from the fact that you can never interpret them completely. While the cognitive usefulness of religious and other mysterious beliefs may be limited (but see Sperber 1975a), it is not too difficult to see how their very mysteriousness makes them 'addictive'.

In the two examples considered so far—Lisa and the sex of plants, Bobby and divine omnipresence—what made the reflective representation a belief was the authority granted to the source of the representation: the teacher or the mother. Laymen accept scientific beliefs on authority too. For instance most of us believe that '$e = mc^2$' with only a very limited understanding of what this formula means, and no understanding of the arguments that led to its adoption. Our belief then is a reflective belief of mysterious content justified by our trust in the community of physicists. It is not very different, in this respect, from Bobby's belief that God is everywhere.

There is a difference though. Even for theologians, that God is everywhere is a mystery, and they too accept it on authority. For physicists, on the other hand, the theory of relativity is not a mystery and they have reasons to accept it which have nothing to do with trust. Well-understood reflective beliefs such as the scientific beliefs of scientists, include an explicit account of rational grounds to hold them. Their mutual consistency and their consistency with intuitive beliefs can be ascertained and this plays an important, though quite complex, role in their acceptance or rejection. Still, even for physicists, the theory of relativity is a reflective belief, it is a theory, a representation kept under scrutiny and open to revision and challenge, rather than a fact that could be perceived, or unconsciously inferred from perception.

Half-understood or mysterious reflective beliefs are much more frequent and culturally important than scientific ones. Because they are only half-understood and therefore open to reinterpretation, their consistency or inconsistency with other beliefs, intuitive or reflective, is never self-evident, and does not provide a robust criterion for acceptance or rejection. Their content, because of its indeterminateness, cannot be sufficiently evidenced or argued for to warrant their rational acceptance. But that does not make these beliefs irrational: they are rationally held if there are rational grounds to trust the source of the beliefs (e.g. the parent, the teacher, or the scientist).

This then is my answer to those who see in the great diversity and frequent apparent inconsistency of human beliefs an argument in favour of cultural relativism: there are two classes of beliefs and they achieve rationality in different ways. Intuitive beliefs owe their rationality to essentially innate and therefore universal perceptual and inferential mechanisms; as a result, they do not vary dramatically and are essentially mutually consistent or reconcilable across cultures. Those beliefs which vary across culture to the extent of seeming irrational when viewed from another culture's point of view are typically reflective beliefs with a content partly mysterious to the believers themselves. Such beliefs are rationally held, not by virtue of their content, but by virtue of their source. That different people should trust different sources of beliefs—I, my educators, you, yours—is exactly what you would expect if they are all rational in the same way and in the same world, and merely located in different parts of this world.

Different types of beliefs, different mechanisms of distributions

Let us now bring together the anthropological and the psychological specu-lations developed so far. If there are different kinds of beliefs, then we might expect them to be distributed by different mechanisms. More precisely, we might expect the distribution of intuitive beliefs, which are a relatively homogeneous kind, to proceed along roughly common lines.

There are grounds to consider that intuitive beliefs in different cognitive domains, e.g. naïve physics, naïve zoology, naïve psychology, have different conceptual structures, see Sperber (1975*b*), Atran (1987) and Atran and Sperber (forthcoming). These differences, however, do not seem to be such as to bring about very different modes of distribution but the distribution of reflective beliefs, which are much more diverse, should take place in many different ways. In this concluding section, I would like to suggest that such is indeed the case.

In all human societies, traditional or modern, with or without writing, with or without pedagogic institutions, all normal individuals acquire a rich body of intuitive beliefs about themselves and their natural and social environment. These include beliefs about the movement of physical bodies, the behaviour of one's own body, the effects of various body–environment interactions, the behaviour of many living kinds, the behaviour of fellow humans. These beliefs are acquired in the course of ordinary interaction with the environment and with others. They need no conscious learning effort on the part of the learner and no conscious teaching effort on the part of others (see Atran and Sperber forthcoming). Even without teaching, these beliefs are easily acquired by everybody. The more fundamental ones are acquired quite early, suggesting a very strong innate predisposition, see Keil (1979), Carey (1982, 1985), Gelman and Spelke (1981) and Hirschfeld (1984).

Some intuitive beliefs are about particulars (particular locations, personal events, individual animals or people) and are idiosyncratic or very locally shared; others are general (or about widely known particulars such as historical events and characters) and are widespread throughout a society. General intuitive beliefs vary across cultures but they do not seem to vary greatly. To mention just one piece of anecdotal evidence, one has yet to find a culture where intuitive beliefs about space and movement would be so different from modern Western ones that the natives would have inordinate problems in learning to drive a car. Much recent work in ethnoscience shows too that cross-cultural differences in zoological, botanical, or colour classification are rather superficial and that, for each of these domains (and presumably for other domains, e.g. artefacts or mental states), there are underlying universal structures, see Berlin and Kay (1969), Berlin *et al.* (1973), Berlin (1978), and Atran (1985, 1986, 1987).

What role does communication play in the construction of intuitive beliefs? The answer is not simple. Intuitive beliefs are (or are treated as) the output of perception and unconscious inference, either the subject's own perceptions and inferences, or those of others in the case of intuitive beliefs acquired through communication. Even when an intuitive belief is derived from the subject's own perceptions, the conceptual resources and the background assumptions which combine with the sensory input to yield the actual belief have, in part, been acquired through communication. So, it seems, both perception and communication are always involved in the construction of intuitive beliefs. Perception is involved either as the direct source of the belief or as its assumed indirect source (which puts a strong constraint on the possible contents of intuitive beliefs). Communication is involved either as a direct source, or, at least, as a source of concepts and background.

What now is the relationship between the relative shares of perception and communication in the construction of an intuitive belief on the one hand, and its social distribution on the other? Is it the case that the greater the share of communication, the wider the distribution? Again, the answer is not that simple. A great number of very widespread beliefs owe their distribution to the fact that all the members of a society, or in some cases all humans, have similar perceptual experiences. However, as already suggested, the resources for perception are themselves partly derived from communication.

Take the widespread intuitive belief that coal is black: were you told it, or did you infer it from your own perception? Hard to know. But even if you inferred it from perception, in doing so you used the concepts of black and that of coal, and how did you acquire those? Regarding 'black', it seems that the category is innately prewired, so that, when you learned the word 'black', you merely acquired a way to express verbally a concept you already possessed, see Berlin and Kay (1969) and Carey (1982). Regarding 'coal', no one would claim that the concept is innate, but what might well be innate is the structure of substance-concepts with the expectation of regular phenomenal features, in particular colour. So, while you probably acquired the concept of coal in the process of learning the word 'coal', acquiring the concept meant no more than picking the right innate conceptual schema and fleshing it out. In the process of fleshing it out, either you were told or you inferred from what you saw that coal is black.

It does not make much difference, then, whether an individual's belief that coal is black is derived from perception or from communication: once the concept of coal is communicated, the belief that coal is black will follow one way or the other. This is generally true of widespread intuitive beliefs. These beliefs conform to cognitive expectations based on culturally enriched innate dispositions and are richly evidenced by the environment. As a result, different direct perceptual experiences and different vicarious experiences acquired through communication converge on the same general intuitive beliefs.

Widespread intuitive beliefs, even exotic ones, are rarely surprising. They are not the kind of beliefs that generally excite the curiosity of social scientists, with the exception of cognitive anthropologists. Among psychologists, only developmental psychologists have started studying them in some detail. Yet intuitive beliefs not only determine much of human behaviour; they also provide a common background for communication and for the development of reflective beliefs.

While widespread intuitive beliefs owe their distribution both to common perceptual experiences and to communication, widespread reflective beliefs owe theirs almost exclusively to communication. The distribution of reflective beliefs takes place, so to speak, in the open: reflective beliefs are not only consciously held, they are also often deliberately spread. For instance, religious believers, political ideologists, and scientists, however they may differ otherwise, see it as incumbent upon them to cause others to share their beliefs. Precisely because the distribution of reflective beliefs is a highly visible social process, it should be obvious that different types of reflective beliefs reach a cultural level of distribution in very different ways. To illustrate this, let us consider very briefly three examples: a myth in a non-literate society, the belief that all men are born equal, and Gödel's proof.

A myth is an orally transmitted story which is taken to represent actual events, including 'supernatural' events incompatible with intuitive beliefs. Therefore, for a myth to be accepted without inconsistency, it has to be insulated from intuitive beliefs, i.e. held as a reflective belief. A myth is a cultural representation; this means that the story is being told, given public versions, often enough to cause a large enough proportion of a human group to know it, that is to have mental versions of it. For this, two conditions must be met. First the story must be such that it is easily enough and accurately enough remembered on the basis of oral inputs alone. Some themes and some narrative structures seem in this respect to do much better cross-culturally than others. The changing cultural background affects memorability too so that the content of a myth tends to drift over time so as to maintain maximal memorability.

Second, there must be enough incentives to actually recall and tell the story on enough occasions to cause it to be remembered. These incentives may be institutional, e.g. ritual occasions where telling the story is mandatory, but the surest incentive comes from the attractiveness of the story for the audience and the success the story-teller can therefore expect. Interestingly, though not too surprisingly, the very same themes and structures which help one remember a story seem to make it particularly attractive.

If the psychological conditions of memorability and attractiveness are met, the story is likely to be well distributed, but in order for it to be a myth, rather than, say, a mere tale recognized and enjoyed as such, it must be given credence. What rational ground do people have to accept such a story as true? Their confidence in those who tell them. Typically, their confidence in elders whom they have many good reasons to trust and who themselves claim no other authority than that derived from *their* elders. The originator of the chain might be a religious innovator who claimed divine authority for a distinctly different version of older myths. Reference to elders provides a self-perpetuating authority structure for a story which already has a self-perpetuating transmission structure. Still, the authority structure is more fragile than the transmission structure and many myths lose their credibility, but neither their memorability nor their attractiveness, and end up as tales.

The belief that all men are born equal is again a typically reflective belief: it is not produced by perception or by unconscious inference from perception. Rather, except for a few philosophers who originated the belief, all those who have held it came to it through communication. Such a belief does not put any significant weight on memory, but it does present a challenge for understanding, and indeed it is understood differently by different people. As already suggested, the fact that it lends itself to several interpretations probably contributed to its cultural success.

Still, the most important factor in the success of the belief that all men are born equal is its extreme relevance, that is, according to Sperber and Wilson (1986), the wealth of its contextual implications in a society which was organized around differences in birthrights. People who accepted, and indeed desired, the implications of this belief found there grounds to accept the belief itself and to try to spread it. However, there was a risk, not in holding the belief, but in spreading it, and so the belief did spread only where and when there were enough people willing to take this risk. In other words, unlike a myth which seems to have a life of its own and to survive and spread, as myth or as tale, in a great variety of historical and cultural conditions, the cultural destiny of a political belief is tied to that of institutions. Ecological factors, more particularly the institutional environment, play a more important role in explaining the distribution of a political belief than cognitive factors.

Consider now a mathematical belief, such as Gödel's proof. Again, all those who hold it, except Gödel himself, arrived at it through communication. However, the communication and hence the diffusion of such a belief meets extraordinary cognitive difficulties. Only people with a high enough level in mathematical logic can begin to work at understanding it. Outside of scholarly institutions, both the means and the motivation to do that work are generally lacking. On the other hand, once the difficulties of communication are overcome, acceptance is no problem at all: to understand Gödel's proof is to believe it.

The human cognitive organization is such that we cannot understand such a belief and not hold it. To some significant extent, and with obvious qualifications, this is the case with all successful theories in the modern natural sciences. Their cognitive robustness compensates, so to speak, for their abstruseness in explaining their cultural success. The fact that successful scientific theories impose themselves on most of those who understand them is manifest to people who don't understand them. This leads these lay persons, quite rationally, to believe that these theories are true and to express as beliefs whatever they can quote or paraphrase from them. Thus Gödel's proof, and scientific theories generally, become cultural beliefs, of different tenor and accepted on different grounds for the scientists themselves and for the community at large.

We might contrast our three examples in the following way: myth is strongly determined by cognitive factors and weakly by ecological factors. Political beliefs are weakly determined by cognitive factors and strongly by ecological factors, and scientific beliefs are strongly determined by both cognitive and ecological factors. However, even this contrast exaggerates the similarities between the three cases: the cognitive factors involved in myth and in science, the ecological factors involved in politics and science are very different. The very structure of reflective beliefs, the fact that they are attitudes to a representation, rather than directly to a real or assumed state of affairs, allows endless diversity.

Notwithstanding their diversity, explaining cultural beliefs, whether intuitive or reflective, and if reflective, whether half understood or fully understood, involves looking at two things: how they are cognized by individuals and how they are communicated within a group, or to put it in slogan form: *culture is the precipitate of cognition and communication in a human population.*

References

Armstrong, D. (1973). *Belief, truth and knowledge.* Cambridge University Press.
Atran, S. (1985). The nature of folk-botanical life-forms. *American Anthropologist,* **87**, 298–315.
Atran, S. (1986). *Fondements de l'histoire naturelle.* Complexe, Brussels.
Atran, S. (1987). Ordinary constraints on the semantics of living kinds. *Mind and Language,* **2**, 27–63.
Atran, S. and Sperber, D. (forthcoming). Learning without teaching: its place in culture. Paper presented at the Workshop on 'Culture, Schooling and Psychological Development'. Tel Aviv, June 1987.
Berlin, B. (1978). Ethnobiological classification. In *Cognition and categorization* (ed. E. Rosch and B. Lloyd). Erlbaum, London.
Berlin, B., Breedlove, D., and Raven, P. (1973). General principles of classification and nomenclature in folk biology. *American Anthropologist,* **75**, 214–42.
Berlin, B. and Kay, P. (1969). *Basic color terms.* University of California Press, Berkeley.
Block, N. (1980). *Readings in Philosophy of Psychology, Vol I.* Harvard University Press, Cambridge, MA.

Bogdan, R. (ed.) (1986). *Belief: form, content, and function*. Oxford University Press.

Boyd, R. and Richerson, P.J. (1985). *Culture and the evolutionary process*. The University of Chicago Press.

Brandt, M. and Harnish, R.M. (eds.) (1986). *The representation of knowledge and belief*. The University of Arizona Press, Tucson.

Cavalli-Sforza, L.L. and Feldman, M.W. (1981). *Cultural transmission and evolution: a quantitative approach*. Princetown University Press.

Carey, S. (1982). Semantic development: the state of the art. In *Language acquisition: the state of the art* (ed. E. Wanner and L. Gleitman) Cambridge University Press.

Carey, S. (1985). *Conceptual change in childhood*. MIT Press, Cambridge, MA.

Dawkins, R. (1976). *The selfish gene*. Oxford University Press.

Dawkins, R. (1982). *The extended phenotype*. Oxford University Press.

Dennett, D. (1978). *Brainstorms*. Harvester Press, Hassocks.

Dretske, F. (1981). *Knowledge and the flow of information*. MIT Press, Cambridge, MA.

Fodor, J. (1975). *The language of thought*. Crowell, New York.

Fodor, J. (1983). *The modularity of mind*. MIT Press, Cambridge, MA.

Fodor, J. (1987). *Psychosemantics*. MIT Press, Cambridge, MA.

Geertz, C. (1973). *The interpretation of cultures*. Basic Books, New York.

Gelman, R. and Spelke, E. (1981). The development of thoughts about animate and inanimate objects. In *Social cognitive development* (ed. J. Flavell and L. Ross). Cambridge University Press.

Harman, G. (1973). *Thought*. Princetown University Press.

Hintikka, J. (1962). *Knowledge and belief*. Cornell University Press, Ithaca.

Hirschfeld, L. (1984). Kinship and cognition. *Current Anthropology*, **27**, 235.

Keil, F. (1979). *Semantic and conceptual development*. Harvard University Press, Cambridge, MA.

Lumsden, C.J. and Wilson, E.O. (1981). *Genes, mind and culture*. Harvard University Press, Cambridge, MA.

Needham, R. (1972). *Belief, language and experience*. Blackwell, Oxford.

Ryle, G. (1949). *The concept of mind*. Hutchinson, London.

Sperber, D. (1974). Contre certains a priori anthropologiques. In *L'Unité de l'homme* (ed. E. Morin and M. Piatelli-Palmarini). Le Seuil, Paris.

Sperber, D. (1975a). *Rethinking symbolism*. Cambridge University Press.

Sperber, D. (1975b). Pourquoi les animaux parfaits, les hybrides et les monstres sont-ils bons à penser symboliquement? *L'Homme*, **15**, 5–24.

Sperber, D. (1985a). *On anthropological knowledge*. Cambridge University Press.

Sperber, D. (1985b). Anthropology and psychology: towards an epidemiology of representations. *Man* (N.S.), **20**, 73–89.

Sperber, D. (1987). Les sciences cognitives, les sciences sociales et le matérialisme. *Le Débat*, **47**, 105–115.

Sperber, D. (1989). L'étude anthropologique des représentations: problèmes et perspectives. In *Les représentations sociales* (ed. D. Jodelet). Presses Universitaires de France, Paris.

Sperber, D. and Wilson, D. (1986). *Relevance: communication and cognition*. Blackwell, Oxford.

Stich, S. (1983). *From folk psychology to cognitive science*. MIT Press, Cambridge, MA.
Tarde, G. (1895). *Les lois de l'imitation*. Félix Alcan, Paris.
Tarde, G. (1898). *Les lois sociales*. Félix Alcan, Paris.
Vygotsky, L. (1965). *Thought and language*. MIT Press, Cambridge, MA.
Wittgenstein, L. (1953). *Philosophical investigations*. Blackwell, Oxford.

Part II

Theoretical Perspectives

3 Social representations as widespread beliefs

Rob Farr

Introduction

A distinct tradition of social psychology has evolved in France in the course of the past 30 years. It is clearly different from the dominant American tradition of social psychology. The difference, according to Herzlich (1972), resides in its being both a European tradition of research and a sociological form of social psychology. Over 80 per cent of the literature is in French. It is unique, in my view, because the objects of study are social representations. Moscovici (1961/1976) started this tradition of research in the late 1950s with his empirical studies of how a knowledge of psychoanalysis had diffused throughout French society and of how its vocabulary had become part of popular culture. *Social representations* (Farr and Moscovici 1984*a*) reflects, in English, some of the rich variety of the original studies carried out, either in the field or in the laboratory, within this French tradition of research. Elsewhere I have reviewed the literature, in both English and French, on social representations (Farr 1987).

In inaugurating a new tradition of social psychology Moscovici did not wish to foreclose any future developments by defining his terms at the outset. The objects of study in Wundt's *Völkerpsychologie* had been language, religion, customs, myth, magic, and cognate phenomena. Durkheim called these entities collective representations. He contrasted them with the individual representations that were of interest to the psychologist. The study of collective representations was part of sociology. Moscovici, in selecting his own key theoretical terms, looked back to Durkheim. To the other forms of collective representation Moscovici added science. His preference for 'social' over 'collective', as the appropriate adjective to qualify 'representations', reflects his interest in understanding modern societies which are much more dynamic and changing than the sorts of society that had been of interest to Durkheim. It also reflects a particular philosophy of science. He believes that phenomena which are central to one discipline, for example as 'collective representations' are to sociology or anthropology, can be explained in terms of phenomena that are central to another discipline, e.g. as 'social representations' are to social psychology.

If Moscovici was reluctant, initially, to define 'social representations' others have been less so. Jodelet (1988), in a recent attempt to delineate the theory, offers the following definition:

'The concept of social representation indicates a specific form of knowledge, i.e. common-sense knowledge, the contents of which reveal the operation of processes that are generative and that (serve) distinct social purposes. More generally, it indicates a form of social thought. Social representations are practical and communicable ways of thinking that are oriented towards an understanding and mastery of the environment (both social and material . . .). As such, they offer specific distinguishing features in regard to how either the contents, or the mental operations or the logic (of social representations) are organized. The social distinctiveness of either the contents or the processes is attributable to: (i) the conditions and contexts in which the representations emerge; (ii) the means by which they circulate; and (iii) the functions which they serve in interaction both with the world and with others (Jodelet 1988, pp. 361–2; idiomatic translation by the present writer).

From the outset, Moscovici has been critical of the purely individual nature of such key theoretical terms in the dominant American tradition of social psychology as attitude, opinion, stereotype, image, etc. By redefining social psychology as the study of social representations Moscovici hopes to resocialize many of these key theoretical terms. Jaspars and Fraser (1984) have already worked out how attitudes and social representations relate to each other. In the course of this chapter I attempt to do the same for opinions and social representations. Both opinions and social representations are instances of what the editors of this book call 'widespread beliefs'.

Social representations and the nature of public opinion

In his 1963 review of research on attitudes and opinions for the *Annual Review of Psychology*, Moscovici expressed the hope that, one day, the concept of social representation would replace those of opinion or image '. . . which are relatively static and descriptive' (Moscovici 1963, p. 252). It is reasonable to infer from this comment that Moscovici, even then, regarded his theory of social representations as being both dynamic and explanatory. He lamented, in the work he reviewed, 'the . . . the lack of a[ny] major theoretical drive toward a new approach to the understanding of reality' (ibid., p. 231). The reality to which Moscovici here refers comprises social, physical, and cultural reality. His own theory is very much within a realist tradition of thought, that is, he advocates the sampling of culture as well as of cognition; of the media as well as of minds; and of objects as well as of subjects. He has produced, as a consequence, a form of social psychology that is ecologically valid, in the full Brunswikian sense of that term, for a particular culture at a particular time. For Moscovici and his associates stereotypes are in the media as well as being in people's minds. They are in the one because they are in the other.

He was impatient, in writing his review, with the many studies he was expected to include that merely reported the results of public opinion polls. He grouped his review of these under the general rubric of 'information gathering'. He expressed the view that '. . . public opinion research would appear to be one of the blind alleys of our science' (ibid., p. 236). He heartily endorsed the view of Albig concerning the past 20 years of opinion research, namely, that 'Methodological refinement has been associated with an atrophy of theoretical thinking' (ibid., p. 236).

Whilst Moscovici himself is very interested in the popularization of science, he was rather scathing in the remarks he made concerning some of the studies he reviewed:

'Science will not gain much through learning that in Minneapolis 12 per cent of the people interviewed link centrifugal force and gravitation. To understand the impact on the public of the spread of scientific and technological knowledge, and the upheaval this implies at linguistic, intellectual, cultural, and symbolic levels, requires other methods than those currently used and other theoretical approaches' (ibid., p. 234).

The alternative methods and theories which Moscovici had in mind in 1963 are now more widely in evidence, three decades later, as a knowledge of French research on social representations diffuses beyond the boundaries of its country of origin (Farr 1987).

There are some critics of the theory of social representations who claim that 'collective representations' are nothing but 'representations' in the minds of the collectivity of individuals who comprise a community. Harré (1985), in his otherwise highly favourable review of the Farr and Moscovici (1984a) volume, makes a distinction between two different meanings of the adjective 'social' when it qualifies 'representation'.

'Something may be social because it is distributively realised in a group, that is each member has "it" but the "it" that each member has is like the "it" of every other individual member. But something may be social because it is collectively realised in a group. For instance, each member may have part of what is required, but the "it" does not come into existence until the group comes together, intercommunicates, assigns roles and rights of display and so on' (Harré 1985).

Harré clearly prefers the latter formulation and he is not convinced that the chapters in the Farr and Moscovici volume, with the possible exception of Jodelet's chapter on changes in the representation of the human body, go much beyond the former formulation. I do not agree that this is an entirely valid criticism but I do agree with Harré that researchers within this tradition ought to be much more explicit in their espousal of the version of 'social' preferred by Harré. Jodelet's reference, in her definition (see above), to the generative mechanisms that lie at the heart of a social representation adequately covers this point, in my opinion.

If Moscovici had been in favour of the 'distributive' notion of collective representations why, then, would he have been so critical of the barrenness of 'mere' public opinion polling? Polling is, par excellence, a sampling of the distribution of opinion within a population of humans. I also think it is clear, in the writings of the 'French school', that representations *are* formed through the very act of communicating, i.e. they are very strongly in favour of the approach advocated by Harré. Moscovici (1961/1976), in his pioneering study of psychoanalysis, for example, noted that when a scientist's notion of reality is made public *then* it becomes a proper object of study for the social psychologist. He was referring, here, to the formulation of a new scientific theory, i.e. psychoanalysis. Elsewhere Moscovici (1984) quoted, with evident approval, Tristan Tzara. 'We think through our mouths.' This compares with the view expressed by the American pragmatist philosopher C.S. Peirce, 'How do I know what I think until I hear myself speak?'. Clearly, then, both for Moscovici and his associates, representations *are* formed through the act of communicating. This, of course, is also the mechanism whereby they become realized collectively.

I think it is fruitful, in this context, to look at the conflict between F.H. Allport (1937) and Herbert Blumer (1948) concerning the nature of public opinion. Allport was strongly in favour of public opinion polling because it accurately reflected his own methodological and theoretical stance in relation to collective phenomena:

'The term public opinion is given its meaning with reference to a multi-individual situation in which individuals are expressing themselves, or can be called upon to express themselves, as favouring or supporting (or else disfavouring or opposing) some definite condition, person or proposal of widespread importance, in such a proportion of number, intensity, and constancy, as to give rise to the probability of affecting action, directly or indirectly, toward the object concerned' (Allport 1937, p. 22).

This is clearly equivalent to Harré's distributive notion of a collective representation. Blumer's critique of public opinion polling is very similar to the one advanced by Moscovici (1963) which was cited at the beginning of this paper:

'. . . those trying to study public opinion polling are so wedded to their technique and so preoccupied with the improvements of their technique that they shunt aside the vital question of whether their technique is suited to the study of what they are ostensibly seeking to study' (Blumer 1948, p. 543).

It is the phenomenon of public opinion that is important, not how it is gauged.

Blumer argues that individuals are not alike in their power to influence public opinion. His discussion of how public opinion forms is similar to Moscovici's ideas on minority influence. 'In so far as public opinion is *effective* on societal action it becomes so only by entering into the purview of whoever, like legislators, executives, administrators, and policy makers, have to act on public opinion' (Blumer 1948, p. 545). Blumer's views about the formation of public opinion are likely to be acceptable to Harré and yet they are also comparable to Moscovici's own views. It is difficult to tell whether it is Moscovici or Blumer who is the more critical and scathing in his attack on 'mere' opinion polling.

'In my judgement the inherent deficiency of public opinion polling, certainly as currently done, is contained in its sampling procedure. Its current sampling procedure forces a treatment of society as if society were only an aggregation of disparate individuals' (Blumer).

Blumer accepts, however, that *voters* constitute a population of disparate individuals. Success in predicting the outcome of elections is hailed, then, as a vindication of the techniques of opinion polling. This, however, is an inadequate model of how public opinion *forms* and here, I am sure, Moscovici would agree. The study of social representations is highly germane to an understanding of how public opinion forms and changes. It is, after all, directly concerned with the study of common-sense knowledge.

Allport and Blumer are not as irreconcilable in their views as, at first sight, they might appear to be. Allport is interested in gauging public opinion and Blumer in identifying how it forms. An issue arises, in some sphere of public life, which cannot be resolved on the basis of precedent or tradition. Hence it becomes an 'issue'. People within the 'public' are divided in their opinion as to how to act and, hence, they debate the issue in public. Interested parties identify themselves and adopt their own, often highly partisan, stances. Each interested party appeals to a wider public and seeks to gain new recruits to their cause. Some premium is placed, in the public debate, on the use of 'rational arguments' and on the production of 'facts' and of evidence. An appeal is made to a wider, disinterested, public who are as yet uncommitted in regard to the particular issue. Opinions are divided. In the course of debate the number of alternative courses of action is whittled down, perhaps, to a choice between two or three possible alternatives.

One can assume, once an issue has been well 'aired' or 'ventilated' in the mass media of communication, that many people, then, have an 'opinion' about it. At this late stage in the process it might be sensible to sample these opinions. F.H. Allport could claim, with some justice, that this was what he meant by describing the issue as of 'widespread importance' in his definition of public opinion. Billig (1987), in his rhetorical approach to social psychology, shows how thinking and arguing are two intimately inter-related social activities. The arguments that, in the public debate, exist at the level of the community are also reflected in the attitudes of the individual participants (Billig 1988). Billig's view is compatible, in my opinion, with the views of Blumer and of Moscovici on the nature of public opinion.

This description of how public opinion forms reflects the experience of journalists and of others who work within the mass media of communication. It concerns, in particular, the role of the newspapers. Much of it stems from the seminal thesis which Park submitted at Heidelberg, in 1904, on *Masse und Publikum* (Park 1972). Park was a professional journalist who played a key role in the development of social science at Chicago. He distinguished between the mass, the crowd, and the public as comprising different types of human aggregate. Blumer took over and developed many of Park's ideas (Blumer 1946). This was the more 'rational' response of social scientists to the apparent 'irrationalism' of the early work of Le Bon and others concerning the psychology of crowds and of Tarde and others on the laws of imitation. It was this earlier tradition of collective psychology which had led to the classic link, within psychology, between abnormal and social psychology (reflected in the *Journal of Abnormal and Social Psychology*, the *British Journal of Social and Clinical Psychology*, etc.). Once an issue has been well aired it might make sense, then, to conduct an opinion poll. Blumer, quite cogently, argues that the public is always divided, engages in debate, and is always striving towards, but never quite achieves, a consensus. He also, rightly, points out that the opinions of some people carry more weight than those of others and that, when it comes to *acting on the basis of public opinion*, people, most certainly, are unequal in their power to influence events. Polling can have an important role to play but the timing of the poll is crucial.

Roiser (1987) is the only person to my knowledge who addresses directly the issue of the relationship between social representations and public opinion. Moscovici (1984) drew a sharp distinction between common-sense knowledge and scientific knowledge. He recalled a time when the latter was derived from the former. Now, he thinks the latter is more often the basis of the former, i.e. we need to be able to represent, in common-sense terms, important scientific phenomena. In the same article Moscovici had contrasted the 'reified universes', in which most research scientists live, with the 'consensual universes' inhabited by most lay people. Social representations, he believed, were to be located in the consensual universe. What Roiser has done is to trace the transition, in the 1930s, from common sense to science in how public opinion is gauged and then to trace the later transition, in the reverse direction, from the 'science' of public opinion polling to its popular representation in the mass media of communication. Whilst this is an important start, much remains to be done in relating social representations to the study of public opinion. This chapter is intended as a further contribution to the same end.

French writers are strangely silent on the all-important topic of how they came to choose the object of their study. There is a great deal of skill in choosing *which* social representation to investigate. Which social representations are worth studying? Here the nature of public opinion may be important. The two candidates for Moscovici's original study were Marxism and psychoanalysis. A knowledge of both had diffused fairly widely in France in the aftermath of World War II. It would, therefore, be possible to pick up 'representations' of the object of study at many different levels within French society and French culture. Whilst France was still nominally a Catholic country, Marxism and psychoanalysis were much more akin to secular religions in terms of the numbers of adherents they attracted. It is interesting to note, however, that a certain percentage of Moscovici's sample of 'workers' did not have any very clear representations of psychoanalysis. The original study was of psychoanalysis. Now, more than a quarter of a century later, Moscovici is studying the social representation of Marxism in contemporary France. Other major studies in France have included the social representation of health and illness; of childhood; of towns and cities; of 'culture' in relation to workers; of the role of women in society; and of changes, over time, in the representation of the human body. These were all social issues which had been well ventilated in the mass media of communication prior to their becoming objects of empirical investigation.

I think the field studies within this French tradition of research are fine examples of what Gergen had in mind when he described social psychology as being history rather than science (Gergen 1973). In these field studies the French are careful to sample and to analyse the information circulating in society concerning the object of their study, i.e. they treat seriously the role of the media in the formation of public opinion. Stereotypes are in the media as well as being in people's minds. An analysis of the contents of the mass media is a distinctive feature of this particular tradition of research in social psychology. French social psychologists are as much concerned with the *formation* of opinion as they are with its *assessment*. Whilst judicious use is made, in the major studies, of opinion polling, the study is a great deal more than just enumerating the *distribution* of individual opinions within the collectivity of individuals comprising the sample or the community. This is why I feel that Harré's critique is slightly wide of the mark and that, basically, there is not as much of a disagreement between himself and Moscovici as he imagines.

Social representations and attitudes

Jaspars and Fraser (1984) comment, with some justice, that the distinctly social nature of 'representations' is not at all clear from the way in which Moscovici first introduced the idea to the English-speaking world:

'If he had used Durkheim's term or had referred to Durkheim's publications on individual and collective representations it would have been evident that what is social about social representations is not that such representations are representations of social reality, or that they are social in origin, but that they are social because they are shared by many individuals and as such constitute a social reality which can influence individual behaviour' (Jaspars and Fraser 1984, p. 104).

Jaspars and Fraser, in what I regard as a seminal paper, give substance to the hope, expressed by Moscovici in 1963, that one day 'social representations would replace the concepts of opinions and attitudes'. They do so in a highly interesting manner. They argue that, if one goes back to the classic study, by Thomas and Znaniecki (1918–20), of *The Polish peasant in Europe and America* then attitudes were, in those days, 'collective representations'. This was true both in theory and in research practice. In their study Thomas and Znaniecki sought to identify the problems that were specific to immigrants from rural Poland as they adjusted to life in metropolitan America. The contrast, therefore, was between the 'values' which were inherent in the dominant American culture and the 'social attitudes' of Polish Americans. For Thomas and Znaniecki, therefore, '. . . attitudes differentiate primarily *between groups* and not between members of the same group' (Jaspars and Fraser 1984, p. 116).

Jaspars and Fraser then proceed to demonstrate how the commonly used techniques for the assessment of attitudes imply a common cognitive representation of the object of study. This representation is almost certainly social both in its nature and in its origins. This is clearly true in regard to Guttman scaling. It is also important, from a historical point of view, because classic techniques for the scaling of attitudes were developed, in the context of social science, at Chicago. Thurstone, of course, was familiar with the distinction between 'values' (more like 'collective representations') and 'social attitudes' (the more subjective side of culture) which, as Jaspars and Fraser note, was being developed, at Chicago, by Thomas and Znaniecki in their study of *The Polish peasant*. In constructing his scales, Thurstone employed a panel of judges in order to determine the scale values of the various statements of opinion in his initial pool of items. As Jaspars and Fraser argue, this was a tacit recognition on his part that attitudes were a form of 'social representation'. Thurstone also conducted a trawl of the mass media of communication in search of a large, initial pool of statements of opinion. Here he was concerned with how the 'object' of the attitude scale he was devising was 'represented' in the media, e.g. divorce, the Church, war and peace, etc. Modern French social psychologists, studying social representations, are similarly interested in a trawl of the mass media.

Jaspars and Fraser then proceed, in their seminal article, to identify Gordon Allport as being the person principally responsible for transforming attitudes from being 'collective representations' (in the sense studied by Thomas and Znaniecki) to being merely 'individual representations'. He achieved this in the course of his, now classic, chapter on attitude for the 1935 Murchison *Handbook of social psychology*. They demonstrate how he progressively 'edited out' the social and collective components in the various definitions of attitude that he considered in the course of his chapter before he arrived at his own definition. He defined an attitude as a predisposition, on the part of the individual, to respond to certain aspects of the environment in a particular way. I think this analysis, by Jaspars and Fraser, is an extremely valuable contribution to the process of resocializing certain key theoretical terms in social psychology. It is important, in my view, to identify precisely *when* and *how* certain key theoretical concepts in social psychology ceased to be social and became, instead, mainly 'individual' concepts. Graumann (1986) has carried out a similar analysis of the contribution to the development of social psychology of Floyd Allport, the brother of Gordon. In his analysis of F.H. Allport's classic textbook of 1924, Graumann has argued that the individualization of the social goes hand in hand with the desocialization of the individual.

Moscovici has been a persistent critic of the purely individual nature of much 'so-called' *social* psychology. In his theory of social representations Moscovici set out with the deliberate intention of 'renewing' the whole of social psychology. He aimed to make social psychology an explicitly social discipline. My only quibble with this ambition is: Why stop with the renewal of social psychology? Why not demonstrate that it is psychology—and not just social psychology—that is the social discipline? This may involve one, as Jaspars and Fraser have demonstrated so ably, in the task of retracing the recent development of the discipline. This can lead to the discovery that, in the past, many of the key theoretical terms in social psychology were more explicitly social than they have been in the past half century of research. Moscovici helped to set this fashion. For some of his key theoretical terms he returned to the writings of such founders of French social science as Durkheim, Tarde, and Le Bon. Such retro-revolutions could well become fashionable (Moscovici 1981).

Culture and cognition

In recent years there has been a growing rapprochment between psychology and anthropology. Michael Cole, almost uniquely amongst American psychologists, has appreciated for quite some time the value of such a rapprochment (Cole and Scribner 1974; Cole and Means 1981). The link between culture and cognition, which was quite explicit in the social psychologies of Wundt, Mead, and Bartlett, has been much better preserved in Soviet psychology than it has been in the psychologies of other European countries or of America. This is due primarily to the continuing influence of Vygotsky in Soviet psychology. Now that psychology is well established as a major cognitive science in these other countries, the rapprochment can proceed apace. American cognitive psychologists were slow, however, to assimilate Piaget. That he was eventually assimilated was due, mainly, to the efforts of Bruner at Harvard in the late 1950s in establishing, jointly with Miller, the Centre for Cognitive Studies. Cognitive theorists in America have been even slower to assimilate Vygotsky. Had they previously taken into account the work of the American philosopher, G.H. Mead, then it would have been comparatively simple for them also to have taken on board the work of Vygotsky. Vygotsky was much more explicitly social and cultural in his treatment of cognition than was Piaget. If Moscovici's theory of social representations were to be accepted generally, then this would greatly accelerate the rapprochment between psychology and anthropology.

Moscovici, in his Foreword to *Indigenous psychologies: the anthropology of the self* edited by Heelas and Lock, states:

'The combination of social psychology and anthropology is for me a symbol and an event. I have been waiting for this for too long not to be overjoyed at seeing it taking shape at last. From time to time what may be called 'retro-revolutions' are observable in the sciences. These are returns to the past—back to problems, ideas or methods which have been forgotten or even banished. They unveil for us a whole aspect of reality which has been neglected, another mode of thought. As a result, an entire field of research is reactivated in what amounts to a revolution' (Moscovici 1981, p. vii).

Jahoda (1982), in his book *Psychology and anthropology*, devotes a whole chapter to a discussion of 'collective representations'. He notes how the links between psychology and anthropology, which go back to the very early days of the emergence of psychology as a distinct discipline, were much closer, then, than were the links between psychology and any other social science.

Jahoda claims that there is no *simple* relationship between collective representations and individual thinking. He warns against making inferences about the thinking of individuals on the basis of an analysis of such collective representations as myths etc. It would be foolish, for example, to jump from a Levi-Straussian analysis of myth to the assumption that individuals think in terms of binary opposites. This is not to deny, however, that the work of Levi-Strauss is important:

'When Durkheim coined the expression "collective representations"—which of course includes myths—he was concerned to show that these played an important role in the regulation and maintenance of social systems and the work of Levi-Strauss may be regarded as an elaboration of this tradition' (Jahoda 1982, p. 226).

Whilst Jahoda remains suitably sceptical about the empirical evidence for the theories of Levi-Strauss '. . . yet it would be foolish to deny any connection between ideas and beliefs held in common by a group of people and their thinking' (p. 236). Jahoda (1988) is also highly critical of the whole notion of 'social representations'. He highlights what he believes to be contradictions and ambiguities in the notion. Moscovici (1988) has responded, in some detail, to these criticisms.

Myth appears in a number of guises in the French tradition of research on social representations. Chombart de Lauwe (1971/78) argues, on the basis of her extensive empirical studies of the social representations of childhood, that they add up to a myth concerning the nature of the child, i.e. that the child lives in 'a world apart'—a world that can be understood only in terms of its contrast to the world of the adult. It was, presumably, one strand in this myth—the sexual innocence of the child—that Freud exploded when he published his essays concerning the nature of childhood sexuality. Jodelet (1989), in her participant observational study of the social representations of mental illness in a rural setting, reports on the re-emergence, in modern France, of myths concerning the contagious nature of mental illness. These myths were widely prevalent, in France, in the Middle Ages. Morin (1969), in his study of the rumours that circulated in Orleans concerning the supposed spiriting away of young girls and their re-emergence in the harems of North Africa as part of the white slave trade identifies, fairly precisely, the anti-semitic nature of the rumours. These modern rumours are very comparable to the anti-semitic myths that once circulated in the region of Orleans in the Middle Ages (Zukier 1987).

There is increasing evidence of this rapprochment between psychology and anthropology. Sperber's contribution to this volume is an interesting pointer to this trend. Shortly after I joined the London School of Economics I gave a seminar in the Department of Anthropology on social representations. The first question I was asked was: 'Is this a form of social psychology in which the *contents* of people's beliefs are treated as being important?'. When I replied in the affirmative my questioner then commented that this research would be of interest to anthropologists. In his Malinowski lecture at the London School of Economics, Sperber (1985) proposed that psychologists and anthropologists ought to collaborate in the study of what he called 'the epidemiology of representations'.

Sperber claimed that the human mind is susceptible to cultural representations in much the same way as the human organism is susceptible to disease. He points out that 'widely distributed, long-lasting representations are what we are primarily referring to when we talk of culture'. He goes on to pose the interesting question, 'Why are some representations more successful in a human population, more contagious, more catching than others?' The answer is to be found in the *distribution* of representations within a society—hence the need for an epidemiology of representations.

'. . . some (representations) are slowly transmitted over generations; they are what we call traditions and are comparable to endemics; other representations, typical of modern cultures, spread rapidly throughout a whole population but have a short life-span; they are what we call fashions and are comparable to epidemics.'

The former type of representation corresponds to Durkheim's concept of 'collective representations'; the latter to Moscovici's concept of 'social representations'.

Sperber contrasts the transmission of infectious diseases, which are characterized by the *replication* of viruses or bacteria, with the transmission of representations. 'Representations, on the other hand, tend to be *transformed* each time they are transmitted' (emphasis added). This is one possible meaning of the adjective 'social' when it qualifies 'representation'. There is, of course, a *mechanical* or *electronic* reproduction of representations in the mass media of communication—this was the original meaning of the term 'stereotype' in regard to print. This *is* relevant to the distribution of representations within human populations. Here the representation is 'collective' in the sense that there are *multiple* copies of it. It might make sense for us to rehabilitate the term 'stereotype' to cover this particular usage, i.e. multiple *identical* copies of the representation. This is entirely consistent with the realist view of science espoused by those researching social representations. As mentioned earlier, stereotypes are in the media as well as being in people's minds and this is why an analysis of the contents of the mass media often forms an integral part of any field study of a social representation. Equally, we can consider the notion of 'transmission' as being equivalent to 'broadcast'. Whilst this does not denote *multiple* copies of the representation it does relate both to the transmission and to the *distribution* of opinions and beliefs within human populations. Whilst the existence of multiple copies of a representation is probably related to its temporal transmission, broadcasting is almost certainly related to its spatial transmission. It is Sperber's emphasis on the transmission and transformation of representations that makes them inherently social phenomena in the sense intended by Moscovici. At the collective level, representations correspond to culture.

On the basis of Sperber's paper and his chapter in this volume there is ample scope for collaboration between psychologists and anthropologists in the study both of representations and of their distributions. 'What pathology is to the epidemiology of diseases, the psychology of thought should be to the epidemiology of representations.' In pursuing the analogy of epidemiology Sperber suggests that 'Psychology is necessary but not sufficient for the characterization and the explanation of cultural phenomena. Cultural phenomena are ecological patterns of psychological phenomena'. Sperber's ideas should be compulsory reading for anyone interested in social representations. They are highly suggestive of the benefits that might flow from a closer collaboration between psychologists and anthropologists.

'Representation' is now one of the hottest theoretical terms in mainstream psychological research. It is important that social psychologists demonstrate to their non-social colleagues in experimental psychology that something significant is added when the adjective 'social' qualifies the term 'representation'. Precisely what it is that is added is, of course, a legitimate topic for debate and it has been a recurrent theme throughout this chapter. The terms of the debate were set by Harré (1985) in his review of the Farr and Moscovici volume. An important part of the answer, in my opinion, is to be found in the Jaspars and Fraser article that appeared in the volume which Harré reviewed. I have tried to address myself, in this chapter, to the issue raised by Harré. I think the text of Sperber's Malinowski lecture significantly advances the debate and sets the agenda for a much closer collaboration, in the future, between psychologists and anthropologists.

'Culture' should be a vogue topic of research in modern cognitive science. I believe it is back in the laboratory (where it was first introduced by Bartlett in the 1920s) except that cognitive scientists have not yet learned to recognize it for what it is. When I spoke about 'social representations' at a workshop in Oxford organized several years ago by the late Jos Jaspars, Robert Abelson responded to my presentation by saying that he had no difficulty in taking on board the idea of 'collective representations'. They were, in his opinion, equivalent to the scripts, plans, scenarios, etc. of modern cognitive science. That they are fairly pervasive within a culture is now firmly established. It is just that cognitive scientists, at least within psychology, have not been particularly curious to identify why and how they came to assume the form that they do. French research on social representations is likely to shed some useful light on these latter issues.

Instead of talking about 'culture' it is more fashionable, today, to talk about 'common sense' and 'lay explanations' (if you are a social psychologist) or about 'real-world knowledge', 'scripts', 'scenarios', or even 'mental models' (if you are a cognitive theorist). We have returned, almost full circle, to Bartlett and his 1932 book on *Remembering*. It is necessary now, at this remove in time, to recall the subtitle of that work: 'A study in experimental *and* social psychology'. In separating his *experimental* from his *social* psychology, Bartlett was merely following a precedent established by Wundt (Farr 1983). Bartlett is now something of a cult figure amongst cognitive theorists. It is important, in my view, that we do not overlook, in the modern context, the social and cultural dimensions of his thinking. Bartlett did, after all, derive some of his inspiration from the Durkheimian tradition of research in France, for example the work of Halbwachs on 'collective memory'.

James once claimed, in a famous essay, that philosophers and psychologists had located far too many 'things' in consciousness that ought, properly, to be restored to the external world of objects, etc. The same, now, is probably true of memory. Halbwachs, very much in the Durkheimian tradition, showed how memories are socially maintained through ceremonial (and custom) which is re-enacted at regular intervals. A great deal of memory is collectively maintained and socially transmitted rather than being inscribed in the tracts of the brain. As Mead (1934) noted a long time ago, it is the act rather than the tract that is important. Work on social representations is highly relevant to the study of memory. It is primarily concerned with showing how the strange or novel becomes assimilated to the familiar (Moscovici 1984). The familiar and the memorable are, indeed, closely related. Bartlett (1932) was concerned with studying these same processes when he traced the successive distortions that occurred in the myth about 'The war of the ghosts' when it was transmitted, serially, from one Cambridge student to another in the 1920s.

Social representation and the sociology of knowledge

In recent years Moscovici and his coworkers have described, fairly consistently, their research as the study of 'social representations'. They are not claiming to study 'collective representations' in the full Durkheimian sense of that term (Durkheim 1898). Whilst sociologists and anthropologists are well-qualified to identify *which* representations are worth studying within a particular culture or society it is best, in the opinion of Moscovici, to leave the empirical study of these representations to the social psychologist. There has been much written, for example, in the sociology of knowledge concerning the importance of studying ideology, yet there have been precious few empirical studies of exactly how an ideology operates. (See Scarbrough's chapter in this volume.)

Moscovici and his coworkers can claim, quite legitimately, to have carried out many empirical studies of social representations. His initial study was of psychoanalysis; his current study is of Marxism. Recently, in *The age of the crowd*, Moscovici (1985) has explored, through a reconstruction of the social psychology of Le Bon, how political leaders 'represent' (in their own minds) the 'masses' they lead. There, Moscovici distinguishes between those sciences (such as collective psychology and political economy) which themselves create history and those other sciences (the majority) that are created by history.

Durkheim's model of society was far too static and traditional to be directly applicable to most modern societies which, by contrast, are highly dynamic and fluid. This is why it is much more appropriate to talk of 'social', rather than of 'collective', representations. Sperber's suggestion about studying the epidemiology of representations allows one to capture the highly nuanced difference between traditional and modern cultures. Moscovici does not accept the social determinism of classic Durkheimian theory. He is, in this respect, much closer to the social psychology of Gabriel Tarde, one of the other founding fathers of French social science. Whilst Tarde, perhaps, is best known for drawing the attention of social psychologists to the key role of imitation in social influence he also stressed the importance of invention and of creativity. Individuals are often the *agents* of change in society. Once an innovation has occurred, then, the laws of imitation might help to account for the distinctive pattern of its adoption. This links up with Sperber's ideas about the transmission of representations.

The clear opposition between the views of Tarde and those of Durkheim emerged in the course of their heated debate in Paris in 1903–4. Moscovici, in his various laboratory studies of minority influence, has established this phase of the social influence process on a much sounder empirical footing. His various case studies of how the ideas of Freud and those of Marx reverberate within contemporary French society and culture are examples of that alternative approach to studying the impact of science to which he alluded in his 1963 *Annual Review* article. Over the years that I have known him, Moscovici has maintained, quite consistently, that social representations are more basic, or operate at a more profound level, than mere attributions. The reasons why he is right are to be found in a little-known monograph which Ichheiser published in 1949, entitled *Misunderstandings in human relations: a study in false social perception* (Ichheiser 1949). The monograph is of considerable theoretical importance in relation to research on social representations (Farr and Moscovici 1984*b*). It was written within a framework of the sociology of knowledge.

For Ichheiser the sources of misunderstanding are to be found in ideology and in collective representations:

'The misinterpretations which consist in underestimating the importance of situational and in overestimating the importance of personal factors, do not arise by chance. *These misinterpretations are not personal errors committed by ignorant individuals.* They are, rather, *a consistent and inevitable consequence of the social system and of the ideology of the nineteenth century*, which led us to believe that our fate in social space depended exclusively, or at least predominantly, on our individual qualities—that we, as individuals, and not the prevailing social conditions, shape our lives' (Ichheiser 1943, p. 152).

The collective representation of individuals as being responsible for their own actions in life is taken over, but in a somewhat modified form, by

Heider (1958) when he discusses attributions concerning 'success' and 'failure'. Heider, similarly, stresses 'intentionality' as being a peculiarly human characteristic. Ichheiser, much more explicitly than Heider, treats this model of man as being a social (or even a collective) representation in the full Durkheimian sense of the term. The antidote to the social impoverishment of much contemporary work in attribution theory is to reinstate Ichheiser and to study *social representations* as they operate in the social world outside of the laboratory. Ichheiser's observations, in Vienna in the aftermath of the Depression (and, later, in America), have an uncannily modern ring about them:

'With millions of people suffering from the shocks of continued unemployment, with business failures one after the other, banks closing, etc., it was vividly revealed to the man in the street that he was not, as he had been led to believe, the master of his fate, because clearly his fate depended upon forces over which he had no control' (Ichheiser 1949, p. 62).

There is evidence, here, of a powerful collective representation at work which continues to operate even when it is no longer appropriate that it should. The inertial force is that of culture. There is quite a dramatic difference between the study of individual representations, as outlined earlier in this chapter, and the study of the individual as a collective representation, as outlined in this final section. Durkheim (1898) was content to leave the former for the psychologist to investigate. Individual representations can be sampled by means of opinion polling. The individual as a collective representation, however, is a *cultural* phenomenon and this is something altogether different (Farr 1990). In those cultures where it is very highly developed, as it is for example in America, it can even exert an influence on the development of the social sciences so that, through its baleful influence, inherently social concepts, such as social attitudes and ideology, can become individualized.

References

Allport, F.H. (1937). Towards a science of public opinion. *Public Opinion Quarterly*, **1**, 7–23.
Bartlett, F.C. (1932). *Remembering: a study in experimental and social psychology*. Cambridge University Press.
Billig, M. (1987). *Arguing and thinking: a rhetorical approach to social psychology*. Cambridge University Press.
Billig, M. (1988). Rhetorical and historical aspects of attitudes: The case of the British monarchy. *Philosophical Psychology*, **1**, 1, 83–103.
Blumer, H. (1946). The mass, the public and public opinion. In *New Outline of the Principles of Sociology* (ed. A.McC. Lee). Barnes and Noble, New York.
Blumer, H. (1948). Public opinion and public opinion polling. *American Sociological Review*, **13**, 542–54.

Chombart de Lauwe, M.J. (1971/78). *Un monde autre: l'enfance. De ses représentations à son mythe*. Payot, Paris.

Cole, M. and Scribner, S. (1974). *Culture and thought: a psychological introduction*. Wiley, New York.

Cole, M. and Means, B. (1981). *Comparative studies of how people think*. Harvard University Press, Cambridge, Mass.

Durkheim, E. (1898). Représentations individuelles et représentations collectives. *Revue de Metaphysique et de Morale*, **VI**, 272–302.

Farr, R.M. (1983). Wilhelm Wundt (1832–1920) and the origins of psychology as an experimental and social science. *The British Journal of Social Psychology*, **22**, 4, 289–301.

Farr, R.M. (1987). Social representations: a French tradition of research. *Journal for The Theory of Social Behaviour*, **17**, 4, 3–29.

Farr, R.M. (1990). Individualism as a collective representation. In *Idéologie et représentations sociales* (ed. J.P. Deconchy). Delval, Cousset (Suisse).

Farr, R.M. and Moscovici, S. (eds) (1984*a*). *Social representations*. Cambridge University Press.

Farr, R.M. and Moscovici, S. (1984*b*). On the nature and role of representations in self's understanding of others and of self. In *Progress in Person Perception* (ed. M. Cook). Methuen, London.

Gergen, K.J. (1973). Social psychology as history. *Journal of Personality and Social Psychology*, **26**, 2, 309–20.

Graumann, C. (1986). The individualisation of the social and the desocialisation of the individual: Floyd H. Allport's contribution to social psychology. In *Changing conceptions of crowd mind and behaviour* (ed. C.F. Graumann and S. Moscovici). Springer Verlag, New York.

Harré, R. (1985). Review of R.M. Farr and S. Moscovici (eds). *Social representations*. Cambridge University Press. *British Journal of Psychology*, **76**, 138–40.

Heider, F. (1958). *The psychology of inter-personal relations*. Wiley, New York.

Herzlich, C. (1972). La représentation sociale. In *Introduction à la psychologie sociale*, Volume 1 (ed. S. Moscovici). Librairie Larousse, Paris.

Ichheiser, G. (1943). Misinterpretations of personality in everyday life and the psychologist's frame of reference. *Character and Personality*, **12**, 145–60.

Ichheiser, G. (1949). Misunderstandings in human relations: a study in false social perception. *American Journal of Sociology Monographs*. University of Chicago Press.

Jahoda, G. (1982). *Psychology and anthropology: a psychological perspective*. Academic Press, London.

Jahoda, G. (1988). Critical notes and reflections on 'social representations'. *European Journal of Social Psychology*, **18**, 195–209.

Jaspars, J. and Fraser, C. (1984). Attitudes and social representations. In *Social representations* (ed. R.M. Farr and S. Moscovici). Cambridge University Press.

Jodelet, D. (1988). Représentations sociales: phénomènes, concept et théorie. In *Psychologie sociale* (2nd edition) (ed. S. Moscovici). Presses Universitaires de France, Paris.

Jodelet, D. (1989). *Folies et représentations sociales*. Press Universitaires de France, Paris.

Mead, G.H. (1934). *Mind, self and society: from the standpoint of a social behavi-ourist*. Edited, with an introduction, by C.W. Morris. University of Chicago Press.

Morin, E. (1969). *La rumeur d'Orleans*. Editions du Seuil, Paris.

Moscovici, S. (1961/1976). *La psychoanalyse: son image et son public*. Presses Universitaires de France, Paris.

Moscovici, S. (1963). Attitudes and opinions. *Annual Review of Psychology*, 231–60.

Moscovici, S. (1981). Foreword to P. Heelas and A. Lock (eds) *Indigenous psycho-logies: the anthropology of the self*. Academic Press, London.

Moscovici, S. (1984). The phenomenon of social representations. In *Social repres-entations* (ed. R.M. Farr and S. Moscovici). Cambridge University Press.

Moscovici, S. (1985). *The age of the crowd*. Cambridge University Press.

Moscovici, S. (1988). Notes towards a description of social representations. *European Journal of Social Psychology*, **18–3**, 211–50.

Park, R.E. (1972). *The crowd and the public and other essays*. University of Chicago Press.

Roiser, M. (1987). Commonsense, science and public opinion. *Journal for The Theory of Social Behaviour*, **17**, 71–91.

Sperber, D. (1985). Anthropology and psychology: towards an epidemiology of representations. *Man* (New Series), **1**, 73–89.

Thomas, W.I. and Znaniecki, F. (1918–20). *The Polish peasant in Europe and America*, 5 volumes. Gorham Press, Boston.

Zukier, H. (1987). The conspiratorial imperative: Medieval Jewry in Western Europe. In *Changing conceptions of conspiracy* (ed. C.F. Graumann and S. Moscovici). Springer-Verlag, New York.

4 Attitudes, social attitudes, and widespread beliefs

Douglas W. Bethlehem

The purpose of this chapter, to adopt for a moment L.L. Thurstone's blunt and forthright style, is to consider whether the concept 'attitude' provides a sufficient structure for the study of widespread beliefs. Ancillary to this major question are a look at what psychology already knows about widespread beliefs, and a consideration of what psychology can peculiarly offer in relation to widespread beliefs and how psychology might approach their study in the future. The first substantive issue to address, then, is the nature of a widespread belief.

Widespread beliefs

This term is not yet a well-defined one, either operationally or conceptually. Clearly, for a *social* science, particularly the study of social psychology, some such concept is of great potential importance. What related concepts have been used in social psychology or allied studies? Four major concepts come to mind: from anthropology, the concept *myth*; from sociology, the concept *norm*; from the sociological side of social psychology, the concept *social representation*; and from the psychological side of social psychology, the concept *stereotype*. These are not, of course, the only concepts that might have been chosen from these fields, but each is an important concept, each is well identified with the field from which it has been chosen and typifies in some respects concepts used in that field.

Myth

'Myth' has a long pedigree in anthropology. Most social and cultural anthropologists today follow Malinowski's sociological analysis of myth as stories and beliefs, usually traditional, which have the function of explaining such universal mysteries as the origin of the earth, justifying cultural practices, and sanctioning certain behaviours. 'Myth is . . . an indispensable ingredient of all culture . . . Myth is a constant by-product of living faith, which is in need of miracles; of sociological status, which demands precedent; of moral rule, which requires sanction' (Malinowski 1925/1974,

p. 146). When the term 'myth' is used today, nothing is implied about whether or not the belief is true.

What myths might we identify, by way of illustration, in modern British society? This question brings us to the shortcoming of the concept: there is nothing approaching an operational definition. Anthropologists in the classical mould might identify myths in a simple society, and no one is in much of a position to gainsay them. The western intellectuals to whom their reports will be addressed are unlikely to know much about 'their' society, and the members of that society are unlikely to read the reports. More to the point, the society is likely to be a simple one, with—given the right informant—a fairly clear body of myths ready to hand. Dealing with a society undergoing rapid social change, or a complex modern society, may prove more problematic. No myth in a complex society is likely to enjoy anything approaching universal acceptance.

A myth—to repeat, nothing is implied about the truth or otherwise of these beliefs—of recent provenance in Britain, and one which is probably waning rapidly as this is written, is that Britain is a small, over-crowded island, being swamped by non-white immigrants. Another, which may again be waning as Britain loses its imperial self-confidence, is that 'British Justice' is the finest devisable by humankind, or, at least, so fine that it has nothing to learn from any other system. A third, confined probably to a minority, is that Rudyard Kipling was a writer only of paeons to the military and imperial establishment and their views. No evidence is offered of the existence of these beliefs or of their widespread nature. The reader will either accept as self-evident that they are widespread beliefs or not: reference to a few newspaper articles, popular writings, or reported speeches, will not convince a sceptic. The first mentioned belief charters hostility to non-white persons, immigrant or native-born British, and calls for curbs on immigration and possibly for repatriation; the second charters such diverse practices as remanding people in custody for many months before trial in very unpleasant conditions and the charging of enormous fees by the best-known counsel, and justifies resistance to change in legal practices; and the third charters a refusal to read Kipling's poetry.

Norms

'Norm' is a concept more equally shared by anthropology and sociology. It refers nonspecifically to a way of thinking or behaving that is regarded within a culture as the right way to think or behave, or a very common way, or the ideal way to think or behave. The first two meanings are clearly within the orbit of widespread beliefs, the third perhaps less so. Norms are classically divided into folkways and *mores*, depending on the moral significance with which they are invested. Folkways are simply ways of doing things which everyone does because it is convenient as well as traditional, and most people would accept that it would be sensible to alter them if more convenient ways of doing the same thing were to emerge. *Mores* are more serious matters: Sumner, who popularized the concepts, cites an earlier author, Lazarus, as defining *mores* as ' "usage in any group . . . generally accepted as good and proper, appropriate and worthy" ' (Sumner 1906, p. 60). Examples from our own society of beliefs which are also norms are the belief that it is right to eat meals with a knife and fork and wrong to eat in any other way; another is that the deliberate infliction of physical cruelty is undesirable in virtually any and all circumstances. These examples of norms—respectively a folkway and a *more*—illustrate the lack of clear definition, and total lack of operational definition, of norms.

Social representation

A concept of more recent provenance from the sociological side of social psychology is *social representation*, discussed by Rob Farr in the previous chapter. The conception seems to have originated—as far as English-speaking social psychology is concerned, at any rate—with Moscovici's (1963) article, in which he defined the term as 'the elaborating of a social object by the community for the purpose of behaving and communicating' (p. 251). Alas, as a glance at a series of review and discussion articles in the *British Journal of Social Psychology* (volume 24, Part 2, 1985) will show, the concept has proved somewhat elusive. Different ways of operationalizing it have been tried, but none meets with anything like universal acceptance or application. Indeed the very ontological status of the concept is subject to considerable debate and not a little unedifying confusion; contrast, for example, Moscovici (1985, 1988) with Potter and Litton (1985) and Jahoda (1988).

Stereotype

The concept of stereotype has occupied an important place in the other, psychological, branch of social psychology. Originally used roughly in its current sense by a journalist and 'pundit' (Lippmann 1956), it has been operationally clothed in a variety of ways. Lately, it has joined the ranks of constructs in individual, cognitive social psychology, being redefined operationally by the likelihood ratio

$$P(characteristic \mid ethnic\ group)/P(characteristic)$$

that is, the ratio (in subjective probability) that a particular characteristic pertains to a person *given* that the person belongs to a particular ethnic group, to the subjective probability that any random person in the world has that characteristic (McCauley and Stitt 1978). Earlier, in a classic paper, Katz and Braly (1958; the original version of the paper was published in 1933) had defined the term in a way which may accord with the idea of a social representation. They had presented Princeton students with lists of adjectives, asking them to mark the adjectives pertaining to members of a particular ethnic group (Germans, English people, 'Negroes', etc.), and noting the degree of intersubjective agreement about which adjectives were thought to be characteristic of which groups. For example, 53 per cent of their students characterized the English as 'sportsmanlike', and the same percentage characterized the Italians as 'artistic', and thus it may be taken that the belief that the English are 'sportsmanlike' was widespread, at least within the group of which Katz and Braly's respondents were representative.

Since then, a number of indices which measures the degree of inter-subjective agreement for stereotypes have been proposed. Freund's (1950) has the advantage of varying between 0 and 1, and the one reported by Lambert and Klineberg (1959), apparently evolved by G.A. Ferguson, is not dissimilar, but is independent of the number of adjectives used (they used a free response technique). Hence stereotype in this sense is a concept which can be used with a fair degree of precision: it is essentially a scientific concept.

Reductionism?

Questions commonly agonized over in social studies confront us at this juncture. They are the questions relating to reductionism. Can one discuss apparently more molar concepts and problems as *merely* summations of more molecular ones? The problem has been much agonized over because more molecular concepts have seemed more fundamental and reductionism has been associated with 'science'. A factor in the confusion over the issue has been the lack of clarity over aims: reductionism may lead to more fundamental concepts in some descriptive or structuralist exercise; but reductionism is less alluring when the goal in mind is the orthodox scientific one of achieving a homologous explanation/prediction, or even where common-sense description is involved. A few examples may clarify the points. In a structural or descriptive sense, lightning may *be* nothing but the phenomena of static electricity—the positive and negative charges leaping the gap between clouds—in that the familiar phenomenon of the bright flash of light and the potentially dangerous electrical activity is always accompanied by the charges behaving in a certain way, and the phenomena connected with the charges and those connected with the flash of light and the potentially dangerous electrical activity are invariably simultaneous. Lightning, I repeat, may in some sense *be* nothing but the charges doing their thing. To the builder of lightning conductors, who must predict where lightning is most likely to strike, and the artist who is painting the storm scene, the charges may be an irrelevance: lightning for them is the chance of being electrocuted or burned and the flash of light. Again, money may in some sense *be* the coins, paper debt, gold kept by governments in certain circumstances, etc., but to the man or woman in the street the concept of money is needed as a device for maintaining verbal and cognitive economy, and the economist wishing to predict the consequences of certain arrangements or alterations in the economic system needs the concept *money*. Yet again, conditioning or learning may *be*, in some sense, chemical alterations in neurons, but the man or woman trying to teach a dog or child to avoid a busy street, as well as the psychologist trying to explain and/or predict the change in rats' habits in laboratories, need the concepts of conditioning and learning. In each case, it is partly a question of which level one chooses to focus on: the molecular view may offer present interest and future promise, but one may wish to concentrate on the relatively molar, that is *lightning* (not electrons), *money* (not coins and credit), *conditioning* (not neurochemistry). Science may be regarded as a drive for cognitive economy, just as thought in everyday life is; the cause of economy is not always served by the explosive growth in complexity which reductionism may bring, even though ultimately reductionism may lead to the devising of more economical and simpler laws and predictions. An optimum balance of complexity and explanatory/predictive power must be chosen for *now*; science is a continual striving, and will never reach the ultimate explanation. The question to which we will have to return is, is it worth trying to explain molar widespread beliefs in terms of molecular attitudes?

Attitudes

Attitude is a concept always reckoned to be of vital importance in social psychology, but its history and definition in the context of the question being considered need examination. A broad history of the term is provided in G.W. Allport's classic article (1954), but we need briefly to retrace its development. Like all scientific terms of any longevity, the meaning of 'attitude' has changed as it has developed.

'Attitude' has always been of fundamental importance in social psychology. As Allport remarks, Thomas and Znaniecki, in their monumental study of migrant Poles (1918–1920/1958), were the first to define social psychology as the study of attitudes ('. . . we shall attempt to show that social psychology is precisely the science of attitudes . . .' (Thomas and Znaniecki 1958, p. 27)). Later they comment that '[Social psychology] may claim to be *the* science of consciousness as manifested in culture' (p. 31). Social psychology, for them, deals with attitudes found in virtually all members of a social group (but which differ across social groups), and which show in the social behaviour of the individuals comprising the group. What must be noted is what they mean by the term 'attitude': to them an *attitude* is the intentional counterpart (*within* the individual, as it were) of a 'social value', and a social value is the meaning put upon any socially recognized object or concept (such as '. . . a foodstuff, an instrument, a coin, a piece of poetry, a myth, a university, a scientific theory . . .' (ibid. p. 21)). The modern aspect of their definition is shown by their insistence that an attitude 'determines real or possible activity of the individual in the social world' (ibid. p. 22).

When Thurstone applied the theory of measurement, which he developed in a brilliant series of papers in 1927, to attitudes (Thurstone 1928), he did what all scientists have to do: he oversimplified in the cause of precision. Science has always to balance comprehensiveness with precision, and there will be some who feel that Thurstone erred on the side of the latter. In order to make the concept manageable, he redefined attitude thus: 'Attitude is the affect for or against a psychological object' (1931/1959, p. 297). In doing so, and in providing a means of measuring attitudes grounded in a coherent measurement theory so excellently suited to studying individual differences and so unsuited to studying cultural differences between groups, he drew the attention of social psychology from attitudes as the intentional counterpart of social values to attitudes as another focus of individual differences. With Likert's (1932) paper, attitude measurement and test theory (an aspect of the science sprung from the individual differences tradition) clearly became different aspects of the same thing. Attitudes' place in social psychology and a firm link with Thomas and Znaniecki were maintained by the assumption that attitudes predict or determine behaviour. But, to underline the point, Thomas and Znaniecki were in the line of Ross, whose pioneering textbook—pioneering at least in having the term 'social psychology' in its title (Ross 1908)—defined the task of social psychology as seeking 'to understand and account for those *uniformities* [my emphasis] in feeling, belief, or volition—and hence in action—which are due to the interaction of human beings . . .' (Ross 1908, p. 1), whereas Thurstone and Likert took attitudes into the lineage of Galton and Binet. A conception of 'social attitudes' had been replaced by a more individualistic concept of 'attitude'.

From the first, the new lineage recognized that there were three, presumably correlated, aspects of attitudes, usually referred to in somewhat archaic terms even today: cognitive, affective, and conative. Though the supposed correlation has not always been easy to demonstrate, there is good evidence to suppose the three aspects to be correlated. Some of this evidence is reviewed by Bethlehem (1985). Indeed, stereotypes on the *individual* level may be regarded as the cognitive component of an attitude. It is not surprising, then, that an entry in Harré and Lamb's dictionary of psychology defines prejudice thus: 'Prejudice is therefore, in psychology, an **attitude** which has two aspects: the *cognitive* . . . and the *affective* . . .'

(Harré and Lamb 1983, p. 487; the entry is by Henri Tajfel). No one not totally naive would expect the correlation to be perfect. Attitude is a scientific concept—that is, one designed to explain and predict—and stands by its usefulness in that regard. The prediction of behaviour is less than perfect, and the explanation is imperfectly coherent, but uncertainty about the future is reduced and a measure of attitudes is a major premiss in a fairly coherent argument whose conclusion relates to individual differences in behaviour, and hence the concept is doing its job.

The genesis of attitudes

We turn aside to consider the genesis of attitudes. The consideration of some alternative bases for attitude formation will necessarily be brief.

Constitutional and physiological factors

There are inherited constitutional and physiological factors in the origin and development of attitudes which can be of great importance. The docility of the ox is brought about by a physiological change, and castration may also diminish aggressive behaviour in humans (see, e.g. Moyer 1971). It appears clear that extroversion is heritable to some extent (see, e.g. Scarr and Weinberg 1984) and extroversion implies impulsivity and a tendency to relatively casual minor acts of aggression. Now, attitudes are shaped partly by behaviour (see below), and if a person is aggressive by reason of his or her hormonal levels or his or her extroversion, then he or she is likely to develop a more positive attitude to aggression. One might speculate further, that a negative attitude to the victim of the aggression might also result, through rationalization.

Again, humans have certain in-built tendencies relating to attitudes. Foods with a sweet taste are naturally reinforcing, and hence 'sweet' is a near universal metaphor for positive evaluation (Osgood 1962); it may be that we have an in-built predisposition to feel anxious and afraid at the sight of mutilated bodies of our conspecifics, as chimpanzees apparently do (Hebb and Thompson 1954). Hence the common negative attitude to the direct infliction of severe injury that vies, it seems, with a positive attitude to some of the results of aggression, to yield the ambivalent attitude to agonistic behaviour so prevalent among humans.

Another example along the same lines is that we have an in-built tendency to like things which reinforce our basic drives; whether this tendency operates through the medium of emotional conditioning is a question that need not detain us here. These things become salient when a drive is strong. In the developed world, few people are actually chronically hungry, but the sex drive is, by its nature and the nature of society, almost constantly subject to arousal. Hence, sexually significant stimuli, which frequently

take the form of scantily clad young women of fashionable shape, are used
to attract attention to, and to influence attitudes towards, everything from
chewing gum to motor cars. However, the fantasies of men kept chronically
short of food centre mainly on food, and their attention when looking at
magazines concentrates on food-related items (Keys *et al*. 1950). Hence
we may speculate that in a hungry society cars would be advertised with
hamburgers on their bonnets.

While some of these links are somewhat speculative, this section serves to
show that inherited, constitutional factors do affect attitudes.

Conditioning and learning

Attitudes are, in part, emotional responses, or potential responses, to
objects, and hence it is clear they are subject to conditioning. Emotions
condition rapidly and often do not extinguish; hence in clinical practice
methods like desensitization by reciprocal inhibition have to be used.

Staats and Staats (1958) demonstrated that emotions, and hence attitudes, can be conditioned quite simply to symbolic representations of
objects, i.e. words in this case, through higher-order conditioning. In what
was presented as a paired-associate learning task, the names of various
nationalities ('Swedish', 'Dutch') or men's given names ('Harry', 'Bill')
were paired with either neutral words, words with positive connotations, or
words with negative connotations (appropriate balances and controls being
built in to the procedure). Subsequently, ratings of the names on an evaluative scale indicated that associations with positively or negatively evaluated
words had themselves acquired a positive or negative evaluation. Criticisms,
once very fashionable, based on 'good subject' explanations of the results
(e.g. Page 1969), seem to have been adequately answered, not least by
demonstrations that (involuntary) GSRs could be conditioned in a similar
way and that these involuntary responses paralleled ratings of the words
(Staats *et al*. 1962; Zanna *et al*. 1970). It is likely that many of our attitudes
are conditioned in this way. Who does not dislike certain names because
they are associated with some disliked person? It is a parent's role to teach
the *right* attitudes to children, partly by associating 'bad' with punishment,
'dirt' with 'bad', swearing with 'dirt', and perhaps some undesirable
acquaintance with swearing by rendering that aspect of the undesirable's
behaviour salient.

Empathy—the tendency to feel a similar emotion to another in response
just to perceiving the other's emotional state—has been recognized by non-
psychologists and psychologists alike, and has formally been demonstrated
by psychologists (e.g. Stotland 1969). Hence, since children empathize with
their parents, that provides an important source of conditioned attitudes,
and since responses conditioned early in life are persistent and easily rein-

stated (Campbell and Jaynes 1966) even after habituation, it seems likely that many of our attitudes originate in that way.

Consistency

This is not the place to argue the importance of consistency theories in psychology or attitude research. It is sufficient for our purpose just to note that it would not be adaptive for a person to act *completely* alogically. A person who says, 'All humans are mortal; I am a human; hence I am immortal' is in for a nasty surprise. Some attitudes must arise through implicit syllogisms something like this: 'Ms X (I was surprised to learn) is a members of political party Y; members of party Y are scoundrels; . . . I do not like Ms X (any more)'.

Self-attribution

Bem (e.g. 1967) has drawn attention to the probability that certain verbal attitudes are probably based on our observations of our own overt behaviour in much the same way as we observe other people's behaviour and make inferences about their attitudes. Since we often do not formulate verbal expressions of attitude until we are asked to do so, it is very plausible that some verbal expressions of attitudes do arise in that way. A remark such as 'I don't know why I watch '*Dynasty*' on television so often, I can't stand it', derives its force from the very fact that it is surprising. One would expect it to be followed up either by an assertion that the speaker intends not to watch the programme in future, or by musing leading to the opinion that '*Dynasty*' really does have something to recommend it.

Attitudes and widespread beliefs

We are now in a position to return to the questions posed at the beginning of the chapter.

Psychology's major contribution to the study of widespread beliefs to date has been the study of ethnic stereotypes, and the indices of inter-subjective agreement that have arisen from their measurement. There is no reason why these indices should not be applied to objects other than ethnic stereotypes, and application of this method may well provide a fairly general way of operationalizing social representations. *Social attitudes*, as discussed above, in connection with Thomas and Znaniecki, have nothing to offer as an explanation of widespread beliefs, since they themselves are part of the *explanandum*. Other than the concepts just mentioned, *psychological* social psychology can offer *attitudes*—in the modern sense—to the study of widespread beliefs.

Do attitudes provide a complete underpinning for myths, norms, and so on? Clearly not. For one thing, reductionism, as has been said above, is generally unsatisfactory. Myths would remain myths, peculiarly themselves, even if they could wholly be explained or decomposed into attitudes: but, in any case, they cannot be so explained or decomposed. There is clearly a relation between myths and norms (taken as representative widespread beliefs), on the one hand, and attitudes, on the other, but the relationship is a loose one. The relationship consists largely in the fact that there must be a certain loose evaluative consistency between the myth and the beliefs and behaviours it explains and charters. Myths about immigrants are such as to provide a loose justification for hostility actually based on other grounds; myths about 'British justice' provide (loosely) a way out of uncomfortable doubts concerning possible miscarriages of justice and the behaviour of the police; and so on. But if we consider larger myths, Bible stories about the Lord choosing the Jews as worthy of His special regard, for example, it becomes clear that any number of myths could have arisen to justify the feeling that the Jews are somehow special. Other myths could charter the determination not to read the poetry of a particular popular poet than the one current about Kipling. As has been said, opinions (and to opinions we may add beliefs in general, myths, norms) imply a certain attitude, but an attitude might map onto many opinions, beliefs, myths, and so on. To take a metaphor from mathematics, attitude is (almost) a function of a given opinion, belief, myth, etc., but the connection from an attitude to opinion, belief, myth, etc., is only a relation.

Turning to norms, attitudes need to be largely consonant with behaviour. Positive attitudes (dormant until challenged) to correct table manners, aspects of medical practice, and so on, doubtless arise from self-observation, tendencies to maintain consistencies among attitudes—a positive attitude to one's family and friends who eat in the received manner—and so on; a negative attitude to extreme physical cruelty may arise partly from an innate horror of blood which takes some time—often as much as a few days—to habituate, partly through empathy with the victim and the consequent self-observation, partly through having a positive attitude to moral saws such as 'do as you would be done by' inculcated in childhood by higher-order conditioning in the way of the Staats and Staats (1988) demonstrations, and partly through the tendency to consistency with other attitudes (such as a negative attitude to injury to oneself). Again, attitudes do not wholly explain these norms by a long chalk. Indeed, in the case of cultural practice, it may be more apposite to say it is the attitude which is explained by the norm.

To take another tack, attitudes may provide a way into widespread beliefs by providing a way of grouping people by their mean attitude level; looking at the distribution of scores on an attitude scale may provide an indication of how widespread an attitude is, and it may be possible to tell by inspection without much further manipulation whether there is more than one sub-culture with respect to attitudes. A distribution may be bi- or tri-modal, for example. Since widespread beliefs may be closely related to attitudes, one may then have an indication of how widespread a belief is.

Conclusion

Our tour of the attitude construct and our inspection of widespread beliefs have led to a few fairly clear conclusions, and they may in a sense be taken as the culmination of the article. What follows this paragraph is in the nature of a series of grace-notes. One conclusion is that reduction of widespread beliefs to attitudes is unlikely to be a valuable exercise even if it were in some sense possible. On the other hand, an attempt at reduction may lead to some interesting observations, provided one is not thinking to *explain away* the phenomenon of widespread beliefs. Finally, attitudes do relate to widespread beliefs. The relation is asymmetrical. A belief, which may be of a widespread nature (a myth, a norm, a stereotype) is likely to map on to one attitude, whereas an attitude may map on to one of many beliefs. Hence we know that a widespread belief implies a particular attitude, and if that attitude is not present, the belief is not likely to be either. Thus attitude scales may possibly be of use in suggesting whether beliefs are common to all members of a group or whether there are subgroups of people with differing beliefs.

To draw towards a finish: it may be that there are other broad categories of widespread beliefs than those dealt with above. 'Ideology' is one possible candidate, and one which in various guises has been of interest to psychology for a considerable time. But it has not proved a fruitful concept in psychology. Ideologies of various kinds have proved elusive when investigators have sought to operationalize them, and their pursuit has been a treacherous enterprise. In a recent review, Kinder and Sears (1985) conclude that 'for a *small proportion* [emphasis added] of the US public, political beliefs are governed by ideology; they are deductions from elaborate and abstract ideas about the nature of government and society' (p. 682). True, as Fraser (1986) pointed out, Himmelweit *et al.* (1981) identified two clusters of attitudes separating Labour from Conservative voters: a cluster on a politico-economic dimension and one on a law-and-order dimension. They have the value of corresponding to the conceptions of most observers of the important points of issue between the Labour and Conservative Parties. But these are scarcely ideologies in the full sense; and issues change in salience over time. It may be that there are basic personality dimensions, constructs enduring over time, which predict political ideology. Ferguson (1941) identified two orthogonal factors, humanitarianism and religionism. Eysenck (1954) suggested tendermindedness–toughmindedness (T) and conservative–radicalism (R). It may be that conservatism is under-pinned, as Wilson (1975) suggests, by 'a generalized susceptibility to feeling threat or anxiety in the face of *uncertainty*' (p. 65). That is, there may be an underlying widespread belief that 'the world is a very dangerous place to live in', which underlies certain attitudes, and other attitudes, of a broadly liberal kind, may be underpinned by a (widespread) underlying belief in the perfectibility of man. But these are very speculative ideas. And the connection to attitudes is tenuous. Moreover, ideology is bound to remain an elusive concept as long as factor analysis, increasingly under suspicion from the mathematically sophisticated, is the principal tool used by investigators. The devastating criticism of Eysenck's T and R dimensions made by Rokeach and Hanley (1956) attests to the dangers of this form of analysis, even were it above suspicion on mathematical grounds.

Finally, the best approach for psychology to adopt in the future for the study of widespread beliefs is a metatheoretical framework of positive scientific endeavour—in other words, a concentration on testable theories. This orientation is the one that is likely to lead to success in the future as it has in the past. For example, the theory of the authoritarian personality (Adorno *et al.* 1950) led to the uniting of attitudes to members of specific ethnic groups with wider social (and widespread, presumably) beliefs: both were entailed by an underlying, quite soundly operationally defined, personality type.

References

Adorno, T.W., Frenkel-Brunswik, E., Levinson, D.J., and Sanford, R.N. (1950). *The authoritarian personality*. Harper & Row, New York.

Allport, G.W. (1954). The historical background of modern social psychology. In *Handbook of social psychology* (ed. G. Lindzey), Vol. 1, pp. 3–56. Addison-Wesley, Reading, MA.

Bem, D.J. (1967). Self-perception: an alternative interpretation of cognitive dissonance phenomena. *Psychological Review*, **74**, 188–200.

Bethlehem, D.W. (1985). *A social psychology of prejudice*. Croom Helm, London.

Campbell, B.A. and Jaynes, J. (1966). Reinstatement. *Psychological Review*, **73**, 478–80.

Eysenck, H.J. (1954). *The psychology of politics*. Routledge, London.

Ferguson, L.W. (1941). The stability of primary attitudes 1. Religionism and humanitarianism. *Journal of Psychology*, **12**, 283–8.

Fraser, C. (1986). *Attitudes, social representations and widespread beliefs*. Paper presented at 21st International Congress of Applied Psychology, Jerusalem.

Freund, J.E. (1950). The degree of stereotypy. *Journal of the American Statistical Association*, **45**, 265–9.

Harré, R. and Lamb, R. (eds). (1983). *The encyclopedic dictionary of psychology*. Blackwell, Oxford.

Hebb, D.O. and Thompson, W.R. (1954). The social significance of animal studies. In *Handbook of social psychology* (ed. G. Lindzey), Vol. 1, pp. 532–62. Addison-Wesley, Reading, MA.

Himmelweit, H.T., Humphreys, P., Jaeger, M., and Katz, M. (1981). *How voters decide*. Academic Press, London.

Jahoda, G. (1988). Critical notes and reflections on 'social representations'. *European Journal of Social Psychology*, **18**, 195–209.

Katz, D. and Braly, K.W. (1958). Verbal stereotypes and racial prejudice. In *Readings in social psychology*, 3rd edn (ed. E.E. Maccoby, T.M. Newcomb, and E.L. Hartley). Methuen, London.

Keys, A., Brozek, J., Henschel, A., Mickelsen, O., and Taylor, H.L. (1950). *The biology of starvation* (Two vols). University of Minnesota Press, Minneapolis.

Kinder, D.R. and Sears, D.O. (1985). Public opinion and political action. In *Handbook of social psychology*, Third edn (ed. G. Lindzey and E. Aronson), Vol. 2, pp. 659–742. Random House, New York.

Lambert, W.E. and Klineberg, O. (1959). A pilot study of the origin and development of national stereotypes. *International Social Science Journal*, **11**, 221–38.

Likert, R. (1932). A technique for the measurement of attitudes. *Archives of Psychology*, No. 140.

Lippmann, W. (1956). *Public opinion*. (Original work published 1922) Macmillan, New York.

Malinowski, B. (1974). Myth in primitive psychology. In *Magic, science, and religion* (ed. B. Malinowski). (Originally published in 1925) Souvenir, London.

McCauley, C. and Stitt, C.L. (1978). An individual and quantitative measure of stereotypes. *Journal of Personality and Social Psychology*, **36**, 929–40.

Moscovici, S. (1963). Attitudes and opinions. *Annual Review of Psychology*, **14**, 231–60.

Moscovici, S. (1985). Comment on Potter and Litton. *British Journal of Social Psychology*, **24**, 91–2.

Moscovici, S. (1988). Notes towards a description of Social Representations. *European Journal of Social Psychology*, **18**, 211–50.

Moyer, K.E. (1971). *The physiology of hostility*. Markham, Chicago.

Osgood, C.E. (1962). Studies on the generality of affective meaning systems. *American Psychologist*, **17**, 10–28.

Page, M.M. (1969). Social psychology of a classical conditioning of attitudes experiment. *Journal of Personality and Social Psychology*, **11**, 177–86.

Potter, J. and Litton, I. (1985). Representing representation: a reply to Moscovici, Semin and Hewstone. *British Journal of Social Psychology*, **24**, 99–100.

Rokeach, M. and Hanley, C. (1956). Eysenck's tender-mindedness dimension: a critique. *Psychological Bulletin*, **53**, 169–176.

Ross, E.A. (1908). *Social psychology*. Macmillan, New York.

Scarr, S. and Weinberg, R.A. (1984). The transmission of authoritarianism in families: genetic resemblance in social-political attitudes. In *Race, social class, and individual differences in IQ*. (ed. S. Scarr). Erlbaum, London.

Staats, A.W. and Staats, C.K. (1958). Attitudes established by classical conditioning. *Journal of Abnormal and Social Psychology*, **57**, 37–40.

Staats, A.W., Staats, C.K., and Crawford, H.L. (1962). First order conditioning of meaning and the parallel conditioning of a GSR. *Journal of General Psychology*, **67**, 159–67.

Stotland, E. (1969). Exploratory investigations of empathy. In *Advances in experimental social psychology* Vol. 4 (ed. L. Berkowitz), pp. 271–314. Academic Press, New York.

Sumner, W.G. (1906). *Folkways*. Ginn, Boston.

Thomas, W.I. and Znaniecki, F. (1958). *The Polish peasant in Europe and America*. (Originally published in five volumes, 1918–1920) Constable, London.

Thurstone, L.L. (1959). The measurement of social attitudes. In *The measurement of values*. (Reprinted from *Journal of Abnormal and Social Psychology* (1931), **26**, 249–69.) University of Chicago Press.

Thurstone, L.L. (1928). Attitudes can be measured. *American Journal of Sociology*, **33**, 529–54.

Wilson, G.D. (1975). *Manual for the Wilson–Patterson Attitude Inventory*. NFER, Windsor.

Zanna, M.P., Kiesler, C.A., and Pilkonis, P.A. (1970). Positive and negative attitudinal affect established by classical conditioning. *Journal of Personality and Social Psychology*, **14**, 321–8.

5 The dynamics of public opinion

Hilde T. Himmelweit

Public opinion and social process

Public opinion is the expression by many individuals—it might be the public at large, particular segments of society, members of an institution, or a crowd—of sentiments, evaluations, or beliefs about societal issues. The term public opinion covers a wide range from evaluations of specific events or policy proposals, e.g. whether the police should be armed, to an examination of the relative priorities the public attaches to widely shared values. Some assessments ask for probabilistic or comparative probabilistic judgements relating, for example, to the economic health of the country a year from now; others assess the public's general emotional state, e.g. apathy, optimism, or other states, or reactions to particular individuals, e.g. leaders of political parties; to groups such as Americans and Blacks, or to institutions such as the City, the monarchy, or Trade Unions. Others elicit the public's attributions, in the case of unemployment, for example, whether this is due to government policy or to structural factors beyond any government's control. Assessment of public opinion ranges from momentary impressions or evaluations, through an examination of beliefs, in the Fishbeinian sense, to the study of broadly held attitudes or the degree to which people subscribe to more enduring values, like patriotism or egalitarianism.

Public opinion differs from privately held opinion in that it needs to be expressed and heard. The scope of public opinion goes beyond the results of systematic questioning of representative samples which began only in the 1930s with the pioneering work of Elmo Roper and Lazarsfeld. Rather, public opinion is manifested when by one means or another 'those in the know', which might be those in power, journalists, the 19th century coffee house clientele, as well as the people themselves hear of what the public thinks or feels. Marsh and Fraser (1989) offer a more extended discussion of conceptions of public opinion.

Not every publicly expressed view would qualify as a public opinion in the sense intended here. For example, people's views on taste or love would not qualify unless these views for some particular reason were thought to have social implications. It is no accident that the popular usage of the term 'public opinion' stems from Jacques Necker, the finance minister of Louis XVI who referred to public opinion as governing the behaviour of investors in the Paris money market (Phillips 1968). Public and private concerns shade into one another: what is a private concern may, in relation to a particular event or person, become a matter for public concern, just as over time, a matter for public concern may change into a private one. An example of the former occurred in Britain where a private matter, choosing a marriage partner, when made by King Edward VIII, became a public issue. A change in the law on abortion, on the other hand, changed what was initially a public matter into a private one. Nor is the shift from public to private concerns, or vice versa, a once-and-for-all affair. If enough pressure is mobilized in favour of amending the law relating to abortion, as has occurred in Britain on several occasions, people's views about abortion again come within the rubric of public opinion. These difficulties of demarcation are not surprising. They reflect the reality of the situation, namely that events occur and views evolve in interaction with others and with the wider society and that both are subject to development and change.

What then distinguishes public from privately held views has less to do with the degree of consensus within the population than with forces, internal or external, creating an imbalance in the customary conduct of affairs. People's views acquire the status of public opinion because they relate to an event, an issue, or a personality of topical relevance.

Public opinion, as defined above, also differs significantly from more privately held views in the role that it, or its perception, plays in the political process. The public's views can have a direct effect on the public's own behaviour and through it on the political process, as for example, through its purchasing and investment behaviour (Katona 1979), or through the support the public gives to, or withholds from, politicians or the management of institutions, whether this be through its vote or other forms of political activity such as strikes.

Equally important is the effect of public opinion, actual or perceived, on politicians and other decision makers. The extent to which public opinion or the opinion of a given relevant public affects policy makers depends on the intensity and consensus of the views expressed, the degree to which they are at variance with policies adopted or proposed, and also on the politicians' dependence, or that of the institution, on the public's goodwill. Such influence might lead to a change of policy, to a delay in presenting a policy, or to a shift in the style or conduct of affairs.

The role of public opinion has occupied thinkers over many centuries. Wieland (1799), the German poet, described it as an opinion that without being noticed takes possession of most heads, and the sociologist, Coolley (1909), a century later as 'no mere aggregate of separate individual judgments, but an organisation, a cooperative product of communication and reciprocal influence'. Seen in this light, public opinion becomes very similar to Moscovici's (1984) social representations which 'enter and influence the mind of each but are not thought out by them, instead re-thought, re-cited and re-presented . . . the product of a whole sequence of elaboration and changes'. This description and those given by Coolley and Wieland are more applicable to the public's constructs about the society rather than to people's off-the-cuff reactions to specific events or issues when these are in the forefront of public debate. But of course how such events are experienced, codified and interpreted is affected by the schemata or social representations current in the society providing what Egon Brunswik (1959) describes as a lens through which reality is viewed.

Since the late 1930s the systematic measurement of public opinion has become a major industry. Some surveys explore issues in depth so as to learn what has given rise to, or lies behind, the expression of particular views and also how views on different issues relate to one another. Others ask for snap judgements by the public concerning preferences for different products, political parties or leaders, or about the public's behavioural intentions. To give but one example, the number of polls commissioned by the news media alone during election campaigns about people's voting intentions, has risen enormously in the last ten years. During the 1979 British general election, the news media published 26 polls, during the 1983 election 46, rising during the 31 days of the 1987 election to a bewildering 130; quite apart from the many private unpublished polls commissioned by the parties themselves.

Many replies to polls are little thought out, given on the spur of the moment, not least in response to the need to have a view. To some extent polls generate as well as reflect public opinion. Whatever the depth or genuineness of the replies, survey or poll data, once published, constitute an event with the potential like other events to affect the public's and politicians' opinions and behaviour. Polls about voting intentions can have an effect on turnout. Two contradictory effects have been described: a band-wagon effect with voters wishing to be associated with the winning party, and an effort effect in that the voters inclined to the party whose majority seems assured may be less likely to make the effort to vote. There has also been concern about the differential effect that polls have in particular on the fortunes of small parties. Here, as was convincingly shown in the October 1974 British general election, a rising trend of support during the campaign for the Liberal party, encouraged potential supporters to vote for it by reducing the perceived risk of a wasted vote (Himmelweit and Humphreys 1974).

Sudden changes in the relative position of intentions to vote for the two major parties can have an affect not only on voting decisions, but also on behaviour external, but related, to the outcome of the election. For example, in the 1987 British election two polls in the last week of the election campaign showed an unexpected but dramatic narrowing of the

Conservative majority over Labour. The result was that those Conservatives inclined to defect to the Alliance (the centre party) did not do so for fear of letting Labour in. There was also heavy selling in the City because of the increased uncertainty about the election outcome.

I have thought it necessary to begin this chapter with a more general consideration of the constituents and role of public opinion, since social psychologists, unlike other social scientists, have been little interested in this topic. Yet the study of the public's views is interesting in its own right and has implications for attitude and attribution theories, for our understanding of inter-group relations, and for the role that events alongside different socializing agents play in the formation of people's cognitions.

The subtle interplay of internal and external factors that affect the public's reactions is brought out well by Williams' (1979) examination of change and stability in value systems which has relevance for an examination of the dynamics of public opinion. Williams points out that a value system serves both to guide anticipatory behaviour and to justify and explain past conduct. 'Values have a cultural content, represent a psychological investment and are shaped by the constraints and opportunities of a social system and a physical environment.' Changes in values are limited due to 'the external "reality constraints" of the aforementioned interpenetrating systems and by the "internal" dimensions of consistency, congruence or appropriateness among the values and beliefs themselves'. Such analysis requires adopting a systems approach, so cogently argued for by McGuire (1985). Nor is this a very new idea in psychology, rather one that has been ignored for a long time. In the 1950s Egon Brunswik (1959) stressed that, for any kind of psychological theorizing, as much time needed to be devoted to an ecological survey independent of the individuals' perception of the environment, as to the study of the individuals themselves. He advocated that particular attention be paid to what he calls the *texture of the environment* and the relation within it of proximal to distant cues.

The approach I am attempting here is the one advocated by Egon Brunswik and by McGuire, namely a more differentiated approach, modelling significant elements and possible modes of interaction. This is an approach less tidy than general theories and less ambitious than striving for universal laws, but one that is more helpful for someone wishing to compare different situations or as a guide to informed observation. This is why Egon Brunswik considers the customary procedure of studying one aspect while keeping others constant inappropriate and proposes instead 'working down', i.e. taking the full complexity of the situation on board and examining subsequently the contribution different factors make by a process of omission, noting the reduction in explanatory power that results.

In the sections that follow, six studies will be referred to frequently to provide illustrative examples. To avoid repetition, a brief description of relevant aspects of these studies is given below.

1. *'How voters decide'* (Himmelweit *et al.* 1985)   A panel study of British men over a 15-year period from age 23–38 (additional information being available about their outlook as adolescents). Their educational and occupational progress was charted and repeated information obtained about their goals and values, their authoritarianism, and their views on a variety of political and social issues. Their vote choice was recorded immediately after each of six successive British general elections. The study continued over a sufficiently long period to make it possible to relate opinion change on selected political issues obtained at 4, 8, and 12-year intervals, to the economic, cultural, and political climate of the society. A re-analysis of the large-scale representative British elections surveys of several elections, including panel studies covering two adjacent elections, made it possible to test the generality of the model of vote choice derived from this small, unrepresentative panel study.

2. *Britain's entry into the European Community*   Two short-term panel studies each involving a sample of over 800 before and after the decision about entry was made. Their purposes were: (1) to examine in a real-life situation the relation of evaluation and beliefs concerning specific aspects of a proposed decision to (a) people's overall attitude, (b) their behavioural intention, and (c) in 1975 when people were asked to vote in a Referendum also to their actual behaviour; (2) to examine the process of adaptation: in 1971 to a decision made on the individual's behalf, by Parliament voting on the issue, and in 1975 to a decision in which the public participated by casting its vote. Interest here lay in whether adaptation to change affected not only individual evaluations and beliefs but also their structure, whether evaluations or beliefs were more sensitive to change, and what were the factors associated with varying degrees of susceptibility to change (Himmelweit 1981).

3. A study of *Generations and Politics* (Jennings and Niemi 1981)   In 1965 a representative sample of high school seniors and their parents in the United States completed questionnaires indicating their hypothetical vote choice and their views on a variety of political and social issues. They were also asked to indicate how their parents or, in the case of parents, their children, had replied. Eight years later in 1973, the young people, now aged 25, were asked many of the same questions as were their parents together with a new cohort of high school seniors.

4. Langton's (1984) study of *persistence and change* in political confidence examines the discounting or reinforcing effect of three important socializing experiences: the family, the school, and the workplace, using as independent variables the subjects' report of the degree of independence and initiative fostered by each experience. He traces the interaction effects of these three experiences on the individual's sense of political efficacy, using interview data from USA and Peru.

5. Kaase and Klingemann (1979) on *antecedent factors leading to a post-materialistic outlook* (Inglehart 1977) and its influence on readiness to engage in less conventional, compared with conventional, forms of political activity.

6. Finally, Lang and Lang's (1983) study of *the battle for public opinion during Watergate* contains a very subtle analysis of the changes in public opinion that occurred in 1972. Initially the public's views followed along predictable party lines. The 37 days of the live broadcast of the hearings, which had an audience comparable to popular entertainment programmes usually broadcast at that time, led to a re-evaluation of the issue and to a general acceptance of the need for impeachment. The authors examine the crucial role played by the media using content analysis and available poll data, the latter being treated sometimes as an independent, at other times as a dependent, variable. The study is a good example of a multi-method systems approach already referred to.

Dynamics of public opinion

Seven types of changes will be considered in this section.

The proportion of 'undecided' or 'don't knows'

Kramer *et al.* (1983), drawing on US archival public opinion data from 1945 to 1982 found a significant reduction in the proportion of uncertain or 'don't knows' as to whether they and their family would survive a nuclear war (from 33 per cent in 1956 to a mere 2 per cent in 1982). In our panel study likewise the proportion undecided about the value of comprehensive schools sharply decreased between 1962 and 1974 due to greater familiarity with this type of school as more came into being and with more media coverage of them, and perhaps more importantly because comprehensive schools during this period became a political football with the Labour Party for, and the Conservatives opposed, to their replacing the existing divided secondary state school system.

Equally, an increase in the percentage who are uncertain can come with experience through awareness of unanticipated side-effects, or with a reduction in the importance for the individual of the institution which is identified with a particular view, e.g. through a reduction in party loyalty, or as in the case of Britain's entry into the European Community, because of a volte-face by the parties themselves.

The degree of polarization or consensus in the public's response

Sarlvik and Crewe (1983) noted, compared with earlier years, a decrease in polarization among the British public and a growing consensus to the right, opposing further nationalization and agreeing that unions were doing more harm than good. An increase in polarization, on the other hand, often occurs where an issue is made the focal part of a party platform, or expressive of an institution's identity.

Relevant here is Marx's view (1846) that ideas of the ruling class percolate 'downwards' rather than that there is a two-way traffic of mutual influence. While Marx overstates the one-sided direction of the spread of an idea within a population, there is a good deal of evidence to support his thesis, as for example in the spread through society of new child-rearing or dietary practices.

The degree as distinct from the prevalence of polarization

Prediction of vote choice from the attitude data of our panel was better than that obtained in a survey carried out by Butler and Stokes (1969). The latter used a three-point response scale (agree, disagree, undecided) while we used a five-point scale which made it possible to show that on many issues people making different vote decisions differed from one another, not in terms of agreement or disagreement, but only in the strength of their support or opposition.

The salience of an issue as indicated by the respondents

Political and economic events and the media all play a part in changing people's agenda as to the relative importance of particular issues. For example, inflation, the key issue in the 1979 British election, was eclipsed by unemployment as the most important issue in the 1983 election, while strikes, also a salient issue in 1979, were hardly mentioned.

The climate of opinion concerning the appropriateness of expressing particular views

An identical response obtained at two different periods in time may signify different degrees of latent support. In our panel study of young men we found that replies given to authoritarian items were very similar in 1962 and 1974. Only on two items were there marked changes. There was a sharp drop in percentage agreement with the view that 'the father is the most important person in the home' and that 'the husband should have the final say in family matters'. The growth of the feminist movement had made the expression of chauvinist views less respectable. Just as after the Holocaust anti-semitic remarks frequently made in some British circles in the 1930s were no longer heard.

This raises the interesting broader question as to the validity of inferring latent attitudes from the expression of beliefs or opinions about sensitive issues. Nor is it solved by reference to the need to allow for social desirability in question wording. The more difficult issue is the following: if society frowns on the free expression of a negative attitude towards an out-group so that questions have to be put in a very muted form, how justified are we in considering variations in replies to indicate differences in the attitude as originally formulated?

The structure of the belief system

When we first sampled the panel's views in 1962 two changes in the law were under debate and were implemented shortly afterwards; namely, legalization of homosexuality among consenting adults, and the abolition of capital punishment. Initially both proposed changes were strongly opposed, an opposition which correlated significantly with opposition to immigration and with some other attitudes forming a cluster of illiberal beliefs. Twelve years later there was a greater acceptance of the law concerning homosexuals and views on this issue ceased to form part of the above illiberal set of beliefs. Not so people's dislike of the abolition of capital punishment, which remained unchanged despite the change in law and continued to correlate highly with opposition towards immigrants. The fixity of views about capital punishment raises intriguing questions as to what it is about an issue that makes it so particularly resistant to change even where attitudes to other issues like those relating to homosexuality, initially equally emotionally charged, are not.

The relevance of an issue or attitude for the decisions to be made

Although there was general agreement that unemployment was the most important issue in the British 1983 and 1987 general elections, the issue played only a very small part in people's vote choice simply because they had no trust in the proposals of any of the political parties to reduce unemployment. We have found it useful to distinguish between consensual and non-consensual issues—consensual issues being those about which there is general agreement, e.g. the need to reduce inflation and unemployment, while opinions are divided about non-consensual issues, as for example about nationalization. While consensual issues tend to be the major issues facing a society, it was the beliefs about the ability of the parties to resolve or even reduce the problem rather than people's indifference to it which made the issue irrelevant when deciding for which party to vote. Beliefs enter the relation of evaluation to behaviour always, but are of particular importance in the case of consensual issues.

There are many other types of subtle changes in public opinion that could be enumerated which are missed by the usual bottom-line measure of opinion change (shifts in the mean or in the percentage agreement), but the above list is sufficient to show that changes in the public's views can be looked at from many different perspectives.

To this list need to be added the following considerations regarding the change: whether it is gradual or sudden; temporary or lasting; restricted to one or two issues or a reflection of a change in the public's general perspective on society of which the issue under investigation is just one facet or example.

Influences on public opinion

Factors shaping public opinion and those making for differential receptivity to change are not independent of one another but operate in a complex interaction that includes feedback effects. But for clarity of presentation it is convenient to separate the two sets of factors. In this section seven factors which shape public opinion are discussed.

The culture, tradition, and norms of a society

The climate of a society gives cohesion to that society, through shared social representations and by means of its laws and customs. It also sets boundaries concerning the expression of particular values or concerning the attitudes and behaviour *vis-a-vis* particular groups and institutions. Each generation seeks to alter the boundaries of the acceptable and the permissible. Such attempts are not necessarily immediately noticeable, do not occur at a uniform rate, are not the same across issues, nor are they necessarily uni-directional. But occur they do. In the 1980s, for example, there appeared to be an enthusiasm, at least in some quarters, to re-erect boundaries, by changes in the law and norms of the society, which in the 1960s some groups, particularly the youth, had been successful at dismantling. In the 1970s sections of society began to react against the consequences of the greater liberalization initiated in the 1960s, affected in part by the harsher economic climate of the day.

Socializing experiences

The socializing experiences provided by family, neighbourhood, school, further education, place of work, peers, marriage, as well as through imposed group membership, for example, trades union closed shops, hospitalization, or imprisonment, or through sought membership of political parties, generate and affect the schemata or social representations people use to evaluate an issue.

Changes in the management of the country or its institutions

These may yield new emphases, a shift in rhetoric as well as changes in norms and conduct including changes in the law.

Political and economic events

These can be dramatic, one-off events like the Falklands War with dramatic consequences on public opinion. One of these was to transform Mrs Thatcher's unpopularity as Prime Minister, unprecedented since polling began, into becoming at the conclusion of that war the most popular Prime Minister. Others are more gradual and continuous, e.g. like rising inflation, unemployment, and a deepening recession.

The demand characteristics of the issue

Much depends on the saliency, novelty and the suddenness of the event occurring, as for example, the stock market crash in October 1987 and on its repercussions, perceived or real, for people's lives. Also important is the extent to which the event has relevance for the entire population or only for a section. The Langs (1983) distinguish between low and high threshold events, the former being events that impinge directly on people's lives. The need to have a view and to give meaning to an event are all relevant factors related to the formulation of public opinion, as is the extent to which a given issue requires action.

The presentation and interpretation of events

Events and issues about which public opinion is sought tend to be outside people's personal experience. Knowledge about them comes at one remove, i.e. through the 'framing' or definition that the mass media in particular give to the presentation and interpretation of the event, including attributions of responsibility and estimates of consequences. Gerbner and colleagues (1980) call it 'symbolic reality' and the Langs (1983) refer to it as the presentation of reality through a 'refraction lens'. It is the various conceptualizations of the event offered (there are nearly always more than one) which for the public become the events to be assessed.

Metaphors play a strategic role here. They can be used to explain a policy or an event, making the unfamiliar familiar, or serve to distance people from the emotional impact of an event as, for example, using the term 'final solution' for the mass killing of Jews by the Nazis. Metaphors can also heighten the importance or danger of the event—for example, at the turn of the century Bagehot described the effect of extending suffrage 'as an unleashing of powerful forces in nature that would destroy the artificially constructed reservoir' to which he likened the British constitution (Rayner 1984). In the case of Watergate, what was initially described as 'the Watergate caper' became the Watergate scandal, and what was initially seen as an isolated act came to be seen as the broader and more significant issue of executive privilege.

The media are not so much agenda setting, which suggests a once and for all situation, as *agenda building*, a process which goes on continuously and may involve several feedback loops with public opinion in turn affecting the agenda.

The Langs see the role of the media in leading to change of views as providing visibility and continuity, and introducing new actors into the situation. In the case of Watergate, the judiciary and other prestige figures judged to be above party politics expressing their views on the media provided an impetus towards reconceptualizing the issue not as one of party politics but as one of national and historic importance. The public's interest in the media exposure in its turn led to a greater readiness by the elite to comment. This in its turn generated more news 'in a cycle of mutual reinforcement that continues until actors and the public tire or another issue moves to the centre of the stage'.

Assigning meaning to an event or issue essential for the creation of a public opinion occurs not only through the media, but also through interested parties or pressure groups and through the reworking of people's views through conversation with others. Both Harré and Secord (1972) and Moscovici (1984) stress the importance of such reworking.

Feedback effects on the public

These are provided through information about the views of significant others as well as about the prevalence of views and their changes by the public at large. The media through the presentation of key figures from different walks of life provide a canvas of views on which the individual can draw, while survey and poll results indicate the degree of social support for particular views. Evidence that many others hold views at variance with those of the individual may lead to what Noelle Neumann (1984) refers to as 'the spiral of silence'. Once sizeable numbers of people believe that because their views are not aired on the media, people do not subscribe to them, they may according to Neumann's theory become reluctant to express them and so inadvertently contribute to a false picture of consensus.

So far, factors shaping public opinion have been listed as if each were operating in isolation from the other. This is not so. The dynamics of public opinion can be understood only if one allows for interaction and feedback effects.

Jennings and Niemi (1981) distinguish between three types of effects to account for changes in people's views.

1. *Period effects* due to the effect of events or their interpretation occurring at the time. In their study, both the children and their parents had after eight years become much less trusting in the honesty and competence of government (Watergate occurred in 1972 and the sample was re-contacted in 1973). The authors assign this change to a *period effect* since a new 1973 cohort of high school seniors indicated even lesser trust.

2. *Life-cycle effects* are those which occur through individuals entering a situation more akin to that of their parents. In that case, any correspondence between their respective views might simply reflect similar experiences and not be the result of socialization. It is important, for example, in the case of political attitudes not to assign to socialization, e.g. to parental attitudes, what is in fact the result of experiences shared by parents and their adult chldren, such as similar working or middle class jobs or similar family responsibilities.

3. The third type of effects are *generation socialization effects* whereby individuals socialized during different periods in the society's history hold different views—the emphasis here is on the climate of the society and that of the family's social and economic circumstances which influenced their outlook and style of child-rearing.

While there was no evidence of a *generation effect* in Jennings and Niemi's study, such an effect was found by Glen (1981) using the Berkeley growth study which compared children born only eight years apart. He found that the older children brought up during the height of the depression and the younger ones after the depression had very different childhood experiences, and the effect of these was seen in their mode of adjustment to society as adults and also in their aspirations and their attitudes to social issues.

Such generation effects are also postulated by Kaase and Klingemann (1979) in their cross-national study when they found that the generation brought up in the 1960s had a less materialistic outlook than did the older generation and also lesser respect for authority and for the conventional channels of political activities. They ascribe the development of a post-materialistic outlook to being brought up during a period of relative economic optimism, which enabled that generation to take economic security for granted.

For period and generation effects to make themselves felt, the differences between the two periods have to be quite marked: economic recession versus economic affluence; peace as against war; being an immigrant as against being born in the country.

Jennings and Niemi's classification of social influence is useful because it draws attention not only to the climate of the wider society and changes in that climate but also to the immediately relevant environment providing experiences which act as lenses through which particular issues are viewed. Socialization experiences are interactive and cumulative. Langton's (1984) study shows that the influence of the various socializing experiences depends on the extent to which they reinforce, undermine, or by-pass one another. He speaks of *discounting* and *enabling* effects with each experience creating a kind of residue, the importance of which varies with the experiences that follow.

Enough has been said to show that one needs to extend one's perception of what constitutes socializing experiences to include the climate of the society and its traditions, external events and their interpretation by the media, experiences which are generally omitted as are the public's perspective on society. Some of these sources of influence create the ground on which new experiences and their formulations make their impact felt. They orient the individual towards particular ways of responding of which awareness that there is something to respond to, is the first requirement.

Susceptibility to change

So far we have considered societal factors which influence public opinion, here we concentrate more on the individuals' susceptibility to change in that opinion and the factors relevant to that susceptibility. Susceptibility varies not only with the demand characteristics of the issue but also with the ready availability of appropriate and shared scripts. At the time of the Falklands War, it was striking that the necessity for the war was so quickly accepted and, once accepted, led to an apparently effortless activation of appropriate, even overlearned, scripts. Deviations from the scripts were criticized as evidence of disloyalty. There was criticism, for example, of the BBC for referring to Argentine soldiers and to British soldiers instead of calling the latter 'our boys'. A content analysis of newspapers and speeches at the time found scripts with which we have become familiar either through personal experience of war or through fictionalized accounts of it. War, in addition, creates strong pressures for conformity leading individuals to conduct conversations and to hold internal dialogues to facilitate coming to terms with the event.

Readiness to change also varies with the continuity with which an issue is kept before the public and the prominence given to it. The Langs point out that the 37 days of hearings concerning the President's involvement in the Watergate affair provided saturation coverage and that such coverage in turn generates more discussions and internal dialogues.

Feather (1974) points out that change in people's schemata occurs when the *cognitive strain* of warding off new experiences or assimilating them to existing schemata becomes greater than incorporating the new by adapting or changing what he calls the individual's abstract structure. Block (1982) in connection with the individual's adjustment to new situations expresses similar views, namely that people assimilate if they can and accommodate if they must.

It follows that attitude or opinion change by a significant number of the population is not a quick affair nor does it occur at a uniform rate. The

Langs point out that much of the evidence about *minimal effects of the media* is derived by examining the effect of a single event, e.g. of a presidential debate in changing people's views about the candidate and that a much longer time perspective is required. Also, if there is no follow-up to a particular event, its role in affecting change will indeed be minimal. Himmelweit (1977) likened the influence of television to a drip effect, imperceptible at first and gaining a foothold only with repetition.

There is also the public's general susceptibility or resistance towards the new. A society, like an individual, finds novelty attractive where it comes at a manageable pace and is not too far 'out'. Where the pace of change in a society is too great, a resistance even to take account of yet another approach or event builds up.

Equally, new experiences may increase readiness to change. In Britain the Second World War, by bringing different social classes in close contact with one another, created a *cognitive thaw* of the stereotypes of each others' attitudes and behaviour which was judged to have been an important factor in paving the way for the acceptance by the middle class of the need for, and subsequent introduction of, the Welfare State.

The degree to which acceptance of a particular view varies will therefore depend on whether it falls on 'prepared soil'. The Langs make this point strongly. In their view, impeachment and hence the resignation of Nixon might not have occurred but for the fact that the ground had been prepared through the emotions released by the Vietnam War, just as in their view France's defeat by the Germans in the war of 1870 contributed to the development and virulence of the public's and the élite's reactions to the Dreyfus affair.

It is also worth remembering that researchers tend to assess people's cognitions and attitudes at a particular moment in the history of their development; these may be amenable to change because they are in the process of formation or because they have become ossified. We had evidence of the former with regard to the two authoritarian statements concerning the man's role in the home. Reference has already been made to the fact that there was a significant stage in our panel's outlook between 1962 and 1974. Yet a four period cross-sectional study we carried out between 1971 and 1982 which included these items showed no further shift in the public's views. This is probably because in 1971 the feminist movement was already in full swing and little happened between then and 1982 that required further re-evaluation.

As already mentioned, a change of attitude may also be facilitated because it coincides with a lessening of the linkage to groups that provide evaluative guidelines. The lessening of party identification and of the role played by social class membership are examples.

There is therefore a societal and a personal life history attached to the expression and significance of each attitude just as there is a history attached to the meaning of a given event and its salience (Himmelweit *et al.* 1985).

In this chapter, I have used the term 'public opinion' to encompass beliefs, cognitions, and evaluations of events, groups, individuals, or institutions as well as values. It would appear that beliefs and cognitions can be changed more readily than evaluations (even though change in these tend to follow a change in cognitions) and that value priorities are relatively more 'ingrained' and hence more difficult to influence. Our political data bear this out. We found that beliefs about the ability of parties to implement policy proposals changed more than did their evaluations of the value of these proposals. In the European Community study, beliefs about the probability of certain things happening if Britain joined or did not join the European Community changed more than did people's evaluations of them.

However, values do change with time. We found that those working-class men in our panel study who had not achieved social mobility in their late thirties had adapted to that situation by decreasing the priority given the goal of personal success by contrast to their working-class colleagues who had become socially mobile, even though at the outset of their working life the two groups attached identical priorities to this particular goal.

Theoretical and research implications

The study of the dynamics of public opinion has implications for a number of issues central to social psychology.

The relation of public opinion to behaviour

The factors already mentioned all play a part in how far and in what way public opinion affects the public's behaviour or the behaviour of others. In the case of voting, the declining role of group influences led to people's views occupying a more important role in their vote choice mediated by past habit of voting for a particular party.

I should like to add to the concept of *cognitive thaw* the concept of *behavioural thaw* denoting that a behaviour previously linked to group membership or adherence to societal norms becomes a matter of individual choice.

But it is not only the fit of people's views to the platform of a particular party which matters, it also depends on their fit to those of available alternative options and on their beliefs about the viability and competence of these options. That is, a change of views will lead to a change in the option selected *only* if the changed view brings the individual within the purview of a viable alternative. A regression analysis, which included measures of the initial fit of the individual's views to each of the parties as well as measures of the extent and direction of change in the voters' attitudes across two elections, proved effective in predicting stability or change in vote, with both *attitude fit* and *attitude change* contributing significantly to the variance (Himmelweit *et al.* 1985).

Another important factor concerns people's beliefs about the likely success of supporting a particular activity. The success of the Civil Rights and the Women's Movement in the United States, initially formed because of a burning sense of injustice on the part of the relevant public, has led to an increase in the readiness with which new pressure groups were formed: the Gay groups, the 70-plus age group, and so on.

Regularities in the relation of events on public opinion and in turn on the public's own behaviour are more readily observed at the *macro-* rather than at the *micro-level.* Katona (1979) found, for example, that individuals' views about the future prospects of the economy did not predict their behaviour well, but that changes in the public's views obtained in successive surveys related meaningfully both to economic indicators and also to independent measures of purchasing and investment behaviour. The reason is of course that idiosyncratic variations, including in this case variations in people's perception of the significance of economic indicators, tend to cancel out where large samples are concerned. Katona also pointed out that changes in optimism about the economy or its obverse took time to develop—about six to nine months—in response to changes in the economic indicators.

The relation of attitude intensity to behaviour also varies with the cost of the behaviour and the assessment of the likelihood of its success, the individual's habit pattern as well as with the perceived social support. The examination of factors relevant to the formation of public opinion and its relation to behaviour points up the narrowness of the Fishbein and Ajzen's (1975) formulation of the relation of attitudes to behavioural intentions and behaviour. They ignore past learning experiences, the role of the particular belief or evaluation sampled within the individual's belief system, and the whole question of attitude fit and attitude shift (Himmelweit *et al.* 1985). Nor do they give proper consideration to alternative and competing available action possibilities.

Far more appropriate is the way Kelman (1974) in his seminal paper conceptualized attitudes. He entitled the paper *Attitudes are alive and well and gainfully employed in the sphere of action.* Judging from subsequent publications by attitude researchers, the paper has had surprisingly little impact despite its originality. For Kelman, 'An attitude is not an index of action, but a determinant, component, and consequent of it. Furthermore it is not an entity that can be separated—functionally or temporally—from the flow of action, but is an integral part of action . . . Action is the ground on which attitudes are formed, tested, modified and abandoned'.

I would add only that the action need not be performed by the individual but can be an action performed by others and that the interpretation of events and action—reality mediated by significant others or by the media—may be as relevant as the actions and events themselves.

The analysis of group identity and group cohesion

The study of public opinion offers another way of examining changes in the significance of group membership by assessing the variance of views within the group relative to those outside particularly where other information points to a change in the significance of the group for its members. It also draws attention to the climate in society and its role in exerting pressure towards conformity or, equally, towards independence—'doing one's own thing'. In the latter case, it is less likely that individuals will define themselves by reference to a group, or identify with the outlook of that group. In the past, when someone from the working class identified with the middle class this was a pointer to his or her outlook and political orientation. Not so today. Indeed, social attitudes which discriminated well between voters for the different parties, discriminated poorly between members of different social classes (Himmelweit et al. 1985).

The need for functional rather than textual equivalence

This is important when using scales whose purpose is to measure relatively enduring orientations (authoritarianism, anomie, locus of control). The content of the items of such scales, with which the subject is asked to agree or disagree, tend to consist of assertions about the prevalence of particular situations, policies, group characteristics, or states of mind and of prescriptive statements with regard to them appropriate at the time. As we have shown, societal changes or changes in the climate of a society may affect the social desirability of agreeing with some assertions or may affect their relevance or indeed their status as opinion, as distinct from a statement of fact. For example, for those living in a dictatorship, a statement such as 'people like myself are quite powerless' will represent a statement of fact more than for those living in a democracy.

The study of mediated reality

It is important to study the way in which a policy, issue, or event is presented by interested parties and by the media. It is necessary, therefore, to examine the content of the media since for the purposes of examining the formation of public opinion, the various interpretations of events are often as relevant as the event itself. Abelson's (1986) description of persuasion as rhetorical vectors that move beliefs in their direction is pertinent here.

The need for a multi-method approach

The studies described here employ a variety of useful research approaches
relatively little used by mainstream social psychologists. These include: the
use of secondary and archival data to increase awareness about societal
changes; the use of secondary data to test the generality of a model or
conclusions derived from a specially designed, focused study of a small
sample; the use of a variety of statistical methods of analysis to throw light
not only on the prevalence of a belief but on belief systems and their
relation to behaviour; multi-dimensional scaling; path analysis; multi-
attribute theory and measures of posterior probabilities derived from
discriminant analyses; macro-analysis which relates survey data to information extraneous to the individual; a multi-method approach to trace the
changing history of a belief within the community by personal accounts,
survey, and poll data as well as by the charting of the events, their framing,
and the elaboration of that framing by significant others (politicians,
journalists, the media using content analysis); examining the feedback loop
that results from the role of the public as both bystander and actor. Incid-
entally, all the studies, apart from that of Himmelweit *et al.* (1985), were
carried out by sociologists and political scientists.

Conclusion

In this chapter I have sought to model the role of social beliefs and the
intricate ways in which such beliefs derive from, and interact with, the
environment which, though it gave rise to the beliefs, does not operate
independently of them. It is affected by and affects the beliefs in a cycle of
mutual dependence. McGuire (1985) stresses the need for such modelling
and for including in it feedback effects. This is, of course, easier said than
done, but I believe it is necessary first to model the process in its complexity
and hence apparent untidiness, adopting Brunswik's desideratum to 'work
down'. This does not mean that for any given problem information needs to
be collected on every facet, but one needs to be conscious of the potential
influence of these facets when deciding to ignore them.

References

Abelson, R.B. (1986). Beliefs are like possessions. *Journal for the Theory of Social
    Behaviour*, **16**, 223–50.
Block, J. (1982). Accommodation and the dynamics of personality development,
    Child Development, **53**, 281–95.
Brunswik, E. (1959). Selected papers. In *The Psychology of Egon Brunswik* (ed.
    K.R. Hammond) (1966), Holt, Rinehart & Winston, New York.

Butler, D. and Stokes, D. (1969). *Political change in Britain*. Macmillan, London.

Coolley, C.H. (1909). Social organization: a study of the larger mind. Reprinted in Cooley, C. (1956). *Two major works. Social organization and human nature and the social order*. Free Press, Glencoe, IL.

Feather, N.T. (1971). Organization and discrepancy in cognitive structures, *Psychological Review*, **78**, 355–70.

Fishbein, M. and Ajzen, I. (1975). *Belief, attitude, intention and behaviour*. Addison-Wesley, Reading.

Gerbner, G., Gross, L., Morgan, M., and Signozelli, N. (1980). The mainstreaming of America: violence profile No. 11, *Journal of Communication*, **30**, 10–27.

Glen, E. Jr. (1981). Social history and life experience. In *Present and past in middle life* (ed. D. Eichhorn *et al.*). Academic Press, New York.

Harré, R. and Secord, P.F. (1972). *The explanation of social behaviour*. Blackwell, Oxford.

Himmelweit, H.T. (1977). Yesterday's and tomorrow's television research on children. In *Communication research—a half century appraisal* (ed. D. Lerner and L.M. Nelson). University of Hawaii Press.

Himmelweit, H.T. (1981). A study of the structure of cognitions and beliefs in relation to the dynamics of change. Report to the Social Science Research Council, London.

Himmelweit, H.T. and Humphreys, P.C. (1974). The Liberal floater. *New Society*, **27**, 585.

Himmelweit, H.T., Humphreys, P., and Jaeger, M. (1985). *How voters decide*, revised and updated edition. Open University Press, Milton Keynes.

Inglehart, R. (1977). *Silent revolution: changing values and political styles among Western peoples*. Princeton University Press.

Jennings, K. and Niemi, R.G. (1981). *Generations and politics*. Princeton University Press.

Kaase, M. and Klingemann, H.D. (1979). Social structure, value orientations and the party system: the problem of interest accommodation in Western democracies. *European Journal of Political Research*, **36**, 367–86.

Katona, G. (1979). Toward a macro-psychology. *American Psychologist*, **34**, 118–26.

Kelman, H. (1974). Attitudes are alive and well and gainfully employed. *American Psychologist*, **29**, 310–24.

Kramer, B., Kalick, S.M., and Milburn, M.A. (1983). Attitudes toward nuclear weapons and nuclear war: 1945–1982. *Journal of Social Issues*, **39**, 7–24.

Lang, E. and Lang, K. (1983). *The battle for public opinion: the president, the press and the polls*. Columbia University Press, New York.

Langton, K. (1984). Persistence and change in political confidence over the life-span: embedding life cycle socialization in context. *British Journal of Political Science*.

Marsh, C. and Fraser, C. (1989). Public opinion and nuclear issues. In *Public Opinion and Nuclear Weapons* (ed. C. Marsh and C. Fraser). Macmillan, London.

Marx, K. and Engels, F. (1846). The German ideology. Reprinted in *The Marx-Engels Collected Works*, Vol. 5, (1976), Lawrence & Wishart, London.

McGuire, W.J. (1985). Attitudes and attitude change. In *The handbook of social psychology*, 3rd edn, Vol. 2 (ed. G. Lindzey and E. Aronson). Random House, New York.

Moscovici, S. (1984). The phenomenon of social representation. In *Social representations* (ed. R. Farr and S. Moscovici). Cambridge University Press.

Neumann, N. (1984). *The spiral of silence*. Chicago University Press.

Phillips, D.W. (1968). Public opinion. In *International encyclopedia of the social sciences*, Vol. 13 (ed. D.L. Sills). Macmillan and The Free Press, New York.

Rayner, J. (1984). Between meaning and event: an historical approach to political metaphors. *Political Studies*, **37**, 537–50.

Sarlvik, B. and Crewe, I. (1983). *Decade of dealignment*. Cambridge University Press.

Wieland, C.M. (1799). *Gespraech unter Vier Augen*. Goeschen, Leipzig.

Williams, R.M. (1979). Change and stability in values and value systems, a sociological analysis. In *Understanding human values* (ed. M. Rokeach). Free Press, New York.

6 Attitudes, social representations, and ideology

Elinor Scarbrough

Introduction

It is surprising that at a time when social and political ideologies play such an important role in human affairs so little interest is being shown in their effects on social conduct and in the definition of conflicts (Moscovici 1972, p. 29).

The most important differentiating feature of human social behaviour is the human use of symbols in social communication . . . the creation and diffusion of ideologies which are produced by, and in turn contribute to producing, new conditions of social life and new modes of social conduct. But . . . the study of ideologies have hardly made their appearance in contemporary social psychology (Tajfel 1972, pp. 3–4).

With these passing remarks both Moscovici and Tajfel intimate that the study of ideology is a proper concern of social psychology. Indeed, in observing that 'even if ideologies and their impact have been widely discussed, they have not been extensively researched' (Moscovici 1984, p. 16), Moscovici might also have arraigned sociology and the study of politics: writings about ideology are commonplace but empirical studies are scarce. But whilst Moscovici and his colleagues may be alert to a lacuna in their discipline, their focus on social representations has not led them to address directly questions of ideology, in particular, what constitutes an ideology and how ideologies bear upon attitudes. None the less, in pointing to the place of social representations in the life of societies, Moscovici promises additional insights on a central question in the study of politics: the place of ideology in political action. The performance of governments, the manoeuvrings of parties, the direction of public policy, the behaviour of electors—all are areas of research where the dynamics of action raise questions of ideology. Equally, they are often questions which the political scientist is not well equipped to tackle; critically, how ideologies come to be formed and how the pervasiveness of ideologies is to be measured. This contribution, then, has a dual focus: to consider what the notion of social representations contributes to the empirical study of ideologies; to clarify the place of ideology in the notion of social representations. Moreover, drawing upon our understanding of political ideologies, we hope to throw some light on questions of ideology in social psychology. These remarks originate in a concern with the dynamics of electoral politics.

Attitudes and political behaviour

The focus on attitudes in studies of electoral behaviour arose directly from the deficiencies of early sociological and social psychological modes of explanation. Sociological models (Berelson *et al.* 1954; Alford 1963; Pulzer 1967) foundered on the failure to identify causal components in the association between demographically defined groups and voting; it remained to be inferred, for example, what it was about being middle class, female, and old that constituted a predisposition, amongst British electors, to support the Conservative party. Social psychological models (Campbell *et al.* 1960; Butler and Stokes 1971) ran aground on the empirical variability of 'party identification' (Campbell and Valen 1966; Thomassen 1976), together with theoretical doubts about a contentless 'affective orientation' towards parties amongst voters (Crewe 1976; Robertson 1976*a*). A third approach, 'the psychology of politics'—as pioneered by Adorno *et al.* (1950) and persisting in the debate on the origins of political extremism (Stone 1980; Eysenck 1982; McClosky and Chong 1985)—is ill-fitted to uncovering the dynamics of electoral choice in polities where relatively few voters support extremist parties.

In face of these difficulties and the evidence of 'issue voting', the focus of research turned to quantifying the electoral impact of political attitudes. That voters are aware of, and have views about the political questions of the day is well attested; after major studies of the American electorate during the 1960s (Nie *et al.* 1976) and the British electorate in the early 1970s (Alt *et al.* 1976), the conventional wisdom that electors are not moved by political issues was laid to rest. But revealing that electors have intelligible attitudes on the events, states, and objects which are the stuff of politics raised two much more difficult questions: how do electors come to form such attitudes? How do electors come to formulate a singular decision for which party to vote, from attitudes on multifarious and diverse questions?

Taking attitudes to be composed of cognitive and evaluative or affective elements, political scientists have, conventionally, characterized attitudes as individual responses to the events, states, or objects which are the stuff of conflicts, or 'issues', in the public domain. Recording responses to singular issues or, at best, eliciting preferences on 'trade-off' issues—for example, between taxation and welfare—the focus of research has been on the structure of attitudes across the issues of the day. Representing 'attitude structure' as the outcome of 'some form of constraint or functional interdependence' between 'two or more beliefs or opinions held by an individual' (Converse 1964, p. 207; Campbell *et al.* 1960, p. 189), the actual measure of 'coherent' or 'structured' political attitudes adopted was the attitude sets of political élites—Congressmen in America, party leaderships in Britain—on matters of public moment. Slipping thus from what is 'functional' for individuals to what is 'functional' amongst political élites entailed not only ignoring what is different about politics for electors and elites but, even more to the point, neglected to consider what it is that lends coherence to sets of attitudes. If structured attitudes are a function of 'constraint' or 'interdependence', what is it that serves to constrain, or render interdependent, responses to the several issues of the day?

Even in times of relative political quietude, such as the Eisenhower years in America or the MacMillan years in Britain, issues are many, diverse, and enjoy no necessary ordering. Moreover, matters of politics do not bear their own hallmarks of intelligibility; even amongst members of parliament, regardless of party allegiance, there was confusion, indeed, disarray, following the Argentine assault on the Falklands. Matters of politics do not arise, or take shape, according to some intrinsic logic; for example, the efforts of Mrs Thatcher's government to implement a monetarist fiscal strategy alongside a nuclear defence strategy were not rooted in necessity. The search for an inherent logic to political issues becomes even more bewildering if we include education reform, expansion of the police force, privatization of public utilities, and support for the American bombing of Libya. In other words, if attitudes across a number of political questions constitute a structure of some kind, the structure cannot be a function of the demands of events, objects, or states appearing in the public domain—that domain is too 'noisy', and too contingent, to yield its own meanings and understandings.

But, to persist with our example, the actions of Mrs Thatcher's government are intelligible—once we turn to the underlying beliefs held in common by the principal actors. It is those beliefs, or rather, that complex of beliefs, that political scientists recognize as an ideology. Pre-empting a later argument, here I simply assert that it is in an ideology that the cognitive and evaluative/affective elements of attitudes are rooted; that political attitudes, in short, are the outcome of bringing to bear on specific events, states, or objects the meanings and understandings embedded in a political ideology. Thus the coherence of monetarist and nuclear strategies is rooted in the vision of robust individuals within a strong state, one face of the neo-liberal ideology propounded by the dominant wing of the modern Conservative party (Scarbrough 1984, pp. 73–6). In other words, what serves to constrain attitudes—or render them 'functionally interdependent'—is the ideology in which they are grounded. Accordingly, 'what goes with what' in structured attitudes is not intelligible until set within the context of the ideology from which separable attitudes emanate. It is just this failure to set attitudes against standing beliefs that makes for the inconclusiveness of so much research on the place of political attitudes in voting (Cf. Särlvik and Crewe 1983; Heath *et al.* 1985).[1]

In this way, the study of electoral behaviour—only one, but a typical concern of political science—has come to question what is being measured in conventional attitude research. And, clearly, our doubts about the analytic status of attitudes are not very different to those expressed by social psychologists, whether challenging the individualism underpinning American traditions in cognitive psychology (Jaspars and Fraser 1984) or pointing to the social nature of understandings, beliefs, and opinions (Codol 1974; Herzlich 1973; Moscovici 1984). On the other hand, reading attitudes as engaging ideology leads us to depart sharply from the approach to attitudes and ideology offered by an alternative view within social psychology. Billig, for example, proposes that 'an attitude refers to a single unit of thought, belief or feeling' related to 'some object, issue or person', whilst an ideology 'refers to a pattern of attitudes' (Billig 1984, pp. 234–5)— a position not dissimilar to that propounded by Michigan scholars a generation ago. Scarbrough (1984, Ch. 2), has offered an extended critique of the 'attitude structure' approach to ideology, and much the same objections apply to Billig's definitions, which can give us purchase neither on what it is that serves to give attitudes a pattern nor from where or what individuals derive their thought, beliefs, or feelings about a specific 'object, issue, or person'. In a world—or, more accurately, worlds of family life, work, political activity, and the like—where reality is the work of its participants in actively constructing and reconstructing meanings and performances (Berger and Luckman 1967; Dawe 1970; Giddens 1976), neither thoughts, beliefs, nor feelings are autonomously formulated.[2] Nor, as we indicated earlier, can the patterning of attitudes be construed as a function of some 'natural order of things' inherent in encounters with specific events, persons, or issues. As Lovejoy puts it: 'The world of concrete existence . . . is no translation of pure logic into temporal terms' (1964, p. 332).

Ideology and political attitudes

From what we have said, however, we might readily fall in with the claim that 'coherent' or structured political attitudes are a function of political ideologies. Covert claims of this kind have been common in studies of

---

[1] A point specifically acknowledged by Heath *et al.* (1985). Searching for an interpretable relationship between issue preferences and voting, they conclude that 'the most effective way of getting the "right" answer is to ignore respondents' own judgements of importance altogether' for what best accounts for electoral choice is 'the fit between the general character of the party and the voter's own general ideology' (pp. 98–9, parenthesis added).

[2] Whilst this position is firmly established in social theory, sociologists have been slow to follow with empirical studies; but see, for example, Bechhofer and Elliott (1968). Within social psychology, the point is borne out in Herzlich's study (1973).

'mass' political attitudes, leading to inferential research in which evidence of structured attitudes has been read as evidence of the pervasiveness, or otherwise, of political ideologies among electors (Campbell *et al.* 1960; Butler and Stokes 1971; Himmelweit *et al.* 1985). And this methodologically odd approach—construing evidence of one kind of phenomenon as evidence of another kind of phenomenon—has arisen directly from the failure to make a conceptual distinction between attitudes and ideology. Portraying political ideologies as the structuring forces underlying coherent, 'structured', political attitudes entails making just such a distinction. We need, then, a working notion of what an ideology is, both to secure the distinction and to indicate how attitudes cannot be read as surrogates for ideology.

The concept of ideology is notoriously problematic. As with other 'essentially contested concepts' (Gallie 1956) it is not readily settled by fiat; the several definitions to hand are not free of ideological ambition. Marxist and non-Marxist writers alike are subject to this stricture. But whereas the ideological purposes of Marxists and neo-Marxists are widely recognized, the purposes of the American positivists are less familiar. Our understanding of adherence to an ideology is to be distanced from the 'army of zealots' approach suggested by, for example, Shils (1968): 'Complete individual subservience to the ideology is demanded of those who accept it, and it is regarded as essential and imperative that their conduct be completely permeated by it.'

Setting aside familiar controversies, we start from the notion of ideology as *a system of beliefs characteristic of a group*, a modest but broadly agreed position (Plamenatz 1971, p. 16). That is, ideologies constitute a set of beliefs which are bound together in some systematic way; the system of beliefs is a property of groups both in the sense that an ideology is generated by an identifiable group and that it may be shared, or used, by others. But adding to the roll of definitions is not enough (Lance-Bennett 1977); to open the way to our later discussion, I shall outline what is entailed in our working notion of ideology. This account is, perforce, highly synoptic; an extended discussion is presented in Scarbrough (1984).

Two features of the social world form the backdrop to our account: the inherent, endemic uncertainty of social life arising from the inter-subjective, reflexive character of social practices; the imperative for action upon social actors (Hollis 1977). Within these bearings, we understand an ideology as 'a *system* of beliefs' by taking seriously the analogy of ideologies as 'maps'. Geertz, for example, asserts: 'ideologies are, most distinctively, maps of problematic social reality' (1964, p. 64). Himmelweit *et al.* (1985) do not address the concept of ideology, but their early discussion of 'ideological thinking' and the 'ideological dimensions . . . of the views of British voters' (p. 17) develops freely into talk of 'the cognitive maps that different sections of the community build up about the society and its institutions'

(p. 235). The first function of the map is to define the terrain of action; in Mannheim's terms, to provide 'a definition of the situation'. As the onto-logical assumptions of an ideology, these belief elements identify the status of actors and delineate the landscape—agents of class struggle for Marxists, individuals under the law for liberals. Secondly, the map identifies destina-tions and marks out routes across the terrain, defining the intertwined goals and values of the ideology. The goals set out, in Rokeach's terms, the value-laden 'preferable end-states of existence' (Rokeach 1976, p. 160); the values designate the moral character of an ideology in the light of the goals. The socialist's goal of equality entails, *en route*, concern for the plight of 'underdogs'; the fascist's contempt for ethnic minorities is rooted in the goal of national purity. But these three kinds of belief elements—the assumptions, values, and goals—lack empirical content, saying nothing about what kinds of acts ease the lot of the disadvantaged or how national purity might be secured. As questions of action lie at the heart of ideologies, the fourth kind of belief constitutes the principles of action, the 'what is to be done' elements of an ideology. In terms of our 'map', they stand as signposts at junctures in the terrain of action: the principle of direct inter-vention points anarchists to act against power centres; the principle of the active state leads socialists to instigate welfare programmes. Finally, ideologies are bound together as systems of beliefs by an epistemological mode; belief elements which provide grounds for trusting the 'map'. Such modes range from the authority of historical texts for Marxists through the informality of 'tradition' in Tory ideology to the experiences of the dis-advantaged for socialists.

Political ideologies thus constitute a *system of beliefs*, rather than any set of beliefs, because a number of different kinds of beliefs have to stand together to allow for confident action in the shifting, and 'meaningless', world of politics. The assumptions, values, and goals provide the grounding for action; the principles of action orient actors about 'what is to be done'. As the political domain is extensive, so political ideologies are wide-ranging belief systems, enabling actors to move on any, and several, of the different fronts of the constituted order. But as general and abstract constructions, ideologies cannot provide specific answers to specific problems; they serve to orient actors, not to determine action. Thus attitudes, even structured attitudes, are not the equivalent of ideologies: attitudes are particular responses to specific challenges; political ideologies are constructions of reality which imbue the politics of the day with order and meaning. Political ideologies constitute the environment in which political attitudes are formed; political attitudes encompass empirical elements of a level of specificity which has no place in ideologies.[3]

---

[3] To illustrate the distortion entailed in reading attitudes as surrogates for ideology, consider the ideological grounds for the opposition of Enoch Powell and Tony Benn to

As a system of beliefs *characteristic of a group*, the second part of our working notion, political ideologies can be readily located in political parties. In everyday terms and in formal studies (Robertson 1976*b*; Budge *et al.* forthcoming), we are familiar with parties in terms of 'what they stand for'. We can identify the leaders and activists of parties, and we may find others who make use of the ideology when faced with the issues of the day; they share the party's version of political reality without taking part in the work of constructing the ideology. But identifying the party as the locus of a political ideology does not resolve questions about the origins of an ideology: what brings together the members of the group which constitutes the party? It cannot be the holding of an ideology in common, for the group cannot be both a function of its ideology and its generative source. Nor can it be the coming together of individuals with similar ideologies; ideologies are not individual belief systems for that would entail all actors defining their own situation and acting autonomously. Political life is not sustainable upon such idiosyncratic, fragmented understandings.

Here the political scientist can turn to the notion of interests. Following Weber's discussion of associative and communal groups (1964, pp. 136–9), the political party can be construed as a group whose members come together to pursue some interest or purpose. Individual interests, however, are specific; to establish a common interest, what is individual has to be rendered general, or 'typified', and here we draw freely from Berger and Luckman's notion of 'typificatory schemes' in everyday interaction (1967, pp. 28–34). For many interest groups this requires only the construction of common understandings, endowing the group with commonality and communality—the 'group ethic' of a 'solidary' social group.[4] What marks out the political party as an interest group—but not only parties—is that its purpose cannot be realized without inserting its claims into the public domain; to secure its interests the group needs to shape, or re-shape, understandings in the community at large. The ethic of the group needs elaboration into a 'map' of the wider community, underpinning claims to control—or, at least, decisively influence—the institutions of the state and, thus, the direction of public life. And in the drive to shape common consciousness where experiences and interests are many and diverse, we again come to understand why ideologies are general and abstract systems of beliefs, not specific answers to particular questions.

This working notion of ideology, however, raises several problems. Ideologies are recognized as social phenomena only in so far as they are

Britain's membership of the European Common Market: for the one, it represented an infringement of national sovereignty; for the other, it represented the political dominance of international capital.

[4] The term 'solidary social group' is not used by Weber himself but it serves to sum up his discussion of groups involving some form of 'communal relationship' (Weber 1964, pp. 136–9).

shared by some group and are concerned with questions in the public domain. The approach can give no account of how members of groups come to those beliefs that constitute ideologies as 'maps', nor how interests are arrived at. The notion of 'rational' interests is challenged, in British politics, by the apparently 'deviant' beliefs of working-class Conservative voters and upper-class socialists (Robertson 1984); conceptual difficulties with 'real interests' make us uneasy about dismissing 'mistakes' under the rubric of 'false consciousness' (Child 1970; Miller 1972). Again, we have no pointers to what we might expect of ideology beyond the ranks of ideologues, yet political ideologies which do not speak to the life of a society would be odd. On the other hand, structural explanations of ideology—largely following Marx in rooting ideologies in the 'contradictions' of the social order (Althusser 1971; Doise 1978; Larrain 1979)—yield constricted, determinist, accounts of political life. Social psychological accounts of ideology are not entirely free of these tendencies: Billig (1982) gives extended attention to the 'contradictions' version of ideology; Rokeach defines ideology as 'an organisation of beliefs and attitudes . . . that is more or less *institutionalised*, or shared with others, *deriving from external authority*' (1976, pp. 123–4, emphases added). We have to turn elsewhere, then, to understand how political ideologies have their roots in the life of a society. It is here that the notion of social representations, as delineated by Moscovici, captures our attention.

Social representations: process and image

Despite having offered several accounts, Moscovici presents social representations as neither a firm concept nor as a theoretically bounded description of empirical phenomena. Indeed, Moscovici uses the term 'social representations' to identify two rather different empirical forms: as the *process* in which individuals and groups construct images of the world; as the *analytic category* identifying images of the world as empirical phenomena. As process, social representations render the world intelligible; as phenomena, social representations are to be distinguished from both theories (notably science) and ideologies. But as process and as phenomena, social representations bear some relationship to both theories and ideologies. On the other hand, social representations as process originate in the nature of social life, whereas social representations as phenomena constitute 'a social reality *sui generis*' (1984, p. 13). It should be noted that while we feel the distinction between social representations as image and as process serves to clarify Moscovici's account, it is not one that Moscovici is prepared to make: 'we cannot make a clear distinction between regularities in representations and those in the processes that create them' (1984, p. 67). From the outset, then, Moscovici's account of social representations presents conceptual difficulties, but the very vagueness of the notion allows us the space, as it were, to explicate a place for social representations in our understanding of ideologies.

Following Moscovici's account, social representations as process constitute 'basically, a system of classification and denotation, of allotting categories and names' (1984, p. 30), with the purpose of making 'something unfamiliar, or unfamiliarity itself, familiar' (1984, p. 24), which arises in the 'concepts, statements and explanations originating in daily life in the course of inter-individual communications' (1981, p. 181). The process of naming is two-fold: to 'anchor strange ideas . . . to set them in a familiar context': to 'objectify' ideas, that is 'to turn something abstract into something almost concrete' (1984, p. 29). Starting with the 'specific representations' that individuals propose 'in the streets, in cafes, offices, hospitals, laboratories, etc.' (1984, p. 16) and elaborated in the 'noisy, public activity' of the 'consensual universes' found in 'clubs, associations and cafes' (1984, p. 21), the process of naming is shot through with values—'neutrality is forbidden by the very logic of the system' (1984, p. 30) for 'words . . . create things and pass their properties to them' (1981, p. 202). Thus social representations as process is a function of 'everyday', informal social life in which individuals and groups actively participate in constructing the images —explanations, meanings, understandings—which serve to orient them in a diverse and fluid world.

As a constituent element of social reality, a social representation is an image of an idea, constructed in language and imbued with meaning (1984, p. 17). Such images are social in that they are formed 'in the course of communication and co-operation' between individuals, they are concerned with 'a collective object' and, most importantly, they are 'shared by all' (1984, p. 13). Members of social groups share many social representations and share them, moreover, as a necessary feature of social life: 'our collectivities could not function today if social representations were not formed' (1984, p. 19). It is the sharing of representations which 'establishes a group identity' (Moscovici and Hewstone 1983, p. 16)—such 'consensual universes' being distinguished from the 'reified universes' of formal roles and institutionalized modes of behaviour by the 'implicit stock of images and of ideas which are taken for granted and mutually accepted' (1984, p. 21). Thus social representations as active images of the world—as distinct from process—constitute both the grounds upon which people understand their world and gives the shifting, intersubjective world a physical reality. To paraphrase Moscovici: 'our psychology contains our sociology in a condensed form' (1984, p. 65).

From this account, we might go on to construe ideologies as extensive but internally structured complexes of social representations. That is, we might restate the component elements of ideologies as different kinds of social representations; the individuals of neo-liberal ideology, for example, being understood as a social representation, or image, of persons, 'tradition' in Tory ideology being a social representation of understandings embedded in historical continuities. In locating ideologies in the 'uncertainty' of social life, our approach accords with Moscovici's assertion that 'in the consensual universe . . . man is the measure of all things' (1984, p. 20). And Moscovici's emphasis on social representations as a property of social groups, or 'consensual universes', closely resembles our account of ideologies as the work of 'solidary' social groups. If portraying ideologies as complexes of social representations involved some reinterpretation of Moscovici's position, we would not be alone. Himmelweit *et al.* (1985), for example, have restated Moscovici's notion in four rather different ways: as 'a common script' shared by members of a society which 'provide an ordered view of social relations and the social order' (p. 203); as 'scripts [which] both reflect social change and are important precursors of such change' (p. 203); as 'cognitive maps . . . [representing] collective responses to the social and political climate of society' (p. 159); and as 'ideologies' (p. 153). Billig (1984), too, deploys four different interpretations of social representations—as 'an ideology' (p. 238), as 'arguments' (p. 244), as 'themes' (p. 247), and as 'symbols' (p. 247). Moreover, in contrast to Himmelweit's suggestion that social representations capture, even promote, the dynamics of social change, Billig suggests that an ideology is constituted in social representations which are 'integrated into a rigid, internally consistent pattern of thought' (Billig 1984, p. 246).[5] Clearly, then, when it comes to questions of social representations and ideologies the field is replete with ambiguity.

In some measure, these ambiguities arise from the self-referential language in which accounts of social representations are couched, compounded by the 'plasticity' of social representations (Moscovici 1984, p. 18). Indeed, for Moscovici, the evolution of a metalanguage—'a common language which will enable [psychologists] to establish a concordance between the forms of thought of individuals and the social content of those thoughts' (1984, p. 52)—is part of the project of social representations. But the dangers here, as with Billig's suggestion that questions of 'ideological consistency' be resolved by 'charting the evasions and elisions of language' (Billig 1982, p. 226) or Potter and Litton's recommendation that social psychologists should 'embed their study within the context of a more general analysis of

---

[5] In focusing largely on Fascism and Marxism, Billig is misleading in pointing to ideologies as 'rigid' modes of thought. Koestler's account of the 'dissonance-reduction' work expected of Communist Party members (Billig 1982, p. 229) is not only belied by the development of modern Eurocommunism (Kindersley 1981) but also needs to be set against the 'loose-jointed' structure of other ideologies, notably Tory ideology. In other words, the 'rigid' character of an ideology is an empirical question.

discourse' (Potter and Litton 1985, p. 89), are two-fold: the insights of social representations might be lost to other social sciences; uncovering 'the structure and the dynamics of representations' (Moscovici 1984, p. 16) might come to focus on the meanings embedded in language, as in discourse theories of ideology, rather than, as Moscovici prescribes, uncovering the relations between social representations and social groups (Moscovici 1983, p. 135).

To return to the suggestion that ideologies might be construed as complexes of social representations. Our purpose in making such a move would be to secure ideologies as *essentially* social phenomena. That is, in this light, the social character of ideologies would extend beyond being shared by some number of people and having as their concern matters in the public domain. Rather, ideologies could be understood as social in being rooted in the processes of social life and in being expressed as images of social reality. Put another way: the seeds of ideologies could be understood to lie in the very nature of the interchanges of everyday life, and the force of ideologies could be understood as setting the forms of everyday life. And in rendering ideologies social both from the beginning and in the end, as it were, we might more readily understand what is social in 'individual' interests and attitudes.

Were we able to make this inferential leap, we could look to social psychologists to uncover the dynamics of social life, capturing the ideological in that which is located in persons. That is, as Moscovici urges, 'splitting representations' (1984, p. 16) would be properly the task of social psychology, leaving sociology and political science to focus on the impact of particular images in social and political life. The need to deconstruct political 'images' and measure their force is real enough: since Graham Wallas suggested that electors need 'something which can be loved and trusted' (Wallas 1908, p. 83), the notion of 'party images' has enjoyed a persisting—but neither specified nor substantiated—place in studies of the British electorate (Butler and Stokes 1971; Särlvik and Crewe 1983; Heath *et al.* 1985).[6] Moreover, the notion of social representations suggests a springboard releasing the concept of ideology from the rigidities of structural approaches and from the distortions entailed in some of the 'epic' claims made for ideologies (cf. Bell 1960; Aron 1967).[7] It would then be—

---

[6] 'People respond to the parties to a large extent in terms of the images they form from the characteristics and style of party leaders and from the party's association with the things governments may achieve' (Butler and Stokes 1971, p. 432). Subsequent studies have not advanced beyond this interpretation of 'party image'; Heath *et al.* have yet to test their claim that voter's ' "synoptic" evaluations' of parties entail questions of ideology (Heath *et al.* 1985, pp. 99, 174–5).

[7] Cf. 'Ideology is the conversion of ideas into social levers' (Bell 1960, p. 370); 'Ideology . . . is a pseudo-systematic formulation of a total vision of the historical world' (Aron 1967, p. 144). Such 'epic' definitions distort our analytic focus both by claiming too much for ideologies and by going no further than definitions.

following Farr's suggestion (1978) that the notion of social representations links the concerns of the social sciences—a joint project to draw the lineaments of social and political life from the 'images' of a society held by persons and groups.

These are tempting possibilities. In the work of Billig and Himmelweit, we have seen social psychologists moving freely between social representations and ideologies; Doise goes so far as to talk of social perceptions and practices as 'ideological representations' (1978, p. 124). But Moscovici's account of social representations yields no grounds for construing ideologies as social representations. This becomes evident from what he writes of the relationship between social representations and ideologies. Nevertheless, following from what Moscovici says of the bearing of ideologies upon social representations, we can locate a place for social representations in the study of ideologies.

Ideologies and social representations

Moscovici does not address questions of ideology directly, but a number of comments in his work suggest that social representations are to be distinguished from ideologies. Yet while social representations and ideologies are different phenomena, they are not unconnected—and it is their connectedness that makes the project of 'splitting representations' particularly interesting for our approach to ideology. But let us consider first the distinctions that can be drawn, from Moscovici's own account, between social representations and ideologies.

From what Moscovici writes, the distinction between 'a consensual universe' and 'a reified universe' is more than a way of distinguishing between his own notion of social representations and Durkheim's 'collective' representations (Moscovici 1981, pp. 186–7, 1984, pp. 16–19). Whilst not dwelling on social life in formal, institutional settings, Moscovici emphasizes the informality of the world in which social representations have their life—that world of 'noisy, public activity' noted earlier. Again, taking his research material from 'samples of conversations normally exchanged in a society' (1984, p. 52), Moscovici points to the place of social representations outside the world of a formal 'set of rules', 'roles', and 'categories' defining the 'global environment' of institutional life (1981, p. 187). But Moscovici is less sure-footed about where ideologies are found. In one mode, he construes 'the true nature of ideology' as being 'to facilitate' the transition from a 'consensual' world to a 'reified world' (1984, p. 23); in another, he associates ideology with formal groups, even institutions, 'a party, a school of thought or an organ of state' (1984, p. 58). Whether, for Moscovici, ideologies are bridgeheads between 'consensual' and 'reified' worlds or are a function of institutions, he clearly suggests that social representations and ideologies are located in different parts of the social world.

Other distinctions, and difficulties, emerge from Moscovici's brief foray into ideology. Taking the status of psychoanalysis in France as a paradigm case, Moscovici likens the evolution of an ideology to that of an official creed: first, the elaboration of a theory by a scientific discipline; then 'the "representative" phase' in which the 'images, concepts and vocabulary' of the theory are recast and adapted; finally, '*the representation* is appropriated (by a party, a school of thought, or an organ of state) and is logically reconstructed so that a product, created by a society as a whole, can be *enforced in the name of science*' (1984, p. 58; emphases added). Here Moscovici himself seems to suggest that ideologies and social representations are one and the same, that the 'images, concepts, and vocabulary' of a scientific theory, after popular restatement and diffusion, constitute a singular representation. But portraying an ideology as '*the representation*' does not align with ideologies as complexes of elements, whatever we call the elements; the richness and scope of socialism, for example, cannot be captured either in the representation of social relations as a function of class structure or in the image of social equality. On the other hand, if an ideology consists of a complex of 'images, concepts, and vocabulary', then social representations are not 'unit' elements to be split, 'just as genes and atoms have been split' (1984, p. 16), but complexes to be decomposed into other 'unit' elements, whatever they might then be called. In which case, we must be perplexed that Moscovici's project is to uncover 'the structure and the dynamics of representations' (1984, p. 16)—not the structure and dynamics of ideologies.

Moscovici's account of ideology is odd too in the twin inferences, embedded in their 'official status', that ideologies originate in formal disciplines and that their force lies in the authority of science. Certainly ideologies have an internal structure, and ideologues—as a matter of intellectual history—often call upon the work of scholars. But the content of an ideology is an empirical question, to be uncovered by charting the system of beliefs elaborated by an identifiable group—which Moscovici appears to acknowledge when claiming that ideologies 'have no specific structure', making them the concern of 'sociology and history' (1984, p. 23). We have to take the structure of ideologies as we find them (Converse 1964, p. 210; Scarbrough 1984, p. 39–40), whereas formal disciplines—'science, art and economics' (1984, p. 25)—are governed by rules of argument and canons of evidence. Moreover, that ideologues may call upon 'science' is slim ground for construing ideologies as formal modes of thought; indeed, what is striking about the major ideologies at large in British politics is how freely ideologues raid disparate disciplines, roam across diverse experiences, and range between different epistemological modes (Scarbrough 1984, Ch. 5).

Furthermore, in proposing that the authority of ideologies lies in their formal structure, Moscovici cannot distinguish between theories and ideologies; if ideologies are theories Moscovici could not, in short, secure a distinction between the 'scientific' and the 'ideological' phases in the evolution of a way of thought.

Quite what relationship Moscovici sees to hold between science, ideology, and social representations is unclear. We have concentrated on what he says of ideology as the popularization of science, but elsewhere he writes of social representations as the direct outcome of 'technical and scientific knowledge transformed into commonsense knowledge' (Moscovici and Hewstone 1983, p. 20). Moreover, whilst suggesting that science and ideologies are on a par as 'unifying systems' (Moscovici 1984, p. 18), he also sees them as 'more and more mutually incompatible' (1981, p. 185).

The work of constructing an ideology is not the work of disseminating scientific knowledge, but the elements of an ideology may change following developments in science. For example, in British politics, Labour ideology —as distinct from socialist—moved, on economic questions, from the principle of state control to the principle of state intervention as Marxist theories were challenged by Keynesian models (Pelling 1985, pp. 62–3). In brief, Moscovici's exemplar yields a curious account of what constitutes an ideology.

The crucial distinction between social representations and ideologies, however, emerges from the relationship Moscovici sees to hold between the two forms. In 'objectifying strange ideas', social representations—as process—'turn something abstract into something almost concrete' (1984, p. 29). As social representations are always 'representations of something or someone' (1984, p. 67), we ask: what is the 'abstract' which becomes concrete in the process? Although Moscovici intimates that 'the unfamiliar' —'a scientific theory, a nation, an artefact' (1984, p. 27)—is the stimulus to social representations, he actually says little about what kind of things provide 'the fire behind the smoke'. On the other hand, Moscovici clearly understands social representations as informed by ideologies; that is, ideologies constitute a resource from which individuals and groups draw in making sense of the unfamiliar. Thus, ideologies provide 'food for thought' for 'the questions they set themselves' (1984, p. 16); 'social representations . . . are based on the stock of theories and ideologies which they transform into shared realities' (1984, p. 19). In which case, some sub-set of the abstract 'something' which is given an (almost) concrete form in social representations is ideological in character. This raises a severe problem for a theory of social representations, but for the moment the point is that, from within Moscovici's account, the ideological is something different to a social representation; as a resource upon which to call in 'fabricating' social representations, ideologies stand—conceptually and empirically—prior to social representations. To emphasize the point: that which is ideological has undergone the process of social representation to emerge in social representation as phenomenon or 'image'; that which was abstract emerges as a social reality. Ideologies and social representations cannot, then, be construed as the same kind of phenomena; we can neither collapse an ideology into a single social representation nor into a complex of social representations, nor can we elevate social representations to the status of ideologies.

Conjectures and problems

That there is a symbiotic relationship between ideologies and social representations—as process and image—is neither a surprising nor a difficult idea. Intuitively, the account is readily intelligible. Certainly, it means that we are not free to render ideologies as social representations or representations as ideologies. Equally, it opens up a new front in uncovering the ideological character of social life, for what Moscovici seems to suggest is that by 'scratching' a social representation we find an ideology underneath. Indeed, he writes something very close to that: 'When we classify a person among the neurotics, the Jews or the poor . . . we reveal our "theory" of society and of human nature' (1984, p. 30). On the other hand, theories, too, are a resource for individuals and groups when they 'think for themselves' (1984, p. 16), and we have identified ideologies and science, or theories, as different forms. In which case, we might infer, the project of social representations is to uncover the 'thinking of a society' in its ideologies and sciences. Thus 'splitting representations' promises to reveal the pervasiveness of particular ideologies, the intersecting of different ideologies, the diffusion of scientific ideas—even the concatenation of science and ideology in the thinking of individuals and groups. Again, Moscovici seems to imply this point: 'The map of social interaction can be read from images, knowledge and symbols' (1973, p. xiii).

On this reading of Moscovici's account, then, we can readily find the place for social representations in the study of ideologies: 'splitting representations' serves to uncover the ideological components in the structuring of social reality. Identifying and analysing social representations as images allows the charting of the ideologies at large in a society, specifying where and in what form ideologies set the terms of attitudes and action. Such images might engage ideology in rather different ways: as the instantiation or the 'condensation' of an entire ideology; the mobilization of some part of an ideology; the conjunction of different ideologies. Identifying which ideologies inform what attitudes, or images, is an empirical task. Meanwhile, social representations as process allow for tracking how ideologies emerge from the life of a society, and how ideologies are individuated in attitudes and action; in short, charting how groups come to generate ideologies, what kind of groups generate what kind of ideologies and what kinds of people use which kinds of ideologies. In other words, rather than setting out to uncover social representations by 'unravelling the meanings of an ideology' (Billig 1984, p. 238), or reconceptualizing social representations as 'linguistic repertoires' (Potter and Litton 1985, p. 89)[8], the project is to uncover ideologies through the work of 'splitting representations'. In this way, the analysis of representations allows us—or, rather, the social psychologist—to cut into what is ideological about the 'realities' of social and political life.

Finally, a word about a problem touched on in what Moscovici writes about the relationship between social representations and ideologies. According to his account, ideologies are resources from which individuals and groups draw in constructing social representations; so ideologies stand prior to social representations and, we may infer, serve to shape responses to the specific 'something or someone' which is the 'fire behind the smoke'. Social representations are to be found in the informalities of 'consensual universes' with their roots in 'daily life'; ideologies appear to be located in such formal groups as 'a party, a school of thought or an organ of state' with their roots in 'science'. But this account suggests a deep ambiguity in Moscovici's position. If ideologies are the work of formal groups, even 'organs of state', then social representations do not have their origins in the spontaneity of 'inter-individual communication'; rather they are epiphenomena, reflecting the institutional and 'scientific' structure of a society. And if social representations are epiphenomena, they do not constitute a 'social reality *sui generis*'. On the contrary, social representations are then a function of the institutional structures of a society—leaving us the problem of accounting for social structures.

Moscovici is not unaware of this problem. He specifically rejects, for example, claims that 'groups and individuals are always and completely under the sway of a dominant ideology which is produced and imposed by their social class, the State, the Church or the school' (1984, p. 15). Again, almost tellingly, he asserts that 'Human beings . . . do not envisage thoughts and words as epiphenomena' (1981, p. 182). None the less, Moscovici neither confronts this difficulty nor is it evident, from within his account, how it might be resolved. The problem clearly has implications for the place of social representations in the study of ideologies; rendering

---

[8] As Potter and Litton do not specify what emerges from social representations as 'linguistic repertoires', their proposal seems odd. If linguistic repertoires are 'recurrently used systems of terms for characterizing actions, events and other phenomena' (p. 89), then social representations would seem to be no more than 'standing images' to be used as occasion demands—an impoverishment of Moscovici's notion, particularly in removing the dynamic of social representation as process. It seems more apposite to construe ideologies as linguistic repertoires.

social representations as reflections of prevailing power structures, the account runs perilously close to structural versions of the ideological character of social life. And clearly it poses a severe problem for Moscovici's wider perspective, both in his concern to distance his own position from that of Durkheim and his concern to root the social construction of reality in the 'thinking for themselves' (1984, p. 16) carried out by individuals and groups.

Two conclusions seem to be warranted by our discussion. The project of social representations clearly offers new perspectives in the study of ideologies. In the methodology of 'splitting representations' there is the promise of tools for quantifying the pervasiveness of particular ideologies and, thereby, uncovering what is ideological in the life of a society. Moreover, in the notion of social representations, as both process and image, Moscovici's project suggests the groundwork for an empirical theory of ideology which is *essentially* social. On the other hand, in not addressing questions of ideology directly, the notion of social representations remains ambiguous, even theoretically fragile. There are other problems which we have not touched on, particularly the part of social representations in creating group identities and the vulnerability of Moscovici's project to becoming another version of discourse theories of ideology. But were the project to succeed in establishing the concordance 'between forms of thought of individuals and the social content of those thoughts', it would sharpen the focus—and ease the lot—of the political scientist intent on grasping the dynamics of ideologies and the force of images in political life. Equally, realizing Moscovici's ambition—to 'reconstruct a general science which would encapsulate a whole galaxy of related investigations' (1984, p. 69)—promises to be an Herculean task. But we might expect the project to be alert to the insights which an understanding of political ideologies yields.

Acknowledgements

I thank Kum-Kum Bhavnani and Colin Fraser for their comments on an earlier draft of this paper.

References

Adorno, T.W., Frenkel-Brunswick, E., Levinson, D.J., and Sanford, R. (1950). *The authoritarian personality*. Harper, New York.

Alford, R.R. (1963). *Party and society*. Murray, Chicago.

Alt, J., Särlvik, B., and Crewe, I. (1976). Partisanship and policy choice: issue preferences in the British electorate, February 1974. *British Journal of Political Science*, **VI**, 273–90.

Althusser, L. (1971). Ideology and ideological state apparatuses. In *Lenin and philosophy*. New Left Books, London.

Aron, R. (1967). *The industrial age*. Praeger, New York.

Bechhofer, F. and Elliott, B. (1968). An approach to a study of small shopkeepers in the class structure. *European Journal of Sociology*, **9**, 180–240.

Bell, D. (1960). *The end of ideology*. Free Press, Glencoe.

Berelson, B.R., Lazarsfeld, P.F., and Macphee, W.N. (1954). *Voting*. University of Chicago Press.

Berger, P.L. and Luckman, T. (1967). *The social construction of reality*. Doubleday, New York.

Billig, M. (1982). *Ideology and social psychology*. Blackwell, Oxford.

Billig, M. (1984). Political ideology. In *Psychology Survey No. 5* (ed. H. Beloff and J. Nicholson), pp. 234–63.

Budge, I., Robertson, D., and Hearl, D. (eds) (1987). *Ideology, strategy and party change*. Cambridge University Press, London.

Butler, D. and Stokes, D. (1971). *Political change in Britain*. Penguin, Harmondsworth.

Campbell, A., Converse, P., Miller, W., and Stokes, D. (1960). *The American voter*. Wiley, New York.

Campbell, A. and Valen, H. (1966). Party identification in Norway and the United States. In *Elections and the public order* (ed. A. Campbell *et al.*) Wiley, New York.

Child, A. (1970). The concept of class interest. *Ethics*, **80**, 279–95.

Codol, J.P. (1974). On the system of representations in a group situation. *European Journal of Social Psychology*, **4**, 343–65.

Converse, P. (1964). The nature of belief systems in mass publics. In *Ideology and discontent* (ed. D. Apter). Free Press, New York.

Crewe, I. (1976). Party identification theory and political change in Britain. In *Party identification and beyond* (ed. I. Budge, I. Crewe, and D. Farlie). Wiley, London.

Dawe, A. (1970). The two sociologies. *British Journal of Sociology*, **21**, 207–18.

Doise, W. (1978). *Groups and individuals: explanations in social psychology*. Cambridge University Press.

Eysenck, H.J. (1982). Left-wing authoritarianism: myth or reality?. *Political Psychology*, **III**, 234–8.

Farr, R.M. (1978). On the varieties of social psychology: an essay on the relationships between psychology and other social sciences. *Social Science Information*, **17**, 503–25.

Gallie, W.B. (1956). Essentially contested concepts. *Proceedings of the Aristotelian Society*, **55**, 167–99.

Geertz, C. (1964). Ideology as a cultural system. In *Ideology and discontent* (ed. D. Apter). Free Press, Glencoe.

Giddens, A. (1976). *New rules of sociological method*. Hutchinson, London.

Heath, A., Jowell, R., and Curtice, J. (1985). *How Britain votes*. Pergamon, Oxford.

Herzlich, C. (1973). *Health and illness*. Academic Press, London.

Himmelweit, H., Humphreys, P., and Jaeger, M. (1985). *How voters decide*. Open University Press, Milton Keynes.

Hollis, M. (1977). *Models of man*. Cambridge University Press, London.

Jaspars, J. and Fraser, C. (1984). Attitudes and social representations. In *Social representations* (ed. R.M. Farr and S. Moscovici). Cambridge University Press.

Kindersley, R. (1981). *In search of Eurocommunism*. Macmillan, London.

Lance-Bennett, W. (1977). The growth of knowledge in mass belief studies: an epistemological critique. *American Journal of Political Science*, **XXI**, 465–500.

Larrain, J. (1979). *The concept of ideology*. Hutchinson, London.

Lovejoy, A.O. (1964). *The great chain of being*. Harvard University Press, London.

McClosky, H. and Chong, D. (1985). Similarities and differences between left-wing and right-wing radicals. *British Journal of Political Science*, **15**, 329–63.

Miller, D. (1972). Ideology and false consciousness. *Political Studies*, **XX**, 432–47.

Moscovici, S. (1972). Society and theory in social psychology. In *The context of social psychology* (ed. J. Israel and H. Tajfel). Academic Press, London.

Moscovici, S. (1973). Preface to C. Herzlich, *Health and illness: a social psychological analysis*. Academic Press, London.

Moscovici, S. (1981). On social representation. In *Social cognition: perspectives on everyday understanding* (ed. J. Forgas). Academic Press, London.

Moscovici, S. (1983). The coming era of social representations. In *Cognitive analysis of social behaviour* (ed. J.-P. Codol and J.-P. Leyens). Martinus Nijhoff, The Hague.

Moscovici, S. (1984). The phenomenon of social representations. In *Social representations* (ed. R.M. Farr and S. Moscovici). Cambridge University Press.

Moscovici, S. and Hewstone, M. (1983). Social representations and social explanations: from the 'naïve' to the 'amateur' scientist. In *Attribution theory: social and functional extensions* (ed. M. Hewstone). Blackwell, Oxford.

Nie, N., Verba, S., and Petrocik, J. (1976). *The changing American voter*. Harvard University Press, London.

Pelling, H. (1985). *The origins of the Labour party*, Clarendon Press, London.

Plamenatz, J. (1971). *Ideology*. Pall Mall Press, London.

Potter, J. and Litton, I. (1985). Some problems underlying the theory of social representations. *British Journal of Social Psychology*, **24**, 81–90.

Pulzer, P. (1967). *Political representation and elections in Britain*. Allen & Unwin, London.

Robertson, D.B. (1976a). Surrogates for party identification in the rational choice framework. In *Party identification and beyond* (ed. I. Budge, I. Crewe, and D. Farlie). Wiley, London.

Robertson, D.B. (1976b). *A theory of party competition*. Wiley, London.

Robertson, D.B. (1984). *Class and the British electorate*. Blackwell, Oxford.

Rokeach, M. (1976). *Beliefs, attitudes and values*. Josey-Bass, London.

Särlvik, B. and Crewe, I. (1983). *Decade of dealignment*. Cambridge University Press.

Scarbrough, E. (1984). *Political ideology and voting*. Clarendon Press, Oxford.

Shils, E. (1968). Ideology. In *The international encyclopaedia of social sciences*. Macmillan, New York.

Stone, W.F. (1980). The myth of left-wing authoritarianism. *Political psychology*, **II**, 3–19.

Tajfel, H. (1972). Introduction. In *The context of social psychology* (ed. J. Israel and H. Tajfel). Academic Press, London.

Thomassen, J. (1976). Party identification as a cross-national concept: its meaning in the Netherlands. In *Party identification and beyond* (ed. I. Budge, I. Crewe, and D. Farlie). Wiley, London.

Wallas, G. (1908). *Human nature in politics*. Constable, London.

Weber, M. (1964). *The theory of economic and social organisation* (ed. T. Parsons). Free Press, New York.

Part III

Studies of widespread beliefs

7 Social categorization, collective beliefs, and causal attribution

Jos Jaspars and Miles Hewstone*

Introduction

In the night of the first of February 1953 an exceptionally heavy winter gale and a spring tide coincided along the coast of Holland. The sea broke through the dikes and flooded 20 per cent of all the land that had been reclaimed by the Dutch in the course of centuries. It was the worst natural disaster that had ever occurred in the country; eighteen hundred people drowned overnight. When the Queen of the Netherlands addressed the nation over the radio a few days later, her speech was preceded by the recitation of a verse from the national anthem, one of the most beautiful poems in Dutch literature. Written at the time of the uprising against the Spanish in the sixteenth century as part of a collection of religious resistance songs, it has the Prince of Orange (William the Silent), in true Calvinist spirit, comfort and encourage the survivors of the first and failed military expedition along the River Maas by advocating resignation to an almighty God. The verse recited in the case of the flood of 1953 evoked this attitude in a way that was very appropriate for the occasion: 'If it had been the will of the Lord at the time, I would have liked to turn from you this heavy tempest, but the Lord above, who governs everything, whom one must always praise, did not desire it'. It served as a poetic, public, and religious explanation comforting the nation and encouraging it to devise a plan to strengthen the dikes once more and shorten the shoreline by 450 miles.

We thought of this unique and historic event when, many years later, some of our colleagues (Lalljee *et al.* 1985) planned to study the role of religious explanations in everyday life and concentrated almost automatically on causal attributions for rare events with negative outcomes. Predictably, the study showed that active members of institutionalized religions invoked divine intervention as an explanation of such events. What struck us more forcefully at the time, however, was that such events would be explained in the traditional analysis of variance ('ANOVA') model of

---

* This chapter is based on the collaborative work of Jos Jaspars and Miles Hewstone. The present form is a substantially revised and somewhat shortened version by Miles Hewstone of a joint paper written mainly by Jos Jaspars for a conference (The Editors).

attribution theory by some interaction of personal and situational factors. God appears to be functionally equivalent to a higher order interaction effect, or an error term, as far as attribution theory is concerned.

This notion is not entirely ridiculous, because in the Law of Tort so-called 'acts of God' are regarded as abnormal contingencies like floods, high winds, high tides, lightning, earthquakes, cloudbursts, and tornadoes, even though a human act may have been a *sine qua non* for the event to occur (Hart and Honoré 1959, p. 152).

These examples seem to illustrate some of the most important short-comings of traditional attribution theory. The rules of causal inference (Jaspars *et al.* 1983*a*) based on John Stuart Mill's conception of inductive logic require the description of a causal field (Mackie 1974), i.e. the set of possibly relevant factors. Mill did not ignore this problem and he devoted a whole book to operations subsidiary to induction. As Mackie (1974) has pointed out, 'there is no need for a finally satisfactory analysis of factors before the eliminative methods can be applied . . . [because] we can start using the methods with a very rough distinction of factors and obtain some correct results, which can be later refined by what I called the progressive localization of a cause' (p. 320). Kelley's (1967, 1973) ANOVA model of causal attribution obviously makes just such a rough distinction of factors which, as Brown and Fish (1983) have shown, is embedded in the structure of language. However, the refinement necessary for the progressive local-ization of a cause has so far not been developed in attribution theory. The model does not tell us that a particular person-by-stimulus-by-circumstance interaction is to be interpreted as divine intervention and not as bad luck or just chance. It seems reasonable to assume that in the progressive narrowing down of the cause of an event, social and cultural factors play a predomin-ant role. We attempted to formalize this role in our earlier, and tentative, theory of social attribution (Hewstone and Jaspars 1984), set out in the form of hypotheses, corollaries, and derivations. In explaining social behaviour or social conditions, we expected that a social categorization of causes would provide the most appropriate refinement of attributions. In addition we expected such attributions to vary as a function of the social category membership of the observer and the actor for cognitive and motivational reasons. It is to be expected therefore that such explanations are shared to some extent by members of the same social category and are affected by social stereotypes and social interaction.

However, it is by no means certain that the actual cognitive process of making causal attributions proceeds, as in science, from the abstract to the concrete. In fact there is some evidence that in everyday life attributions proceed in exactly the opposite direction (Jaspars 1983; Jaspars *et al.* 1983*b*). Expectations appear to rule out certain logical possibilities right from the start, thereby simplifying the causal inference process but carrying with it the risk of biases or even errors in certain situations. Following Kelley (1967), two different cases of attribution, which depend on the amount of information available to the perceiver can be identified. In the first case, the attributor has information from multiple sources and can perceive the covariation of an observed effect and its possible causes. In the second case, the perceiver is faced with a single observation and must take account of the configuration of factors that are plausible causes of the observed effect. The notion of covariation applies to the first, rather 'pure', case and, as Ross (1977) has pointed out, involves the application of essentially logical rules. In his words, it can be carried out by a 'mere statistician'. The use of configuration concepts (such as schemata) is far more social, demanding 'considerable insight about the nature of the man' (Ross 1977, p. 181). In seeking to highlight the social, and more specifically the collective, nature of causal attribution, we shall focus the present discussion on those cases where the perceiver lacks the information, time, or motivation to examine multiple observations. We will first discuss the role of social categorization in attribution, leading to a discussion of the knowledge base of such attributions in the form of social schemata, and conclude with the collective nature of such explanations.

Social categorization and attribution

John Stuart Mill (1872/1973) proposed his system of inductive logic as a connected view of the principles of evidence and the methods of scientific investigation. He realized that his four methods of experimental enquiry needed operations subsidiary to induction. In particular he suggested that a classification of natural groups according to kind and series was necessary (Book IV, Chapters VII and VIII). His solution is, however, in part unsatisfactory and begs the question in other respects. 'The end of classification', he argued, 'as an instrument for the investigation of nature is to make us think of those objects together which have the greatest number of important common properties and which, therefore, we have oftenest occasion, in the course of our inductions, for taking into joint consideration' (Mill 1973, Book IV, Chapter VIII). He admitted that 'In our first attempts we are likely to select for that purpose properties which are simple, easily conceived and perceptible on a first view, without any previous process of thought', and he added that natural categories arise from 'spontaneous tendencies of the mind, by placing together the objects most similar in their general aspect' (Mill 1973, IV, VII, 2).

These remarks do not get us very far, although they contain some ideas which are reminiscent of more recently developed concepts like saliency (Taylor and Fiske 1978) and cognitive heuristics (Kahneman et al. 1982), which have been discussed in connection with the study of attributional processes. In science we can, of course, take Mackie's (1965) view that the process of inductive inference is self-corrective. Classification of conditions according to irrelevant factors will not provide us with satisfactory explanations and the process of inductive enquiry will continue by trial and error until a satisfactory explanation is reached. Although such an arbitrary iterative process is conceivable, it is highly unlikely that we proceed in this fashion either in science or in common sense, which brings us back to the original question which Mill was unable to answer satisfactorily: how do we proceed from the notion of general abstract causes to concrete or natural and specific conditions which are regarded as necessary and sufficient for the occurrence of an event we observe?

In order to see how such narrowing down might take place, it is perhaps useful to go back to the first attribution experiments based on Kelley's (1967) ANOVA model, which relates directly to Mill's methods of experimental enquiry. In virtually all studies using vignettes (e.g. McArthur 1972) subjects in the experiment are not given any explicit information which would allow them to classify actors, stimuli, or occasions. The distinctions made are between the actor and everyone else, between this stimulus and every other stimulus of a particular kind, and between the present and the past. Obviously we can introduce in all three cases a further classification of actors, stimuli, and temporal occasions. In fact, that would be more or less standard procedure in the case of an experimental investigation, guided by hypotheses about the effects of personal, situational, or temporal factors. Hence the problem of narrowing down the causal inference process of the subjects can be resolved in a trivial sense by providing them with more information about the attributional dimensions of consensus, consistency, and distinctiveness (see Hewstone and Jaspars 1983). If subjects do not go beyond the information given, we would expect them to detect the covariation between the introduced categorization and the behaviour to be explained. In the scientific analysis of experimentally obtained data, the categorization would allow for a further decomposition of variance between and/or within observed actors, so that the source of variance could be located more precisely.

Since the actor in a behavioural event is, of necessity, either male or female, attributional information which mentions the name of the actor is almost always categorical, but this is usually ignored, since the subjects are only told about the behaviour of the actor and the behaviour of 'everyone else', rather than the behaviour of the other members of the same sex category. Obviously this information could be further specified by indicating whether we are concerned with everyone else belonging to the same *social* category (e.g. sex) or not. Since the distinction between the actor and everyone else is nested within the distinction between *social* categories, any explanation involving the person is confounded with a *social* category. To give but one example: when we are told that Sue is afraid of the dog, and we also know that she has always been afraid of this dog, and is afraid of any other dog, we could then add either that no one else is afraid of the dog or that all other girls (or no boys) are afraid of the dog. In the former case, attribution theory suggests a *person* explanation (something about Sue) but in the second case an explanation in terms of the *social* category would be expected (Sue is afraid because she's a girl). However it is also clear that the *person* explanation in the first case is confounded with an explanation that implies unique qualities of the person and characteristics of whatever *social* category we use to partition the consensus information. *Any* person *explanation therefore always implies also a* social *category explanation*. Because traditional attribution theory has not been developed beyond the abstract formal level of an inductive inference it has never occurred itself with such implications, although Kelley (1973) was aware of the fact that consensus information presented a special case of attributional information.

A question which arises from this social extension of the inductive logic model of causal attribution is, of course, what the effect would be on attributions if *social* category consensus were more clearly specified. Instead of informing the subjects that no one else showed the behaviour, they could be told that no one else belonging to the same *social* category showed the behaviour. In this case the information would exclude explanations in terms of the social category; hence person attribution, in the case of low category consensus, should increase. This is exactly what Hewstone and Jaspars (1983) reported. Compared with the original McArthur study, in which consensus information was kept general, Hewstone and Jaspars found that categorized consensus information was two to three times more important.

Using a recently developed inductive logic model of attribution, the introduction of categorized consensus can be considered in more detail. This model (see Hewstone and Jaspars 1987) treats causes as necessary and sufficient conditions for the occurrence of an event, and specifies the attributions logically implied by patterns of consensus, consistency, and distinctiveness information. Explicitly comparing the studies by McArthur (1972) and by ourselves (Hewstone and Jaspars 1983), it then becomes clear that the major effect of categorized consensus is on stimulus attribution. Under general consensus, stimulus (entity) attribution conforms to the notion of a cause as a necessary and sufficient condition. Under categorized consensus (e.g. 'all boys . . .') stimuli were seen as a cause when they were sufficient conditions.

In all these experiments, however, subjects were not offered the opportunity to explain the behaviour in terms of the social category to which the actor belonged. Had this explanation been available, we would have expected that high category consensus and low general consensus would lead to a category rather than a person attribution. It is this kind of situation which arises in the case of social stereotypes, where behaviour is observed or assumed to covary with social categories. Stereotypical information can be introduced into vignette studies of attribution by using items which are stereotypical to one group of actors, or another. Hewstone and Jaspars (1988) showed that such social beliefs did indeed affect attributions, but only in the absence of the more explicit consensus, varied systematically across vignettes. Subjects in the McArthur-type study seemed so concerned with 'logically' extricating covariation of cause and effect from each vignette, that they gave little attention to more social information.

It is thus evident that social categorization can affect causal attributions, even in rather artificial and implicitly logical laboratory paradigms. More striking evidence for the social and collective nature of attribution has been gleaned from studies of intergroup attribution, to which we now turn.

Intergroup attribution

By 'intergroup attribution' we refer to how members of different social groups explain the behaviour, and the social conditions, of members of their own and other social groups (Hewstone 1988; Hewstone and Jaspars 1982, 1984). In a previous publication (Jaspars and Hewstone 1982), we pointed out that intergroup attribution can easily result in explanations in terms of social categories while the same behaviour in an in-group situation will lead to a situational explanation. When an Englishman does not extend his hand to greet a Polish visitor to Britain who is used to this custom, the latter may attribute the former's response as a sign of some personal quality of English people, such as aloofness. Exactly the same behaviour would seem to an Englishman to be quite common, consistent, and indistinctive and hence requiring no explanation at all.

The first empirical study to explore intergroup attributions was that of Taylor and Jaggi (1974), carried out in southern India against the background of conflict between Hindu and Muslim groups. The basic hypothesis of the study was that observers (Hindu adults) would make internal attributions for other Hindus (i.e. in-group members) performing socially desirable acts. The reverse was predicted for attributions to Muslim out-group members (see Table 1). The predictions were clearly borne out by the data.

Because of the importance of this study, a conceptual replication was carried out in south-east Asia (Hewstone and Ward 1985). A first study used Malay and Chinese students in Malaysia. Malays behaved as expected, by making internal attributions for the positive behaviours of their own group members, but for negative behaviours by the Chinese. This is clear ethnocentric attribution, with the effect for in-group favouritism actually far stronger than that for out-group derogation. Contrary to predictions,

Table 1 Ethnocentric attributions (after Taylor and Jaggi (1974); reprinted from Hewstone and Jaspars (1982*a*))

	Type of actor	
Type of behaviour	In-group	Out-group
Positive	Dispositional	Situational
Negative	Situational	Dispositional

the Chinese also favoured the Malay actors, at the expense of their own group. A second study was then carried out in neighbouring Singapore. The Malays retained the tendency to make internal attributions for positive behaviour by their own group, but they did not make significantly different attributions for positive and negative behaviour by the Chinese. The Chinese did not significantly favour either group. The results of these two studies (see Fig. 1) clearly go beyond Taylor and Jaggi's (1974) study, reminding us of the need to consider such factors as group status and the background to intergroup relations. However, the results of these and other studies (reviewed by Hewstone and Jaspars 1982, 1984) support the notion that the behaviour of in-group and out-group members can be, and often is, explained very differently.

We want to consider now the extent to which such attributions are based on social knowledge. Given the cognitive *Zeitgeist* in social psychology, we start by examining the cognitive bases of intergroup attribution, highlighting the role of expectancies and schema-based attribution.

Schema-based attribution

As attribution theory has become increasingly influenced by 'social cognition' research (see Fiske and Taylor, 1984), so researchers have looked at how the naïve or intuitive scientist makes use of 'knowledge structures'— beliefs, theories, propositions, scripts, and schemata—that filter incoming social information (Nisbett and Ross 1980). A knowledge structure approach to attribution is based on the knowledge that people have of the world. The most important knowledge structure for explaining how people make attributions would seem to be the schema. A schema has been defined, simply, as 'a cognitive structure that represents organized knowledge about a given concept or type of stimulus' (Fiske and Taylor 1984, p. 140); or, in more detail, as:

'an abstract or generic knowledge structure, stored in memory, that specifies the

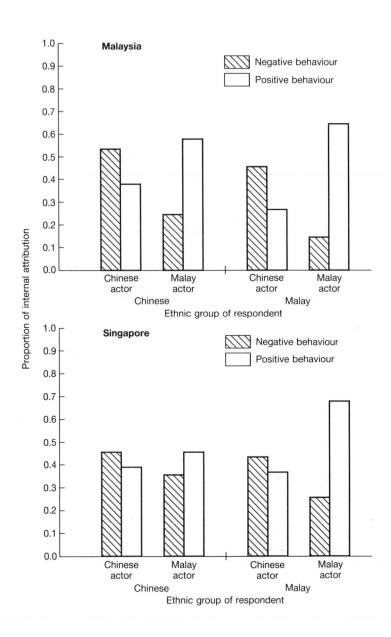

Fig. 1. Ethnocentric attributes

defining features and relevant attributes of some stimulus domain, and the inter-relations among those attributes' (Crocker *et al.* 1984, p. 197).

This knowledge structure has implications for social information processing, including perception, memory, and inference. Since cognitive social psycho-logists (e.g. Hamilton 1979) began to think of stereotypes as 'structural frameworks' or 'schemata', in terms of which information is processed, a number of implications for the study of social attribution have emerged. This approach emphasizes the way that people's prior concepts and theories shape how they view the data that they seek to explain. Knowing from previous research that schematic cases are judged faster, more easily and more confidently than cases not fitting a schema (e.g. Lurigio and Carroll 1985), it has been suggested that, in explaining schema-consistent (or expect-ancy-confirming) behaviour, perceivers may simply rely on dispositions implied by the schema, not even bothering to consider additional factors (Hamilton 1979; Pyszczynski and Greenberg 1981). Given that schema-based social information processing is fast and relatively efficient, one can think of expectancy-confirming attributions as following a strategy of 'minimum causation' (Shaklee and Fishhoff 1982), whereby the search for possible causes of an effect is terminated once an effect has been adequately explained (see Pryor and Kriss 1977; Smith and Miller 1979).

The schematic approach does seem to illuminate some interesting aspects of intergroup attribution (see Hewstone 1988), including the role of attribu-tions in belief perseverance and change, and the stage at which social beliefs influence attributional information processing. However, for a perspective that is supposedly 'knowledge-based', the schema approach has had much more to say about the process than the contents of social attributions. It is an unfortunate consequence of the rise of 'social cognition' that the content of social knowledge has often been ignored. The rationale for this focus is the belief that social and cognitive contents are culturally, temporally, and situationally bounded, but that cognitive processes are universal (Taylor and Fiske 1981). This view is perhaps most strongly stated in Kruglanski's (1979) claim that a unitary ('epistemic') theory of process should restrict itself to the process of knowledge acquisition, which is assumed to be invariant across content domains. It is in exploring the nature and contents of the social knowledge underlying attributions that studies of collective beliefs can make a valuable contribution.

Social knowledge and attribution

Two decades of research in artificial intelligence have shown conclusively that computer programs based on formal reasoning methods alone are incapable of providing intelligent solutions to even moderately complex problems. Virtually all expert systems for which computer programs have been written rely primarily on knowledge painstakingly culled from human experts (Lenat 1984). The great flaw of formal reasoning methods is that they are subject to a combinatorial explosion and, particularly in the case of inductive problems, *do not contain information that enables them to decide which variables are important and which are not*. It is therefore crucial that such programs should become able to reduce the random search for solutions by drawing upon other 'sources of power', such as knowledge of the world's regularities, rules of thumb, reasoning by analogy, parallel processing, and so on (Lenat 1984).

We face exactly the same problem in the study of attribution processes, i.e. the detection of causes based on information about effects. Such expert systems consist of hundreds of 'if–then' rules of thumb which constrain the search by guiding the program towards the most likely solution. However, the weakness of such systems is, as Lenat points out, that *they do not learn from experience* and *from one another*. Obviously one way of learning from experience is through formal reasoning based on observed covariation and hence it would seem vital for any model of human attribution processes to include such rules of causal inference in addition to knowledge of the social world. In part, knowledge of the world can be encoded in the same form as knowledge based on inference and can be used in combination with it or utilized to reduce the problem space. However, in order to allow for the attribution of (behavioural) effects to specific causes it will also be necessary to encode the information in terms of natural, social categories. A list of such categories can normally be generated by subjects when asked to suggest *possible* causes for behavioural events without any covariational information, but social psychologists have rarely asked about where these 'natural' social categories come from. One approach which has asked, and begun to answer, that question is the social representations approach, which is considered in the following section.

Collective beliefs and social explanations

While attribution theory has come to be a cornerstone of American social psychology (see Jones 1985), a number of social psychologists in Europe have approached the study of common sense using the notion of a social representation, a term introduced to social psychology by Moscovici (1961) via Durkheim (1898). Durkheim started using the term 'représentations collectives' in about 1897, to refer to characteristics of social thinking as distinct from individual thinking (see Lukes 1975). Moscovici used the term 'représentations sociales' in an ambitious attempt to conceive of the way knowledge is represented in a society and shared by its members in the form of common-sense 'theories' about various aspects of life and society. It is not necessary, in this volume, to contrast available definitions, but a useful definition to adopt, given the link between social representations and causal attribution, is one that acknowledges the essentially explanatory nature of social representations:

'By social representations, we mean a set of concepts, statements and explanations originating in daily life . . . They are the equivalent, in our society, of the myths and belief systems in traditional societies; they might even be said to be the contemporary version of common sense' (Moscovici 1981, p. 181).

It is surprising and unfortunate that the study of attributions and of social representations has developed in almost complete isolation. Surprising, when one considers that Fauconnet (1928)—a forerunner of attribution theory, acknowledged by Heider (1944)—as a former student of Durkheim, considered the attribution of responsibility to be a social fact, and part of the system of collective representations. Unfortunate, because Moscovici argues that, 'studies of social representations [like attribution theory] have been concerned from the beginning with the problem of causality, but from a different angle' (1981, p. 200). Following Hewstone (1989), social representations can contribute to an understanding of what attributions are; when, how, and why they are made; and where they come from. These contributions will be briefly summarized in the remainder of this chapter, to emphasize the social and collective nature of attribution.

What are attributions?

Eschewing the simple dichotomies of internal versus external and causes versus reasons, a recent answer to the question of 'what' attributions are is offered by work on perceived causal structures. By these Kelley (1983) refers to the way people perceive the temporal flow of life's events to be structured causally. Kelley shows that people's explanations for their separation in marriage (Fletcher 1983), cardiac patients' perceptions of the causes of their heart attacks (Cowie 1976), and policy makers' arguments (Axelrod *et al.* 1976) reveal a temporally ordered network of interconnected causes and effects.

Antaki (1981, 1986), who has argued for the importance of 'ordinary explanations' of social behaviour, has recently tried to break down open-ended, unstructured interviews into causal structures. His criterion for a causal structure underlying a given event was, 'that set of causes elaborating the explanation of a given event through one or more paths' (1986, p. 217). To follow his example, someone might see 'unemployment' as having two causal paths—world recession and the policy of a political party—one of which is traced back to one prior cause (changes in patterns of world trade), the other branching into, say, two causes (the appeal of policies to the electorate and the party leader's own economic beliefs).

Given that much of the research on social representations has involved unstructured interviews, as well as content-analysis of the mass media (e.g. Herzlich 1973; Moscovici 1961–76), one could easily envisage an analysis of socially shared causal structures. Returning to the suggestion made earlier in this chapter, the behaviour which is attributed to the person can potentially also be attributed to the social category of which the person is a member (cf. Deschamps 1977, 1983), this would *also* imply that the category could be used to explain the actor's characteristic (something about the person) that was originally seen as the cause of the behaviour. In other words, since the social category may be defined as the necessary condition for some quality of the person, which in turn is seen as a necessary and/or sufficient condition for the behaviour, a *causal chain* can be established. We would therefore expect that explanations spontaneously offered should reflect such causal chains rather than single cause–effect links which the ANOVA model of causal attribution implies. Such causal chains have been identified in the research by Windisch (1978) and by Hewstone *et al.* (1982), but research now needs to study the extent to which such causal structures are socially shared. Following studies of social representations, the importance of language in naturally occurring explanations should not be ignored. As Ostrom (1981) has noted, we know very little about 'the actual vocabulary of causality in common use' (p. 418).

A new direction for research would be to investigate the use of metaphor in common-sense explanations. Lakoff and Johnson (1980) argue for the prevalence of metaphorical language as well as thinking, because the unfamiliar is rendered familiar, as Farr and Moscovici have claimed about social representations in general (1984, pp. ix–x). The study of ordinary-language images of the European Community conducted by one of us (Hewstone 1986) revealed the extent to which complex economic notions were understood, or at least represented, by the simplifying imagery of butter 'mountains' and milk 'lakes'. Yet we know of no work specifically aimed at studying metaphors used in social explanations.

When do people make attributions?

Weiner's (1985) review of 'spontaneous' causal attribution pointed to unexpected outcomes as often producing extensive causal analysis (see also Hastie 1984; Pyszczynski and Greenberg 1981), a conclusion that is also consistent with Mackie's (1965, 1974) philosophical treatment of the 'causal field' or context in which judgements of probable cause are made (see Einhorn and Hogarth 1986). Mackie has argued that judgements of causal relevance are generally related to the degree that a variable is a 'difference-in-a-background'. Thus factors that are part of some presumed background or 'causal field' are judged to be of little or no causal relevance, while 'differences-in-a-background' (e.g. unexpected events) arouse spontaneous causal thinking (see also MacIver 1942).

Obviously, the next question one asks is: where do expectancies come from? The notion of social representation would suggest that we look for the source of expectations in social representations. Moscovici (1981) actually stated this view explicitly:

'A theory of social causality is a theory of our imputations and attributions, associated with a representation . . . any causal explanation must be viewed within the context of social representations and is determined thereby' (p. 107).

And, as Farr (this volume, Chapter 3) points out, Moscovici has long maintained that social representations are more basic, or operate at a more profound level, than 'mere' attributions.

In arguing for the role of social representations in determining when people make attributions, we almost merge into offering an answer to another question, that of how people make causal explanations.

How do people make attributions?

As we noted earlier, there has been a great deal of attribution work on knowledge structures and schematic processing (see Wyer and Srull 1984), yet Nisbett and Ross (1980) acknowledge that there has been surprisingly little research on the beliefs shared by large numbers of people in a group or culture. The research on social representations has, of course, studied exactly such socially shared beliefs and the link between them and schemata has been neatly made by Eiser (1986): 'Despite the schema concept's wide applicability and inclusiveness, the basic question of where schemata come from has often been avoided' (p. 243). Eiser goes on to emphasize that many of our schemata are acquired from and shared with other people. In this way the concept of social representation can help to explain how attributions are made.

Moscovici and Hewstone (1983) have suggested that whereas science is mainly concerned with asking why or how, social representations are mainly concerned with answering 'because'. People share strong expectations about events, social behaviour, and their outcomes: 'Jews are to blame because . . .'; 'the poor are exploited because . . .'; 'blacks are inferior because . . .'. Thus social representations impose a kind of automatic explanation. Causes are singled out and proposed prior to a detailed search for and analysis of information. Without much active thinking, people's explanations are determined by their social representations. Where the social representations approach differs from the schema approach is in stressing the socially shared knowledge base—its content and social origins

—on which attributions are found and not merely the *process* of schema-based attribution.

Why do people make attributions?

Numerous writers have suggested that attributions serve psychological and social functions (see Bains 1983; Forsyth 1980; Tetlock and Levi 1982), but these needs have mostly been explored in intra- and inter-personal domains. Focusing on attributional functions suggested by the social representations approach would suggest a rather different set of phenomena from those normally treated by attribution theory. These might include such beliefs as witchcraft, studied from an anthropological perspective by Evans-Pritchard (1937) and from a historical perspective by Thomas (1971).

The reader may be tempted to classify witchcraft explanations as characteristic of some form of 'primitive' causality. Poliakov's (1980) analysis, however, refers to the fascination of human beings for an elementary and exhaustive causality—a 'first cause'. He provides evidence for the operation of a pattern of thought—so-called 'causalité diabolique'—which has occurred at several periods of history. The 'demons' blamed for catastrophes have been Jesuits, Marxists, freemasons and, of course, Jews, these groups being seen as responsible for a 'world conspiracy'.

Billig (1978) analysed the ideology of the British (extreme right-wing) 'National Front' party and located it firmly within the traditions of the conspiracy theory, a tradition that provides explanations for a multiplicity of events:

'In essence . . . the explanations are simple: events do not have multiple causes and the chance factor in history is discarded. All events are traced back to deliberate decisions taken by conspirators' (p. 315).

However, as Billig notes, a search for troubling events does not of itself lead to a conspiracy interpretation. He provides a picture of one racial bigot's perception of black people in Britain as the cause of a whole series of ills:

'I do honestly connect the mass immigration of coloured people with a general running down of standards in the country: education, law and order and all this sort of thing . . . society's changed so badly. I look back on those days [of his youth] with a sort of feeling. And I know then that they were all white faces around me. You relate one problem with another obviously' (p. 320).

As Billig remarks, this respondent's contentment with such a simple causal explanation means that he has no need to embark upon a conspiracy interpretation of politics, until and unless he is spurred on by the latent anti-semitism of National Front propaganda to trace the causal chain further backwards and to answer such questions as 'whether there is a conspiracy to flood Britain with immigrants?' (Billig 1978, p. 322).

The functions of a conspiracy theory are easy to see. Someone or some group is held responsible. The 'simple' explanation for Britain's national decline implies the repatriation of black people as the 'solution'; the 'complex' explanation implies the need to attack world Jewry. Ultimately, both types of explanation procure the attributor at least the illusion of control. As the historian Thomas wrote of witchcraft explanations:

'The great appeal of witch-beliefs, as against other types of explanation for misfortune, was, therefore, that they provided the victim with a definite means of redress. They did not merely offer the intellectual satisfaction of identifying the cause of the mishap; they made it possible to take immediate steps to have things put right . . .' (Thomas 1971, p. 650).

Bains's (1983) analysis of societal explanations and the need for control points out that almost all magical and superstitious beliefs attribute negative events to controllable causes. This is just as true for Nazi propaganda (Carr 1969; Herzstein 1980)—which Bains describes as a 'package of control'—as for the seemingly bizarre explanations current in the Dark Ages. Merkl's (1975) study of Nazi autobiographies provides evidence for a particular kind of obsessional, paranoid causality and he reports that 16 per cent of the Nazi party believed in a world Jewish conspiracy.

Thus some of the societal functions of attribution are illuminated by a social representations approach. At the same time, the 'why' of explanations is seen to feed back into the 'what', to suggest further attributional studies of propaganda which would point to the origins of socially shared explanations.

Where do attributions come from?

Following Wells (1981) one can distinguish between two ways in which people have come to think about causal forces in their social environment. 'Original processing' refers to the direct observation of relationships, such as the covariation between two events, and has been studied in detail by attribution theory (Alloy and Tabachnik 1984; Crocker 1981). 'Socialized processing' concerns how people learn about causes and adopt cultural hypotheses through language-based communications. This latter process is something that has been largely ignored in attribution theory, but has been studied as an aspect of social representations.

Following Moscovici and Hewstone (1983), this socialized processing or 'common sense' appears in two ways. 'First-hand knowledge' is the corpus of knowledge spontaneously produced by the members of a group; 'second-hand knowledge' is built up from recent discoveries and theories. It is the latter kind of knowledge that will be emphasized here, as a transformation of scientific and technical knowledge, diffused through the media. Moscovici (1976) coined the term 'amateur scientist' (as distinct from Heider's 'naïve scientist') to convey the picture of the layperson as influenced by, and showing varying interest in, scientific developments and new theories. Once transformed, these new ideas can have an impact on common-sense explanations. This was shown in Moscovici's (1961–76) study of how ideas about psychoanalysis permeated through French society, and how Freud's ideas, once transformed or vulgarized, influenced people directly. Moscovici discusses those people who had used psychoanalysis to explain the behaviour of themselves and others. In his sample, 22 per cent of school pupils and 45 per cent of students reported having tried to analyse and interpret the reactions of others by using these new ideas (p. 187).

Following Moscovici and Hewstone (1983), many common-sense explanations may be the result of a transformation of scientific explanations and it may be at least as important to know how social knowledge is transformed as to know how individuals process information. However, questions about the origins of attributions have concerned researchers far less than the four questions considered immediately above. This can be illustrated with reference to a celebrated attributional phenomenon.

The 'fundamental attribution error' (Ross 1977) refers to the tendency to attribute behaviour to the actor's dispositions and to ignore powerful situational determinants of the behaviour. A number of possible, and not mutually exclusive, explanations for this tendency are considered by Nisbett and Ross (1980)—perceptual–cognitive factors (representativenesss, availability, and anchoring heuristics), linguistic factors (what word describes situations that typically elicit generous behaviour?), and domain-specific theories. In fact, Nisbett and Ross prefer an explanation in terms of a general 'dispositionalist theory' that is 'thoroughly woven into the fabric of our culture' (p. 31), and that is present in classic novels as well as philosophical positions. Reading their history, Farr and Anderson (1983) note that Heider was much influenced by Ichheiser (1943) and that the latter traced this dispositionalist 'misinterpretation' back to the nineteenth century ideology of 'individualism' (see Lukes 1973) and the collective representation of the person. What is regrettable is that cognitive accounts of the 'fundamental attribution error' (e.g. Moore *et al.* 1979; Sherman and Corty 1984)—valuable though they are—should have so overshadowed the fact that people's implicit theories about the causes of behaviour give too much weight to dispositionalist causes, and that these theories come from somewhere.

In sum, as Farr (this volume, Chapter 3) has noted, the social representations approach is as much concerned with the formation of attributions, as with their assessment. We need to follow the social representations school and carefully analyse the information circulating in society concerning the behaviours or events to be explained.

Conclusion

In this chapter we have attempted to develop the implications of a genuine social approach to the study of causal attribution. We began by examining the role of social categorization in 'narrowing down' causal inference processes, and by showing how an explanation of behaviour in personal terms may be confounded with an explanation in terms of social categories. We then briefly referred to evidence of intergroup attribution, suggesting that a schematic approach did throw light on some aspects of this type of social attribution, but was limited in its emphasis on processes of social cognition. Knowledge of the world must form a part of any theory of social attribution and it was suggested that the social representations approach was valuable in illustrating how widespread beliefs have an impact on causal attributions—by influencing what we study as attributions: when, how, and why they are made; and where their origins lie.

Clearly, there are many challenges ahead for the social extension of attribution theory, such as how perceivers combine prior expectations, configurational information, or real-world knowledge with new information derived from observed covariation. These challenges suggest that an ultimate theory of social attribution will be prototypically social-psychological, ranging from cognitive-psychological processes to collective beliefs, shared among many people. Traditionally, attribution theory has focused on the psychological aspects of attribution; this chapter serves as a reminder that the social aspects are just as important if we are to understand fully the nature of common-sense explanations.

References

Alloy, L.B. and Tabachnik, N. (1984). Assessment of covariation by humans and animals: the joint influence of prior expectations and current situational information. *Psychological Review*, **91**, 112–49.

Antaki, C. (ed.) (1981). *The psychology of ordinary explanations of social behaviour*. Academic Press, London.

Antaki, C. (1986). Ordinary explanation in conversation: causal structures and their defence. *European Journal of Social Psychology*, **15**, 213–30.

Axelrod, R. (ed.) (1976). *Structure of decision: the cognitive maps of political elites*. Princeton University Press.

Bains, G. (1983). Explanations and the need for control. In *Attribution theory: social and functional extensions* (ed. M. Hewstone). Blackwell, Oxford.

Billig, M. (1978). *Fascists: a social psychological view of the National Front*. Harcourt, Brace and Jovanovich, London.

Brown, R. and Fish, D. (1983). The psychological causality implicit in language. *Cognition*, **14**, 237–73.

Carr, W. (1969). *A history of Germany, 1815–1945*. Weidenfeld and Nicholson, London.

Cowie, B. (1976). The cardiac patient's perception of his heart attack. *Social Science and Medicine*, **10**, 87–96.

Crocker, J. (1981). Judgement of covariation by social perceivers. *Psychological Bulletin*, **90**, 272–92.

Crocker, J., Fiske, S.T., and Taylor, S.E. (1984). Schematic bases of belief change. In *Attitudinal judgment* (ed. J.R. Eiser). Springer, New York.

Deschamps, J.-C. (1977). *L'Attribution et la catégorisation sociale*. Peter Lang, Berne.

Deschamps, J.-C. (1983). Social attribution. In *Attribution theory and research: conceptual, developmental and social dimensions* (ed. J. Jaspars, F.D. Fincham, and M. Hewstone). Academic Press, London.

Durkheim, E. (1898). Représentations individuelles et représentations collectives. *Revue de Metaphysique et de Morale*, **6**, 273–302. (Translated as 'Individual and collective representations', in E. Durkheim (1974). *Sociology and philosophy*. The Free Press, New York.)

Einhorn, H.J. and Hogarth, R.M. (1986). Judging probable cause. *Psychological Bulletin*, **99**, 3–19.

Eiser, J.R. (1986). *Social psychology: attitudes, cognition and social behaviour*. Cambridge University Press.

Evans-Pritchard, E.E. (1937). *Witchcraft, oracles, and magic among the Azande*. Oxford University Press.

Farr, R.M. and Anderson, A. (1983). Beyond actor/observer differences in perspective: extensions and applications. In *Attribution theory: social and functional extensions* (ed. M. Hewstone). Basil Blackwell, Oxford.

Farr, R.M. and Moscovici, S. (1984). *Social representations*. Cambridge University Press, and Maison des Sciences de l'Homme, Paris.

Fauconnet, P. (1928). *La responsabilité*. Alcan, Paris.

Fiske, S.T. and Taylor, S.E. (1984). *Social cognition*. Random House, New York.

Fletcher, G.J.O. (1983). The analysis of verbal explanations for marital separation: implications for attribution theory. *Journal of Applied Social Psychology*, **13**, 245–58.

Forsyth, D.R. (1980). The functions of attributions. *Social Psychology Quarterly*, **43**, 184–9.

Hamilton, D.L. (1979). A cognitive-attributional analysis of stereotyping. In *Advances in experimental social psychology*, Vol. 12 (ed. L. Berkowitz). Academic Press, New York.

Hart, H.L.A. and Honoré, A.M. (1959). *Causation in the law*. Clarendon, Oxford.

Hastie, R. (1984). Causes and effects of causal attribution. *Journal of Personality and Social Psychology*, **46**, 44–56.

Heider, F. (1944). Social perception and phenomenal causality. *Psychological Review*, **51**, 358–74.

Herzlich, C. (1973). *Health and illness: a social psychological analysis*. Academic Press, London.

Herzstein, M. (1980). *The war that Hitler won*. Abacus, London.

Hewstone, M. (1986). *Understanding attitudes to the European Community: A social-psychological study in four member states*. Cambridge University Press and Maison des Sciences de l'Homme, Paris.

Hewstone, M. (1988). Attributional bases of intergroup conflict. In *The social psychology of intergroup conflict: theory, research and applications* (ed. W. Stroebe, A. Kruglanski, D. Bar-Tal, and M. Hewstone). Springer Verlag, New York.

Hewstone, M. (1989). Les représentations sociales et la causalité. In *Les représentations sociales* (ed. D. Jodelet). Presses Universitaires de France, Paris.

Hewstone, M. and Jaspars, J. (1982). Intergroup relations and attribution processes. In *Social identity and intergroup relations* (ed. H. Tajfel). Cambridge University Press and Maison des Sciences de l'Homme, Paris.

Hewstone, M. and Jaspars, J. (1983). A re-examination of the roles of consensus, consistency and distinctiveness: Kelley's cube revisited. *British Journal of Social Psychology*, **22**, 41–50.

Hewstone, M. and Jaspars, J. (1984). Social dimensions of attribution. In *The social dimension: European developments in social psychology* (ed. H. Tajfel). Cambridge University Press and Maison des Sciences de l'Homme, Paris.

Hewstone, M. and Ward, C. (1985). Ethnocentrism and causal attribution in Southeast Asia. *Journal of Personality and Social Psychology*, **48**, 614–23.

Hewstone, M. and Jaspars, J. (1987). Covariation and causal attribution: a logical model of the intuitive analysis of variance. *Journal of Personality and Social Psychology*, **53**, 663–72.

Hewstone, M. and Jaspars, J. (1988). Implicit and explicit consensus as determinants of causal attribution: two experimental investigations. *European Journal of Social Psychology*, **18**, 93–8.

Hewstone, M., Jaspars, J., and Lalljee, M. (1982). Social representations, social attribution and social identity: the intergroup images of 'public' and 'comprehensive' schoolboys. *European Journal of Social Psychology*, **12**, 241–69.

Ichheiser, G. (1943). Misinterpretations of personality in everyday life and the psychologist's frame of reference. *Character and Personality*, **12**, 145–60.

Jaspars, J. (1983). The process of causal attribution in common sense. In *Attribution theory: social and functional extensions* (ed. M. Hewstone). Basil Blackwell, Oxford.

Jaspars, J. and Hewstone, M. (1982). Cross-cultural interaction, social attribution and inter-group relations. In *Cultures in contact: studies in cross-cultural interaction* (ed. S. Bochner). Pergamon Press, Oxford.

Jaspars, J., Hewstone, M., and Fincham, F.D. (1983a). Attribution theory and research: the state of the art. In *Attribution theory and research: conceptual, developmental and social dimensions* (ed. J. Jaspars, F.D. Fincham, and M. Hewstone). Academic Press, London.

Jaspars, J., Fincham, F.D., and Hewstone, M. (ed.) (1983b). *Attribution theory and research: conceptual, developmental and social dimensions*. Academic Press, London.

Jones, E.E. (1985). Major developments in social psychology during the past five decades. In *Handbook of social psychology* (Vol. 1) (3rd edn) (ed. G. Lindzey and E. Aronson). Random House, New York.

Kahneman, D., Slovic, P., and Tversky, A. (ed.) (1982). *Judgment under uncertainty: heuristics and biases*. Cambridge University Press.

Kelley, H.H. (1967). Attribution theory in social psychology. *Nebraska Symposium, on Motivation*, **15**, 192–238.

Kelley, H.H. (1973). The processes of causal attribution. *American Psychologist*, **28**, 107–28.

Kelley, H.H. (1983). Perceived causal structures. In *Attribution theory and research: conceptual, developmental and social dimensions* (ed. J. Jaspars, F.D. Fincham, and M. Hewstone). Academic Press, London.

Kruglanski, A.W. (1979). Causal explanation, teleological explanation: on radical particularism in attribution theory. *Journal of Personality and Social Psychology*, **37**, 1447–57.

Lakoff, G. and Johnson, M. (1980). *Metaphors we live by*. University of Chicago Press.

Lalljee, M., Brown, L.B., and Hilton, D. (1985). Invoking God's agency: God explanations, explanations for failure to do one's duty to God and images of God. Unpublished manuscript, University of Oxford.

Lenat, D.B. (1984). Computer software for intelligent systems. *Scientific American*, **251**, 204–13.

Lukes, S. (1973). *Individualism*. Basil Blackwell, Oxford.

Lukes, S. (1975). *Emile Durkheim: his life and work: a historical and critical study*. Penguin, Harmondsworth.

Lurigio, A.J. and Carroll, J.S. (1985). Probation officers' schemata of offenders: content, development and impact on treatment decisions. *Journal of Personality and Social Psychology*, **48**, 1112–26.

McArthur, L.A. (1972). The how and what of why: some determinants and consequences of causal attributions. *Journal of Personality and Social Psychology*, **22**, 171–93.

Mackie, J.L. (1965). Causes and conditions. *American Philosophical Quarterly*, **2**, 245–64.

Mackie, J.L. (1974). *The cement of the universe: a study of causation*. Clarendon, Oxford.

MacIver, R.M. (1942). *Social causation*. Harper Torchbooks, New York.

Merkl, P.H. (1975). *Political violence under the Swastika*. Princeton: Princeton University Press.

Mill, J.S. (1973). System of logic (8th edn). In *Collected works of John Stuart-Mill* (Vols. 7 and 8) (ed. J.M. Robson). University of Toronto Press. (Original work published in 1872.)

Moore, B.S., Sherrod, D.R., Liu, T.J., and Underwood, B. (1979). The dispositional shift in attribution over time. *Journal of Experimental Social Psychology*, **15**, 553–69.

Moscovici, S. (1961). *La psychanalyse, son image et son public*. (Second edn, 1976.) Presses Universitaires de France, Paris.

Moscovici, S. (1981). On social representations. In *Social cognition: perspectives on everyday understanding* (ed. J.P. Forgas). Academic Press, London.

Moscovici, S. and Hewstone, M. (1983). Social representations and social explanations: from the 'naïve' to the 'amateur' scientist. In *Attribution theory: social and functional extensions* (ed. M. Hewstone). Basil Blackwell, Oxford.

Nisbett, R. and Ross, L. (1980). *Human inference: strategies and shortcomings of social judgment*. Prentice-Hall, Englewood Cliffs, NJ.

Ostrom, T.M. (1981). Attribution theory: whence and whither. In *New directions in attribution research* (Vol. 3) (ed. J.H. Harvey, W. Ickes, and R.F. Kidd). Erlbaum, Hillsdale, NJ.

Poliakov, L. (1980). *La causalité diabolique*. Calmann-Lévy, Paris.

Pryor, J.B. and Kriss, M. (1977). The cognitive dynamics of salience in the attribution process. *Journal of Personality and Social Psychology*, **35**, 49–55.

Pyszczynski, T.A. and Greenberg, J. (1981). Role of disconfirmed expectancies in the instigation of attributional processing. *Journal of Personality and Social Psychology*, **40**, 31–8.

Ross, L. (1977). The intuitive psychologist and his shortcomings: distortions in the attribution process. In *Advances in experimental social psychology* (Vol. 10) (ed. L. Berkowitz). Academic Press, New York.

Shaklee, N. and Fischhoff, B. (1982). Strategies of information search in causal analysis. *Memory and Cognition*, **10**, 520–30.

Sherman, S.J. and Corty, E. (1984). Cognitive heuristics. In *Handbook of social cognition* (Vol. 1) (ed. R.S. Wyer and T.K. Srull). Erlbaum, Hillsdale, NJ.

Smith, E.R. and Miller, F.D. (1979). Salience and the cognitive mediation of attribution. *Journal of Personality and Social Psychology*, **37**, 2240–52.

Taylor, D.M. and Jaggi, V. (1974). Ethnocentrism and causal attribution in a South Indian context. *Journal of Cross-Cultural Psychology*, **5**, 162–71.

Taylor, S.E. and Fiske, S.T. (1978). Salience, attention and attribution: top of the head phenomena. In *Advances in experimental social psychology* (Vol. 11) (ed. L. Berkowitz). Academic Press, New York.

Taylor, S.E. and Fiske, S.T. (1981). Getting inside the head: methodologies for process analysis in attribution and social cognition. In *New directions in attribution research* (Vol. 3) (ed. J.H. Harvey, W. Ickes, and R.F. Kidd). Erlbaum, Hillsdale, NJ.

Tetlock, P.E. and Levi, A. (1982). Attribution bias: on the inconclusiveness of the cognition-motivation debate. *Journal of Experimental Social Psychology*, **18**, 68–88.

Thomas, K. (1971). *Religion and the decline of magic*. Penguin, Harmondsworth.

Weiner, B. (1985). 'Spontaneous' causal thinking. *Psychological Bulletin*, **97**, 74–84.

Wells, G. (1981). Lay analyses of causal forces on behavior. In *Cognition, social behavior and the environment* (ed. J. H. Harvey). Erlbaum, Hillsdale, NJ.

Windisch, U. (1978). *Xenophobie*. L'Age d'Homme, Geneva.

Wyer, R.S. and Srull, T.K. (ed.) (1984). *Handbook of social cognition* (three Vols). Erlbaum, Hillsdale, NJ.

8 Social beliefs and intergroup relations: the relevance of some sociological perspectives

Willem Doise
(Translated by Elizabeth Mapstone, University of Oxford.)

Levels of explanation and theoretical pluralism

To assimilate information is to organize it. There may perhaps exist highly structured scientific domains in which the explanatory principles used by researchers are sufficient in themselves to produce an ordering of all new information applicable to these domains. At first sight, however, this does not appear to apply to social psychology: the enormous mass of new information which accumulates each year in various journals, essay collections, and monographs is widely disparate. Nevertheless, certain major themes, such as differentiation and group formation, or autonomy and interdependence in interpersonal relations, do permit some organization of this particular area in the social sciences. Furthermore, these different polar themes are complementary, since in-depth investigation of one of these themes entails reference to its opposite; there can be no group formation without differentiation, no interdependence of individuals without autonomy and vice versa (see Doise *et al.* 1978).

Another way of organizing the vast amount of research in social psychology takes into account the nature of the explanatory principles involved as well: these are the explanatory principles which relate to an individual's organizational processes, to interpersonal dynamics, to asymmetrical social positioning in the context of social relations, and to the impact of social norms and representations. Elsewhere (Doise 1984) I have already demonstrated how important this distinction of levels of analysis is if we wish to account for the specificity of different studies of intergroup relations. It should also be remembered that we have distinguished among these four levels of analysis only so that we may demonstrate the need to articulate them at a theoretical level.

This articulation of principles of analysis is especially necessary in the field of intergroup relations, and for a number of different reasons. First, it is a field in which it is clear that anthropologists and sociologists have developed their own heuristic analytical principles, which should be taken into account by social psychologists when elaborating their own explanations. In the following two sections, some of the interdisciplinary foundations of the study of intergroup relations will be presented in more detail. A second reason for integrating several explanatory principles in intergroup research is more conjectural, and arises from the fact that in recent years a social psychological theory of intergroup relations has already begun the work of articulation of levels of analysis, by showing how individual motivation is expressed differently in different intergroup contexts. I am referring of course to the theory of social identity presented in a number of papers by Tajfel and Turner (e.g. Tajfel 1981; Turner 1984); their concept of a continuum running from, at one end, the interpersonal and at the other, the intergroup, will constitute the departure point for the ideas proposed here.

Universals and particulars

Tajfel (1981) emphasized more than once the need to make a conceptual distinction between interpersonal behaviour and intergroup behaviour. Interpersonal behaviour is held to be determined by the personal characteristics of the individuals in the interaction and thus leads to a great deal of diversity and variation, whereas intergroup behaviour is said to be characterized by conformity as it takes account only of the category memberships of the individuals concerned, and ignores their more personal characteristics. It is important to remember that this distinction is explicitly related to two different ideological systems. Individualistic belief in social mobility will lead to mainly interpersonal behaviour, and is contrasted with the opposing belief which looks for change in the relations between categories of individuals. Tajfel goes so far as to give some indication of the historical and sociological conditions most favourable to the growth of one or other of these general beliefs, and his experimental work attempts essentially to determine the relative importance of strategies which maximize common good for both the in-group and the out-group, or for in-group alone, and strategies which try above all to create a difference in favour of the in-group.

There is a problem, however, with the link between Tajfel's general ideas, as summed up above, and their experimental operationalization. Even though this problem is not specific to the research carried out by Tajfel and his team, it is their work which will allow us to expose the problem very clearly. If it is the case that particular sociological and historical conditions lead to the development of a belief in social mobility or in social change, how can one claim to study these ideas and their effects in the laboratory, on demand? If these beliefs can be so easily activated by the experimenter, it must be because they are in some sense already present in the individuals when they enter the experimental situation. We must therefore concede that the generating principles for these two beliefs can coexist, at least in our day, but it seems probable at other times as well: the experiment thus only produces the particular transitory conditions which lead to their different actualization. I have a very specific notion of what an experiment in social psychology can achieve (see Doise 1986a, Ch. 5); here I will explain the underlying assumptions it entails at the level of the concept of the person.

This concept is both universalist and particularist at the same time. I will explain, first by returning to ideas in social psychology and then by looking at ideas provided by an anthropologist. If, along with Tajfel, Turner, and many other social psychologists (see for example Beauvois and Joule 1981) we want to investigate the processes which intervene in different or opposing ideologies, and if for this purpose we turn to children in secondary school or to university students, it follows that we must believe that the processes which operate in the interactions evoked experimentally are of the same nature as the processes which account for the behaviour characteristic of different historical conditions. The notion of articulation of levels of analysis can help clarify such a universalist concept of the human and the social: several elementary but fundamental processes organize our individual experience, but interpersonal dynamics interfere with these processes, as do the dynamics of asymmetric social and status relations within a particular global social context. Furthermore general beliefs about the nature of social relationships operate on these psychological processes. This idea is universalist because it assumes that the same elementary personal and interpersonal processes are widely diffused, but are combined and articulated constantly in a particular way and have content of specific values. This is, of course, a postulate, I might almost say a belief, which constitutes the very foundation of experimentation in social psychology. Without it, experimentation could have no meaning except in a homogeneous cultural context, if it were possible to delimit such a milieu. However, the crucial importance of this idea goes well beyond the possibility and the plausibility of experimentation: I believe that it is also of central importance for the possibility of mutual comprehension between individuals who have had different social experiences. If such understanding is to some extent possible, if translation from one language into another can make sense, it must be because people function with similar mental processes, that they understand the dynamics of interactions and of social situations because they are guided by similar schemata, perhaps even turn to similar hierarchical value systems which permit linguistic barriers and cultural frontiers to be crossed. While to deny this kind of universality is to deny the possibility of interpersonal communication, to accept it is not to imply uniformity and identity of social and cultural facts. The multiplicity of possible articulations between processes at the same level and between different levels leads to the creation of an indefinite number of particular social processes, just as the organizing principles common to one language permit the generation of innumerable particular statements. It is important to emphasize the fact that the foundations of such universals and particulars cannot be the human neurophysiological organization alone, but that they are above all constituted by processes of a social nature.

This issue, which is of unparalleled importance for any general study of intergroup relations, has been treated in a profound manner by Louis Dumont (1967, 1977, 1983). Many readers will be familiar with his two books, one on the caste system in India and the other on individualistic economic ideology in the West. But it is in a volume entitled *Essays on individualism* that he brings together his conclusions through a comparison of these two important studies. The central theme of these essays is essentially the problem of that which is shared and that which is specific to the individual, the problem of the universal that is human and the particular that is cultural.

If it has been true that a universalist belief has governed our investigations of other cultures, since this concept is a part of our culture and based, according to Dumont, on individualism, the concept of the other culture as a specific whole which is different from our own became necessary as a consequence. Intercultural understanding requires an acceptance of and examination of concrete differences within a universalist perspective, such as, for example, relations of opposition, which are to be found in the opposing and asymmetric social relationships that are the universal elements of all cultures. An example in the West was the traditional opposition between spiritual power and temporal power, where the latter is subordinate to the former in ecclesiastical matters and the former to the latter in civilian life. This kind of opposition, marked by crossed asymmetries, is also characteristic of a caste system. It is true that cultures ascribe different values to the holistic and the individualistic principles, and an asymmetric opposition is to be found at this level as well: the caste system values holism more highly and in modern Western culture individualism is the predominant value, but each of these cultures also values the other pole at different and subordinate levels (see Dumont 1967, paragraph 118).

Research in social psychology carries with it a concept of the person and of the social which has implications at all levels, from the psychological to the ideological. When anthropology looks at the universal and the particular in human beings, it develops models which are important for the study of intergroup relations. In both cases certain basic postulates, or if you prefer, general beliefs guide the work, motivate and provide the justification for detailed research into specific processes. What is essential about these general concepts is that they are invoked as the universal principles underlying those symbolic or ideological dynamics which govern all processes of social interaction in various different situational or cultural contexts. In a sense, they are at one and the same time the explanatory principles and the phenomena to be explained: in addition, they tend to treat the problem of the links between intrapersonal, interpersonal, relational, and social processes as though it has been somehow solved. Let us now look at how sociologists approach this question.

Sociological perspectives

Here I will restrict myself to presenting the findings of a study of the articulation of levels of analysis in the work of four Parisian sociologists, who were chosen because they represent different kinds of articulation.

Boudon's purpose was to apply sociological processes to the results of individual intentions (Boudon 1977, 1981, 1984). The concepts of individual action and of intentional behaviour constitute the logical atoms of his methodological individualism. He then proceeds to develop models designed to explain how rational acts at the level of the individual give rise to irrational effects at the collective level. This is what happens, for example, when an academic qualification becomes devalued after a very large number of students succeed in obtaining it. He provides a great many examples of effects at the level of the group which do not appear to correspond to the intentions of the individual actors. However, it remains a fact that understanding these collective effects is based essentially on an understanding of individual intentions, that is, on a psychological analysis.

'the fact that numerous examples of sociological analysis resort implicitly to an introspective type of method to describe the behaviour of actors is important. It shows that the sociologist reserves the right to resort to a universalist psychology. It implies, therefore, that the particular characteristics of the situation and of the context where the observed is placed will not affect his psychology to the point where his behaviour becomes unintelligible to the observer. If the behaviour of the observed appears to the observer to be difficult to comprehend, it is not due to the fact that their 'psychologies' are different but, for example, because certain elements of the system of interaction to which the observed belongs elude the observer' (Boudon 1981, pp. 37–8).

More recently, Boudon (1984) returned to this theme when commenting on Weber.

Even if this approach does not explicitly deal with the issue of intergroup relations, it has been given here because it is an extreme example of the expression of a universalist concept. This concept is so strong that Boudon does not feel it necessary to be explicit about his notions of the psychological functioning of the individual in the books cited. The only psychology to which Boudon resorts seems to be that of a universal and interchangeable individual known to all, or at least to all sociologists. His analyses dealing with the intentions of the individual do not begin to conceive of any need for a psychology of individual differences. In spite of or because of the extreme importance attributed to the individual in the explanation of the social, this sociologist thinks he can do without any specific investigation of individual dynamics. This does not however prevent the very simplicity of these analyses from throwing a sometimes very useful light on important intergroup phenomena, such as, for example, the differential investment in a group cause by members of a majority or a minority group. Each member of a group may be tempted to leave to the other the responsibility of working for the cause. But this tendency to inaction is not the same in members of a numerous group and those whose group is very small:

'Naturally, all things being equal, this incentive not to act is much stronger when the latent group is relatively large in size. If I belong to a latent group of 2000 people, my contribution to a possible collective action is likely to have a negligible effect. On the other hand, it will be quite likely to involve me in serious costs (the loss of time, etc.). The same will not hold where a latent group is relatively small. Here everybody's involvement matters. This effect of size explains why, in the situation where a small number of individuals are opposed to a much larger latent group, the *power* of a 'small' group can be greater than that of the larger group' (Boudon 1981, p. 125).

But differential effects like these are only explained by the operation in each and every one of the same principles of calculation applied to the different situations. These calculating principles are in a sense universal and supposed to be understood by the sociologist.

Because he is more interested in the articulation of different levels of analysis, Crozier's research seems to me to be of greater importance for social psychology in general, and for the social psychological investigation of intergroup relations in particular. In the book by Crozier and Friedberg (1980), a theory is proposed which suggests that the strategies and decisions of individuals and of groups cannot be looked upon as simple phenomena of adaptation to a social environment, because they also attempt to a certain extent to create that environment. The strategies of social actors must first be studied as a negotiation of the social constructs within which they function and which they constantly modify by their interactions.

A central idea in this book about actors and systems is that of a game. This idea is intended to recall that the actions of social actors always develop within a structured field of operation, but does not mean in any way that the strategies that they may develop are completely restricted. On the contrary, several passages in this book describe, with supporting examples, an important strategy of participants in games which occur within an organization or between organizations: they keep for themselves 'zones of uncertainty' by clever use of elements in the situation. This concept of social life, and especially of life in organizations, as a game which creates zones of uncertainty means that many traditional ideas like those of attitude or of role, or indeed any which permit the making of sure predictions, become inadequate.

One important idea in the study of intergroup relations is that of 'criss-cross regulation', a concept which has proved a useful aid in understanding how the French *departmental* system operates.

'Integration and coordination are always accomplished by a person whose activity and source of legitimacy are of a different order from those of the parties being integrated and coordinated . . . Criss-cross regulation insures that an upper echelon in a given channel will not have to bear the brunt of direct pressure from its lower echelons, and conversely, that a lower echelon can escape the overbearing domination of its superior. The intervention of third parties, who are experts in a different kind of "technique", as it were, makes it possible to avoid the sources of conflict and tension occasioned by direct negotiation. Everyone is protected against loss, even if an error should be committed' (Crozier and Friedberg 1980, pp. 133 and 141).

The following section will show that social psychology is still too rarely interested in relations between groups in terms of the processes which involve such crossed relations. But we should note at this stage that general beliefs or cultural approaches in themselves have been found to be inadequate, and that it is essential to articulate their study with the dynamics of situational and individual processes. While attitudes, beliefs, general opinions, or ideologies no doubt exist, they are constantly being modified and transformed by systems of interaction.

Having presented two rather 'individualistic' sociologists, we shall now show that advocates of more 'holistic' ideas do nevertheless choose to articulate their analyses with theories of individual or interpersonal dynamics. This is the case with Touraine. His book, *The self-production of society* (1977), is a highly theoretical work which systematizes a set of ideas about the nature of society itself. Most of the classic ideas in sociology are freshly illuminated by this work. Touraine succeeds in articulating the new ways of understanding society, brought about by the changes, upheavals, and revolutions which are so characteristic of modern society, with the notion of social movement.

Three principles intervene in the definition of a social movement: the principle of identity, the principle of opposition, and the principle of totality. These three principles should be defined in relation to one another.

'*The principle of identity* is the definition the actor gives of himself. A social movement cannot be organized unless this definition is conscious; but the formation of the movement largely precedes that consciousness. *It is conflict that constitutes and organizes the actor . . . The principle of opposition* must be defined in the same way. A movement cannot be organized without being able to name its adversary, but its action does not presuppose that identification. *The conflict causes the adversary to appear*, as it shapes the consciousness of the actors confronting one another . . . Finally, no social movement can exist that defines itself solely by conflict. All possess what I term a *principle of totality*. The labor movement only existed because it did not consider industrialization solely as an instrument of capitalist profit but had the will to construct a noncapitalist, an anticapitalist, industrial society, freed from private ownership of the means of production and capable of a higher development. The principle of totality is nothing but the *system of historical action* of which the adversaries, situated within the double dialectic of the social classes, are disputing the domination' (Touraine 1977, pp. 311–13).

The aim of sociological intervention is to help militant groups create a social movement. A whole procedure is developed, designed to actualize the principles of identity, opposition, and totality, and implying a well-defined logic in the succession of situations. The groups to be subjected to intervention would be made up of representatives of different tendencies in a social struggle and, right from the start of the intervention, these groups would be confronted by representatives of hostile groups. Such confrontations facilitate the articulation of two of the principles of social movements: that of identity and that of opposition.

There remains the principle of totality. Bringing this into play is mainly the job of the sociologists:

'Just as confrontation represents the I–O (Identity–Opposition) dimension of a social movement, so too the meeting with the *researchers* represents the I–T (Identity–Totality) dimension, for the researcher causes the stakes of a conflict to emerge, and he cannot be identified with the actor and even less with his adversary' (Touraine 1981, p. 143).

The distancing which is thus made possible should allow the participants in a struggle to take on the proper character of a social movement, whether their struggle is relative to some claim, to some organization, or some institution.

It is true that the social identity studied by social psychologists has not necessarily a great deal in common with the principle of identity of a social movement. Nevertheless, at the level of intervention, in the situation created by the sociologist, it is confrontation with the adversary which is supposed to bring about work on identity. Researchers are expected to take care with the smallest details of the psycho-sociological processes. 'The interlocutor may sometimes be too strong, sometimes too weak for the group. In the latter case, two persons should work with the group instead of one' (Touraine 1981). Different effects may occur as a consequence of the confrontation: reinforcement of the identity of the group, but also internal cleavage and redefinition of the opponents. A separation of roles between the researchers becomes, in this case, very important: one, the agitator, will support the group by recalling, for example, militant activities of the past and their importance for public opinion, the other, the secretary, will hardly ever intervene but will in a sense constitute the group memory by recording a complete account of proceedings and typing out summaries which will be used later for activating the principle of totality.

One conclusion seems inevitable following this brief presentation of Touraine's work: an authentically 'holistic' concept, which looks at society as a whole, led the sociologist to elaborate a theoretical framework, which finally brought him to the need to integrate his social study with a study of interventions in particular situations of particular interactions between individuals. These studies postulate the existence of representations which society, and the social movements which make it up, elaborate on the level at which systems of historical action are oriented. Principles of identity, of opposition, and of totality, which can be set working and studied in concrete interactional situations, govern these representational processes. Thence the importance and relevance of the recent work by Touraine for the study of the function of representations and beliefs in the interactions of groups.

No less relevant for such research is the work of Bourdieu, which shows how an equally 'holistic' sociological approach also comes to articulate its sociological analyses proper with the investigation of individual processes.

Bourdieu was first known for his two books with Passeron (Bourdieu and Passeron 1964, 1977) which describe how a culture in general, and the educational establishment in particular, tend to reproduce the established social order. Despite a growing democratization of access to higher education, and precisely because of the inflation of academic qualifications and the established differentiations within the university establishment, this theory of social reproduction remains relevant today (Bourdieu 1978b). But so that the reader may better understand by what means the reproduction of social differences operates, I will first present the ideas developed in articles in the journal *Actes de la récherche* of which Bourdieu is director, and which were later published as a book (Bourdieu 1979).

A key notion in these articles is that of *field*: this refers to a group of social objects which are structured by a set of hierarchical and opposing relationships, and whose share of the available social value capital is determined by this structure. Parisian *haute couture*, the diplomas and degrees produced by the educational establishment, and the domain of French linguistics are all such fields. Within these fields, the value hierarchy is at stake in a general struggle: the oppositions which are characteristic of a field are the same as those which exist between classes or sections of classes in a society. This gives rise to an important notion: that of *structural homology*, which means that relations inside a specific field are of the same kind as relations between classes in the field of relations of production. In addition, positions in a class, or section of a class, are generally expressed in a way which is censured and misconstrued through the defence of their positions presented by certain agents of a given field, who at the same time continue to obey the specific laws which govern the distribution of values in their field. Since these laws are recognized by the agents of a field, it makes sense to speak of *recognition* and *misrecognition* (as translated in Bourdieu and Passeron 1977): for a field to function, the laws which decide the distribution of values within the field must be known and accepted by the actors within the field, but their link with other interests, that is, their expressive interest must be denied. The object of social science is to study the structure of a field, the homology, and the links of its internal relations with the dominant relations of power and production which are part of a society.

But this conceptual system needs to be supplemented by theories about individual dynamics. These theories are more systematically presented in various books, and their core is constituted by the concepts of 'habitus' and 'disposition'.

The sociology of the educational system comes down mainly to an investigation of the establishment of habitus:

'Only when it is seen that a group's integration rests on the (total or partial) identity of the habitus inculcated by PW (pedagogic work) i.e. when the principle of the homology of practices is located in the total or partial identity of the practice-generating grammars, is it possible to escape from the naïveties of the social philosophies of consensus. Such sociologies, in reducing group integration to the possession of a common repertoire of representations, are unable, for example, to apprehend the unity and the integrative function of practices or opinions that are phenomenally different or even contradictory but produced by the same generative habitus' (Bourdieu and Passeron 1977, p. 35).

When it comes to explaining the links between economic and social changes, appeal is made to the same key concepts, which are 'statistically measurable in the form of regularities independent of individual wills' (Bourdieu 1978*a*, p. 92).

Elsewhere (Doise 1986*b*) I have examined the relations between the notion of habitus and that of social representation. Here it suffices to emphasize the fact that the sociologist who most underlines the weight and continuity of sociological determinism is also the one who talks most about the psychological functioning of individuals, though all the while scarcely borrowing a single theoretical concept from his colleagues in psychology or social psychology.

The postulates which govern the scientific work of these four Parisian sociologists are often different, even in opposition to one another. Boudon strongly defends an individualistic approach, which is intended to be universalist when it reduces individual psychological processes to elementary calculations. A vision of this kind is scarcely sufficient to illuminate the complexity of intergroup relations, even though it does occasionally shed an interesting light on certain aspects of these relations. Crozier, who emphasizes the need to look upon the strategies of social agents as part of a high-level game in which the aim is constantly to modify whichever of the rules of the game are embedded in the situation, by this very approach develops a model of the person which is essentially interactionist and anti-reductionist. This means that the researcher must investigate each situation in a way that takes account of the interaction of strategies and the modifications of intent, motivation, and meanings given to this situation. Social psychologists must remember that their subjects also try to give their own meaning to the experimental situation.

But these meanings should not be thought of as arbitrary improvizations, but rather as so many variations on the themes presented by the experimenter, or, to use the terminology of Crozier and Friedberg, as games that subjects will construct out of the game proposed for the experiment.

The two other sociologists cited have more holistic convictions. Touraine, with his theory of the interlinking of the principles of identity, of opposition, and of totality, develops a very general conceptualization, but the important point is that he makes it concrete by going on to study interpersonal interactions, which are of course analysed in their historical and sociological context. Bourdieu gives us the important example of a conception which links the schemas permitting understanding between individuals to the principles of organization which also govern social relations. The two main threads in his work, the one ethnological and the other sociological, both nevertheless give rise to the same general concept of individual processes, and demonstrate once again how a holistic concept can account for social particulars as well as social universals.

Research in social psychology

General concepts intervene in the operation of social processes, and more precisely in the operation of intergroup relations, just as they intervene in their explanation.

One of Tajfel's great merits was that he showed that it was possible to carry out experiments to demonstrate the dynamics of general beliefs. A number of books (Tajfel 1978, 1981, 1982, 1984) report the results of research by Tajfel and his former colleagues, as well as by other researchers inspired by his approach or who worked within a similar perspective. Here we will simply indicate more than half a dozen different directions being taken by researchers into a number of new problems, new approaches which nevertheless are important for the understanding of the function of general concepts in the dynamics of intergroup relations.

Our own intergroup research has dealt mainly with the processes of accentuation in the representation of differences between groups and of similarities within groups. However, a detailed analysis of early published results (Deschamps and Doise 1978) and more recent results (Deschamps

1982; Deschamps and Lorenzi-Cioldi 1981) permits a more precise formulation of the issue by demonstrating that these phenomena, originally investigated at the level of the group, may at the same time be accompanied by an increase in differentiation between one's self and other members of the in-group. This asymmetry between homogenization of the out-group and differentiation between self and the in-group is of great importance for understanding the function of the concept 'individualism' (see also Park and Rothbart 1982).

When situational circumstances extend the individualistic approach as far as members of the out-group, the latter become less the target for discrimination and are treated more as members of the in-group (Wilder 1978).

A sociological process, found in the research already cited (Deschamps and Doise 1978) seems to favour individuation in the in-group: boys but not girls differentiate between self and other members of the in-group. Deschamps (1979) has related this asymmetric process to a distinction between dominant and dominated groups: the former apply to the latter a collective homogenizing definition while reserving for themselves, and also to a certain extent for other members of the in-group, a higher level of individual autonomy. This theory accords well with the results of research on attribution, which attributes more autonomy to members of those social categories with greater prestige (see Doise *et al.* 1978, Ch. 11). Deschamps *et al.* (1982) have also explored these asymmetric processes in a school context. They produced results which illustrate the functions of habitus and of disposition, to use the terms proposed by Bourdieu and Passeron (1964, 1977).

Attributions of ability and of intent are made differently between individuals depending upon whether they share or do not share the same membership categories. This is the case where members of different ethnic groups meet (Taylor and Jaggi 1974) and is certainly true for images that Westerners have of other cultures (see for example Preiswerk and Perret 1975). This kind of asymmetry may also serve to maintain a positive self image, although this process is not unaffected by the reality of social differences, as has been clearly shown by Bolzman *et al.* (1987) and was pointed out by Hewstone and Jaspars (1984, p. 398):

'Under certain conditions social attributions will not function to provide a positive ingroup identity, e.g. certain minority-majority group relations (where the minority group perceives no alternatives to the existing system). In this case, members of the "objectively" inferior group will make attributions which tend to devalue the ingroup and favour the outgroup.'

Judgements in attribution thus reflect a sociological objectivity, and in this sense we are dealing with an 'internalization of the objective situation' (Bourdieu 1978*a*, p. 92) or with 'incorporated social situations' (Bourdieu

1979, p. 545). But individuals or groups of individuals may affect this social objectivity. Research into social influence, and more particularly into minority influence, shows us how. Moscovici (1980) particularly distinguishes the process of influence brought about by a majority or by power, and the processes set in operation by a minority. In the first type of case, the targets of influence try first to maintain good relations with the source of influence and pay attention above all to elements in the replies given by the agent of the majority influence so as to be able to adopt them. Responses modified for relational reasons disappear when the relations cease. When it comes to a minority source, the relational dynamics are less strong, and before formulating a response the subject is therefore able to take a more independent look at reality. Turner (1984) and Mugny (1984) have recently tried to articulate the study of social influence with that of intergroup relations by manipulating identification with the source of influence. Many of the results reported by Mugny show that we need to distinguish influence directly linked to the source's message and an influence which is only indirectly linked. These effects frequently operate in opposite ways and, in our opinion, show that dynamics other than that of identification intervene. A source with which one identifies less, that is, a source which is an out-group, may have a distinctive effect which is more durable and more related to its objective position. Mugny *et al.* (1983) demonstrated such an effect in Switzerland when they reported that a 'humanitarian' message in favour of foreigners had a more lasting effect on young Swiss youngsters when it emanated from a minority group of foreigners than when it came from a minority group of compatriots. Only a universalist concept, or more precisely, a principle of totality in Touraine's sense can, in our opinion, explain such results. A general belief could be stronger than categorical identity.

Universal beliefs intervene also in the dynamics of negotiations between groups, especially where there is mediation by a third party. Touzard (1977) has analysed the role of mediation in the solution of intergroup conflicts. In a certain sense, the mediator in a conflict situation must represent those values of the society which show the way the negotiation should go. It is thus very important that the mediator have a clear picture of her/his own role and intervene in a manner which accords with the nature of the conflict; an overly technical mediation may neglect the ideological and symbolic aspects of a conflict or vice versa. An ill-adapted mediation style may accentuate the conflict and make the solution even more difficult. In other words, the mediator must take account of the general ideas which are actualized in the situation.

The power of sanction enjoyed by a third party playing a mediating role may be a determining factor. The difficulties of relations between groups, and above all, the spiral of distrust which tends to develop, are well known to those who participate in such relations. But what guarantees can there be that this spiral can be broken? Ng (1981) created a situation in which members of two groups had to divide payments between the groups and observed the usual discrimination in this condition. On the other hand, in a new condition, the experimenter led subjects to believe that they were alone in deciding the allocation to be given to their group and to members of the other group. Discrimination in favour of the membership group was practically absent in this condition, as subjects could not expect discriminatory behaviour on the part of the members of the other group. This suggests that it would be in order to counter possible discrimination on the part of the other group that the in-group behaves unfairly towards it. More recent research by the same investigator (Ng 1984) demonstrates the need to integrate the study of specific intergroup processes with investigations into the effects of a general belief in equity, as these new results show that the effects of equity and the effects of categorization can be in some conditions of equal importance. Similar results have often been found in intergroup experiments by the Bristol team (Billig 1973; Bornstein *et al.* 1983; Branthwaite *et al.* 1979; Turner 1980, 1983) but can scarcely be said to have been incorporated into the thinking of Tajfel and his colleagues, who appear to be more interested in the principles of identity and of opposition than in the principle of totality, to use Touraine's terminology.

One concept which continues to be important despite recent criticisms (see for example Deschamps and Brown 1983) is that of the supra-ordinate goal, first put forward by Sherif. Certainly, investigation into the effects of a common goal needs to be articulated with investigation into the effects of social identity. If evoking a common identity (Kramer and Brewer 1984) can play an important role in safeguarding community resources, it is not enough to explain 'the tragedy of the commons' to borrow the title of the book by Hardin (1968). Study of this problem, which has been barely begun by social psychologists, requires an approach which will integrate several levels of analysis and which will necessarily integrate the investigation of general ideas and ideology. This kind of research implies also a new approach to the problem of ethics which social psychologists have for too long neglected, leaving it to a number of developmental psychologists who follow in the footsteps of Piaget (1965) or Kohlberg (1963). The problem of a general concept of the person will of necessity be posed to social psychologists who work in this area, but this is not a reason to neglect it: on the contrary.

One idea still insufficiently exploited in the study of intergroup relations is that of complementarity. When looking at Peabody's (1968) research into intergroup images, we pointed out (Doise 1978) that all the evidence suggested that societies establish, not just a single set of hierarchical concepts or values to evaluate different groups, but rather several of these sets which then allowed different groups to retain a positive identity in different contexts. Van Knippenberg (1984) recently looked at this problem of complementarity by reporting empirical results (Van Knippenberg *et al*. 1981) which found confirmation in an experiment by Mummendey and Schreiber (1983). These investigations usefully supplement the Bristol team's theory of social identity, and at the same time provide a social psychological illustration of the concept of hierarchical opposition developed by Dumont.

However, this kind of asymmetrical and crossed intergroup dynamic is not the only way in which established concepts and values can be modified. An important contribution by Lemaine (1984) was to show, by both experiment and by case study of scientific innovation, how groups invent new criteria or new combinations of criteria of judgement and evaluation. We can understand why it is that this writer also refers to Crozier and Friedberg (1980) when he suggests that individuals and groups cannot be considered as being simply the plaything of extrinsic social determination or as functioning just in terms of dominant or widely diffused ideas.

Conclusion

The reader may perhaps feel that this chapter has produced more information about the beliefs of researchers than about the beliefs of social actors in general. This would not be entirely inaccurate, because we have tried to put in focus the concepts being used by investigators as well as those general ideas which they have been investigating. But these two kinds of concept do not exist in separate universes, and it is for this reason that we thought it a good idea to present a more general picture of the different theories now being used in the investigation of social beliefs relevant to the dynamics of intergroup relations.

Dumont's distinction between holistic and individualistic concepts and Tajfel's distinction between interpersonal and intergroup behaviour are not only categories of meaning belonging to scientists, they are also keys to understanding the dynamics of important beliefs as they intervene in everyday life. The same applies to the principal concepts that we have borrowed from the sociologists. We believe that empirical research, as practised by social psychologists, must turn more and more to this kind of general idea about systems of belief, while continuing to explicate the specific conditions in which the different beliefs operate. The example of Tajfel's work shows that social psychologists would find it advantageous to pursue this dual goal, but this can be done only by articulating systematically the different levels of analysis, and by reflecting on the status of those general ideas which intervene as much in terms of explanatory principles as in terms of phenomena to be explained.

References

Beauvois, J.L. and Joule, R. (1981). *Soumission et ideologies*. Presses Universitaires de France, Paris.

Billig, M. (1973). Normative communication in a minimal intergroup situation. *European Journal of Social Psychology*, **3**, 339–43.

Bolzman, C., Mugny, G., and Roux, P. (1987). Comparaisons entre groupes de statut social different: attributions sociocentriques ou logique d'une représentation sociale? *Social Science Information*, **26**, 129–54.

Bornstein, G., Crum, L., Wittenbraker, J., Harring, K., Insko, C.A., and Thibaut, J. (1983). On the measurement of social orientations in the minimal group paradigm. *European Journal of Social Psychology*, **13**, 321–50.

Boudon, R. (1977). *Effets pervers et ordre social*. Presses Universitaires de France, Paris.

Boudon, R. (1981). *The logic of social action* (translated by D. and G. Silverman). Routledge & Kegan Paul, London.

Boudon, R. (1984). *La place du désordre*. Presses Universitaires de France, Paris.

Bourdieu, P. (1977). *Outline of a theory of practice* (translated by R. Nice). Cambridge University Press.

Bourdieu, P. (1978*a*). *Algeria 60*. Cambridge University Press.

Bourdieu, P. (1978*b*). Classement, declassement, reclassement. *Actes de la Recherche en Sciences Sociales*, **24**, 2–22.

Bourdieu, P. (1979). *La distinction, critique sociale du jugement*. Les Editions de Minuit, Paris.

Bourdieu, P. and Passeron, J.C. (1964). *Les heritiers*. Les Editions de Minuit, Paris.

Bourdieu, P. and Sayad, A. (1964). *Le deracinement*. Les Editions de Minuit, Paris.

Bourdieu, P. and Passeron, J.C. (1977). *Reproduction in education, society and culture*. Sage, London.

Branthwaite, A., Doyle, S., and Lightbown, N. (1979). The balance between fairness and discrimination. *European Journal of Social Psychology*, **9**, 149–63.

Crozier, M. and Friedberg, E. (1980). *Actors and systems, the politics of collective action* (translated by A. Goldhammer). University of Chicago Press.

Deschamps, J.C. (1979). L'identité sociale et les rapports de domination. *Revue Suisse de Sociologie*, **6**, 109–40.

Deschamps, J.C. (1982). Social identity and relations of power between groups. In *Social identity and intergroup relations* (ed. H. Tajfel). Cambridge University Press.

Deschamps, J.C. and Brown, R. (1983). Superordinate goals and intergroup conflict. *British Journal of Social Psychology*, **22**, 189–95.

Deschamps, J.C. and Doise, W. (1978). Crossed category memberships in intergroup relations. In *Differentiation between social groups* (ed. H. Tajfel). Academic Press, London.

Deschamps, J.C. and Lorenzi-Cioldi, F.(1981). 'Egocentrisme' et 'Sociocentrisme' dans les relations entre groups. *Revue Suisse de Psychologie*, **40**, 108–31.

Deschamps, J.C., Lorenzi-Cioldi, F., and Meyer, G. (1982). *L'echec scolaire. Elève modèle ou modèles d'élève*? Editions Pierre-Marcel Favre, Lausanne.

Doise, W. (1978). *Groups and individuals. Explanations in social psychology*. Cambridge University Press.

Doise, W. (1984). Social representations, intergroup experiments and levels of analysis. In *Social representations* (ed. R.M. Farr and S. Moscovici). Cambridge University Press.

Doise, W. (1986a). *Levels of explanation in social psychology* (translated by E. Mapstone). Cambridge University Press.

Doise, W. (1986b). Les représentations sociales: définition d'un concept. In *L'étude des représentations sociales* (ed. W. Doise and A. Palmonari). Delachaux et Niestlé, Paris.

Doise, W., Deschamps, J.C., and Mugny, G. (1978). *Psychologie sociale experimentale*. A. Colin, Paris.

Dumont, L. (1967). *Homo hierarchicus*. Gallimard, Paris.

Dumont, L. (1977). *Homo aequalis I*. Gallimard, Paris.

Dumont, L. (1983). *Essais sur l'individualisme*. Editions du Seuil, Paris.

Hardin, G.J. (1968). The tragedy of the commons. *Science*, **162**, 1243–8.

Hewstone, M. and Jaspars, J.M.F. (1984). Social dimensions of attribution. In *The social dimension*, Vol. 2 (ed. H. Tajfel). Cambridge University Press.

Kohlberg, L. (1963). The development of children's orientation toward a moral order. I: sequence in the development of moral thought. *Vita Humana*, **6**, 11–33.

Kramer, R.M. and Brewer, M.B. (1984). Effects of group identity on resource use in a simulated commons dilemma. *Journal of Personality and Social Psychology*, **46**, 1044–57.

Lemaine, G. (1984). Social differentiation in the scientific community. In *The social dimension, Vol. 1* (ed. H. Tajfel). Cambridge University Press.

Moscovici, S. (1980). Toward a theory of conversion behaviour. In *Advances in experimental social psychology*, Vol. 13 (ed. L. Berkowitz). 209–39.

Mugny, G. (1984). The influence of minorities: ten years later. In *The social dimension*, Vol. 2 (ed. H. Tajfel). Cambridge University Press.

Mugny, G., Kaiser, C., and Papastamou, S. (1983). Influence minoritaire, identification et relations entre groupes: etude experimentale autour d'une votation. *Les Cahiers de Psychologie Sociale*, **19**, 1–30.

Mummendey, A. and Schreiber, H.J. (1983). Better or just different? Positive social identity by discrimination against, or by differentiation from outgroups. *European Journal of Social Psychology*, **13**, 389–97.

Ng, S.H. (1981). Equity theory and the allocation of rewards between groups. *European Journal of Social Psychology*, **11**, 439–43.

Ng, S.H. (1984). Equity and social categorization effects on intergroup allocation of rewards. *British Journal of Social Psychology*, **23**, 165–72.

Park, B. and Rothbart, M. (1982). Perception of out-group homogeneity and levels of social categorization: memory for the subordinate attributes of in-group and out-group members. *Journal of Personality and Social Psychology*, **42**, 1051–68.

Peabody, D. (1968). Group judgments in the Philippines: evaluative and descriptive aspects. *Journal of Personality and Social Psychology*, **10**, 290–300.

Piaget, J. (1965). *The moral judgment of the child*. Keagan Paul, Trench & Trubner, London.

Preiswerk, R. and Perret, D. (1975). *Ethnocentrisme et histoire*. Editions Anthropos, Paris.

Tajfel, H. (1978). *Differentiation between social groups: studies in the social psychology of intergroup relations*. Academic, London.

Tajfel, H. (1981). *Human groups and social categories*. Cambridge University Press.

Tajfel, H. (1982). *Social identity and intergroup relations*. Cambridge University Press.

Tajfel, H. (1984). *The social dimension. Vols 1 and 2*. Cambridge University Press.

Taylor, D.M. and Jaggi, V. (1974). Ethnocentrism and causal attribution in a South Indian context. *Journal of Cross-Cultural Psychology*, **5**, 162–71.

Touraine, A. (1977). *The self-production of society*. University of Chicago Press.

Touraine, A. (1981). *The voice and the eye. An analysis of social movements* (translated by A. Duff). Cambridge University Press.

Touzard, H. (1977). *La médiation et la résolution des conflits*. Presses Universitaires de France, Paris.

Turner, J.C. (1980). Fairness or discrimination in intergroup behaviour? A reply to Branthwaite, Doyle and Lightbown. *European Journal of Social Psychology*, **10**, 131–47.

Turner, J.C. (1983). Some comments on . . . 'the measurement of social orientations in the minimal group paradigm'. *European Journal of Social Psychology*, **13**, 351–67.

Turner, J.C. (1984). Social identification and psychological group formation. In *The social dimension, Vol. 2* (ed. H. Tajfel). Cambridge University Press.

Van Knippenberg, A.F.M. (1984). Intergroup differences in group perceptions. In *The social dimension, Vol. 2* (ed. H. Tajfel). Cambridge University Press.

Van Knippenberg, A.F.M., Wilke, H., and De Vries, N.K. (1981). Social comparison on two dimensions. *European Journal of Social Psychology*, **11**, 267–83.

Wilder, D.A. (1978). Reduction of intergroup discrimination through individuation of the outgroup. *Journal of Personality and Social Psychology*, **36**, 1361–74.

9 The political and social beliefs of adolescents

Raymond Cochrane and Michael Billig

Introduction

Much of the work on the political attitudes of young people looks at what is commonly called 'political socialization'. This is unfortunate because the very concept of political socialization often draws attention to the continuities of social life, at the expense of overlooking the discontinuities. The concept of socialization, when applied to political attitudes or commitments, implies the task of successive generations is to learn the political and social beliefs appropriate to their familial and social environment. In this respect, successful socialization implies the intergenerational transmission, with modification, of political beliefs and attitudes. At the back of much of this work, is the image of a society reproducing itself across generations with the basic elements remaining essentially unchanged. However, a crucial feature of capitalist society may be discontinuity, rather than continuity. As Marx and Engels wrote in *The Communist manifesto*: 'The bourgeoisie cannot exist without constantly revolutionising the instruments of production, and thereby the relations of production, and with them the whole relations of society' (Marx and Engels 1968, p. 38). If we are to take seriously this diagnosis, then we should expect constant change in social relations, and under conditions of constant change, one would expect social relations, and social attitudes, to take more indeterminate forms than might be expected from reading some of the writings on 'political socialization'. For our theories to capture the social psychological dimensions of this indeterminacy, we need a perspective which can encompass discontinuities and contradictions.

Furnham (1985) suggests that traditional research on young people's political and social beliefs can be organized around four issues. Perhaps of least interest to a social psychologist have been the studies of political knowledge and the determinants of the extent of knowledge, for example, age, social class, contact with mass media. More centrally there have been studies of the structure of political beliefs. Typically, it has been asked what dimensions underlie adolescents' political views, whether these are similar to those found in adults, and what factors influence adolescent political beliefs. So, for example, Sidanius and colleagues (1986) have examined the dimensions along which the specific sociopolitical beliefs of Swedish school children could be laid. They found three factors (political-economic conservatism, xenophobia, and punitiveness) underlay responses to the items on a 'conservatism' scale. They went on to show that scores on these dimensions were related to parental political ideology and the nature of parent–child interactions and emotional relationships.

Third, there have been studies of the transmission of political views from parents to their children and, in some cases, to their grandchildren. Generally, it is found that party preference is more predictable across generations than are specific political attitudes (e.g. Jennings and Niemi 1971).

Fourth, studies have looked at demographic correlates of the political and social beliefs of adolescents. Furnham's own study compares the views of 17-year-old boys and girls, and of English and South African adolescents. He found that girls were less conservative than boys and that white South African high-school students were more conservative than were English students. Not surprisingly, perhaps, the South African students were more likely to be opposed to equality, the African liberation movements, and mixed marriages, but more likely to support white superiority, Christianity, and fluoridation.

To such a typology we would add that there have also been studies of attitudes towards the political system (e.g. belief in efficacy, trust, and the utility of democracy itself) rather than beliefs about particular political issues; studies of personality and political beliefs (e.g. the Authoritarian Personality hypothesis that particular socialization experiences produce particular political views); and studies of 'life span' versus generational or cohort influences on changes in political values (for example, the studies of Ingelhart (1977) on the materialism/post-materialism value dimensions).

Underlying most of these approaches to adolescent politics and political socialization is the concept of political attitudes—what factors influence the development of attitudes, and what are the structures of attitude systems? Implicit in most studies based on the attitude construct is the assumption of striving for cognitive consistency. For example, balance and equity theories assume that individuals are motivated to bring a harmonious consonance to their thinking (see Billig 1986d, for a discussion of the assumption of mental unity and its role in equity theories; see also Tajfel 1982). Frequently the assumption is not expressed as an overt motivational premise, but nevertheless, it is assumed that individuals bring some sort of internal order to their attitudes, beliefs, affective reactions, and cognitive interpretations. Thus, social psychologists studying political beliefs will frequently refer to 'belief-systems' or 'value-systems' or 'attitudinal systems', as if internal representations of the world are systematized, and it is unquestioned that such notional 'systems' have psychological reality. Moreover, it is assumed that the psychological significance of beliefs about the social world is derived from their position in such internalized systems. In consequence, the task of social psychologists studying political beliefs, attitudes, ideologies, etc. appears to be to uncover the structures of these systems (e.g. Sidanius and Ekehammar 1979), rather like transformational linguists who have set themselves the goal of laying bare the deep grammatical structure supposedly underlying actual utterances. Just as idealized transformational grammars have all the substance of ghostly platonic essences, so the 'systems' of social psychologists may reflect the psychologist's desire for systematization rather than any psychological reality.

With the current emphasis in social psychology on cognitive approaches, there has been a tendency to translate some of the assumptions of attitudinal theory into the language of cognitive theory. Thus, instead of talking about 'belief-systems', cognitive social psychologists prefer to talk of 'schemata' for interpreting the social world. Cognitive social psychologists assume that individuals are equipped with schemata, which allow them to process information about the social world and to determine the selection, retrieval, interpretation, and recall of information. In consequence, the assumption of inner unity runs just as strongly in cognitive social psychology as it ever did in attitudinal theory; for there are assumed to be biases in schematic processing, which lead to the constant confirmation of assumptions (Billig 1985a, 1986b, 1986d).

The assumptions of cognitive social psychology can be applied to the issue of political beliefs. For example, Hamill et al. (1985) and Sharp and Lodge (1985) have written about 'partisan schemata'. The assumption is that supporters of different political parties have different sets of interpretative schemata for interpreting political events. There is also the assumption that there is some organizational structure to political beliefs, for example, Conover and Feldman (1984) write that they 'propose a schematic model of how people organize their beliefs about the political world' (p. 95).

If one assumes that there are definable 'belief systems', or 'political schemata', which lie at the core of political beliefs, then political socialization can be seen principally as a matter of acquiring a particular systematization or organization of beliefs. For example, investigators of political socialization have examined how the young generation incorporate the political styles of thinking of their elders (e.g. Jennings and Niemi 1981; for a thoughtful review, see Braungart and Braungart 1986). There is a temptation to consider adolescent political thinking principally as a matter of acquiring a particular, culturally available, block of attitudinal systematizations. Coincidentally, some Marxist theories of ideology make similar assumptions. For example, Althusser (1971) sees the issue of ideological 'reproduction' in terms of the education of the young generation into definable ideological habits: at the root of this notion is the assumption that such ideologies are internally consistent (see Billig *et al.* (1988) for details of the assumptions of internal consistency in many sociological theories of ideology and also for comparisons between theories of ideology and cognitive social psychology).

The assumption of inner ideological unity has tended to direct researchers' attention to the consistent factors of social beliefs, rather than looking for inconsistencies. It is possible that the same assumption underlies the work of some of the proponents of social representation theory. In this respect the criticisms of Litton and Potter (1985) and Potter and Litton (1985) are interesting. Among other criticisms, they specifically take issue with Moscovici (1981) for concentrating upon the ways in which social representations are said to reduce uncertainty and produce social cohesion. Potter and Litton (1985) propose a valuable alternative approach, which is based upon the concept of 'linguistic repertoires' and the analysis of discourse. When such an analysis concentrates upon the contradictory repertoires at the disposal of the same person, then the discourse approach of these critics of social representation theory is very close to what here is being described as a rhetorical approach. If Potter and Litton are correct in their critique of social representation theory, then these contradictory elements are better investigated from a discourse, or rhetorical, perspective.

In contrast to many contemporary social psychological approaches to the study of widespread social beliefs, the rhetorical approach assumes neither an inner organizational system, nor an internal unity. Instead there is the assumption that often people will express themselves in different ways, that common-sense will contain contrary themes, and that the expression of contrary themes is a sign of neither ignorance, nor unresolved psychological tension, nor disingenuity concealing the 'true' attitude which lurks just beyond the reach of the social psychologist's measuring instrument. The rhetorical approach will be presented in more detail later in this chapter.

Background to our studies

In 1978, we were asked whether we would take part in a Social Science Research Council (now Economic and Social Research Council) initiative on 'young people in society'. A report commissioned by the SSRC had highlighted a distinct lack of research on the psychology of adolescence and the SSRC response was to set aside some money for research on this topic. They identified several areas where they felt research would be profitable, and the way in which young people come into contact with the political system was one of them.

Our project originally had the very broad objective of examining the political identifications and attitudes of adolescents and to relate these to a variety of aspects of their own experience. What we hoped would be one of the most interesting aspects of the project was our intention to compare information gained about adolescent political views by the use of traditional survey methods with that gained by ideographic methods. We assumed that the latter approach would yield information which could be used to complement the survey data and enable us to gain a more complete psychological appreciation of the political attitudes and beliefs of young people.

The study began in the autumn of 1979 with a questionnaire survey of about 1500 fifth formers in West Midlands schools.* Some of the items were purpose designed while others were taken from questionnaires used in a number of previous studies. The questionnaire tapped many aspects of political identification and beliefs (such as party choice, knowledge of politics, attitudes towards the political systems, political views, class identification, etc.). After completing the basic analysis of these data we embarked upon a series of small group discussions of political issues with another cohort of fifth formers in the same schools. A series of half a dozen tape-recorded discussions was held with each of about 20 such groups over a period of a year. As far as possible, sessions were contrived to be discussions between peers with minimal intervention from us. The questionnaire survey was repeated with a third cohort of fifth formers in 1982.

Several political and social changes occurred during the course of the study which led to discrepancies in the measures of beliefs derived from the original questionnaire survey and the attitudes that were being expressed in the small group discussions.

First, there was the rapid growth in the level of unemployment in the West Midlands following the Conservative victory in the 1979 general election, and this undoubtedly influenced the way many of the young people involved in our study felt about politics. Whereas in 1979–80 only 4 per cent of the fathers of our respondents were unemployed, by 1981–82 this figure had grown to 15 per cent. Employment prospects for school leavers deteriorated even faster, and to such an extent that hardly any of the fifth formers who left several of the schools we studied obtained immediate employment (for an account of the effects of unemployment on young people's lives, see Coffield *et al.* 1986).

Secondly, between conducting the survey of the political views of adolescents and completing the group discussions, the Social Democratic Party (SDP) emerged as a political force. Obviously, the advent of the SDP was unforeseen by us, but what we found more surprising was its ready appeal to our young respondents, who, by and large, would not be considered as belonging to the natural constituency of the SDP. We tried to examine some of the reasons behind the willingness of adolescents to give their allegiance to the emergent party.

* The questionnaires used in this study and all the data collected using them have been deposited with the ESRC Survey Data Archive, University of Essex.

Thirdly, at the same time as support was shifting from the traditional parties to the SDP, it was also shifting to the National Front (NF) and other fascist parties. Whereas in our first survey, carried out in 1979–80, NF support was confined to a small minority, it soon became apparent in the discussion groups which followed that survey that identification with the NF as a party, and even more with its policy of the forcible expulsion of non-Whites from Britain, was becoming widespread, and that this was often accompanied by unashamed racist opinions, openly expressed (Billig and Cochrane 1981; Cochrane and Billig 1982).

Partly as a result of, and partly as a response to, the three changes above there appeared to be a steady growth of a strong feeling of pessimism, hopelessness, and a poorly articulated, but nevertheless real, conviction that things in general, and the life circumstances of our respondents in particular, had slipped out of control. Not out of their own control, because that had never been the case, but a pervasive feeling that no one, and certainly not the political leaders of the country, had a grip on the way events were turning out. These feelings were partly, no doubt, a realistic interpretation of what was happening to an area which, for generations, had known relative economic prosperity and full employment but which, almost overnight, became an unemployment blackspot. But other factors also contributed to the feelings. There were, for example, the well-publicized and oft-repeated statements by the government that our recession was only a reflection of a world-wide slump which Britain, as a single country, could not influence. There was also the indirect impact of some of the SDP's propaganda which gave legitimacy and credibility to the notion that the old political system was failing and was unable to meet the challenge of problems the size of Britain's.

A corollary of these developments was a marked decline in support for the major political parties which previously, it could have been assumed on the basis of their class position, the adolescents in our samples would have supported. The decline in class-based party allegiance and voting among adults has been well documented by Butler and Stokes (1974), Crewe *et al.* (1977), and Himmelweit *et al.* (1985). What communicated itself to us very strongly during our conversations with the young people was the failure of the Labour and Conservative parties to inspire any idealism, hope, or belief in their ability to reverse the economic and social decline on which, it was generally believed, Britain had embarked. These perceptions were shared by party supporters and non-supporters alike. There also appeared to be a strong tendency to respond to the perceived lack of control over events by accepting apparently simple, often nationalist, sometimes authoritarian, solutions to economic problems and again these shared beliefs cut across party identifications.

The studies

The clearest evidence of the shift away from allegiances to traditional political parties is found in a direct comparison of responses to the first and second questionnaires, separated by only two years, and administered in exactly the same schools. On both occasions respondents were asked for which party they would vote if they were old enough. Table 2 reveals a dramatic decline in support for the Conservatives and a marked shift away from Labour. The Alliance (Liberal/SDP) gained support but so did the National Front and British Movement. Indeed, by the time of the second survey, in the winter of 1981–82, over 30 per cent of the white fifth-formers in our sample expressed some support for these two parties; for comparative data, see Hagendoorn and Janssen 1986.

In fact, information about party identification was not the most interesting data we gathered by any means. Although allegiances were sometimes firmly held, they were not held with enthusiasm—indeed many participants in discussion made no bones about indicating their boredom with 'politics', which they invariably defined as party politics. In addition, many of the widespread views outlined above were held more or less independently of party identification—especially those which were concerned with race. However, there was often considerable interest in expressing ideas and beliefs concerning social issues which were very definitely political even if not so defined by the holders. Some examples of the nature and extent of the widespread political attitudes which surfaced in the group discussion will be used as the raw material for the remainder of this chapter.

Much of the material concerns race issues. This reflects not so much the amount of time devoted to race in the discussion groups but the lively and interested discussion this topic provoked. More than with any other issue,

Table 2   Percentage support for political parties by fifth form pupils in six West Midland schools

Party	1979–80	1982
Communist	1.0	1.3
Conservative	34.6	16.7
Labour	51.5	43.2
Liberal/SDP*	6.3	24.6
NF/BM	6.6	14.2
Base $N=$	1200	1045

* SDP not included in 1979–80 survey.

when race was being discussed the groups, or at least the all-white groups, became animated and there were often several people trying to talk at once. Race is also an apposite topic because it emerged that the majority of participants were speaking the same language and were evidently sharing sets of perceptions and expectations.

A fifth-form girl summed up her views about politics by saying, 'I don't understand politics very well, but I think we should get rid of all the blacks and put them back where they belong'. It would, perhaps, not have been surprising that a skinhead British Movement supporter should have complained about blacks and Pakistanis taking all the jobs, but the girl quoted here said she was intending to vote for the SDP when she was old enough. Racist themes occurred in the comments of other SDP supporters, and in the comments of Labour and Conservative supporters as well, but were usually associated with an outright rejection of the fascist parties as being extreme and anti-immigrant. Indeed the emphasis on moderation and the recitation of the dangers of extremist intolerance preached by the SDP leaders struck a chord with the adolescents involved in our study.

The extent of SDP support did cause us some surprise. Our samples of young people were largely from working-class backgrounds and were, in terms of traditional political allegiances, rather unsophisticated and even cynical. The increase in support for the Alliance was quite spectacular and in quantitative terms reflects quite accurately the impact of the SDP on adults as revealed by their showing in the general election of June 1983. Our discussions with the school samples, however, showed that their support for the SDP had some paradoxical elements in it, in addition to the question of race, and suggested that the rise of the popularity of the SDP was not a simple reflection of a desire for moderation, but also contained many elements of the very mood which its leaders sought to combat.

The comments of our SDP supporters suggested that there were many contradictions in their views. Some SDP supporters sympathized with one fifth former, aspiring to become an accountant, who said, 'I don't agree with right or left-wing politics . . . so I believe in a democratic system with not too much emphasis on right or left-wing politics'. But this was likely to be accompanied by a blanket condemnation of all politics and politicians. Politicians were described by SDP supporters as being 'high and mighty', 'upper class', seeking only 'power, popularity, and money'.

Noticeable in this attitude was an impatience with political discussion. Another quote from an SDP supporter illuminates this: 'most politicians know nothing about what they are talking about; they argue with each other for hours on end and at the end of it they get nowhere'. More forcibly, one sympathizer said that 'if the MPs want to play at politics, lock them in a nice padded room and let them play'. This type of attitude incorporated contrasting themes drawn from radical and reactionary rhetoric as it expressed simultaneously populism and an anti-democratic authoritarianism. This extended from a simple rejection of party politics, 'I think that instead of different parties, fighting to get in, they should take the best people out of each party and make one big party', to obvious authoritarianism, 'I think all the powerful politicians should form a really powerful party and put Britain back on its feet again'.

This line of thought led inexorably to the logic that what Britain needed was a strong populist government formed from one powerful party that did not have to bother with argument, dissent, and elections and could get on with running the country. This party was to be the SDP.

This state of mind has been termed by Lipset (1960) 'extremism of the centre'; it is an attitude which seeks to replace democratic discussion by some sort of united national will. It seemed unlikely that people with those beliefs would, in the long run, be satisfied by the contrived moderation of Dr David Owen. It seemed to us that a serious question hung over the future political affiliations of those young SDP supporters who had projected their anti-political and populist yearnings on to the SDP. Having broken the mould once, it was possible that they would be receptive to further unconventional political choices (Billig and Cochrane 1982b).

In fact there were other ways in which the 'moderate' supporters of the SDP were similar to the 'extremists' of the National Front. We identified in our questionnaire data what might be called a 'populist' dimension running through the views of both NF and SDP supporters (Cochrane and Billig 1982). This was made up of a variety of opinions which could be considered to comprise an aspect of extremism. Supporters of the fascist parties and the SDP, for example, were more likely to express the view that violence was sometimes justified in achieving political ends, they were strongly anti-authority, anti-establishment, and tended to believe that the trade unions were too powerful and should be cut down to size. At the same time, the supporters of non-traditional parties were more politically alienated than the supporters of the Labour and Conservative parties; that is they believed that they were completely powerless and that politicians took no notice of what ordinary people like them thought.

Just as views concerning the SDP were far from simple and far from being consistent either with the stated aims and objectives of the party, or with the range of views expressed by its supporters, so were attitudes to the Labour party equally problematic. The electoral decline in support for Labour after 1979 was reflected in the attitudes of our young sample. Whereas adult dissatisfactions with the Labour party were, at that time, being attributed to the party's internal quarrelling, fear of extremism, and feeble leadership, the youngsters in our sample had little knowledge of, and even less interest in, these events. A not uncommon response to questions about the views of Tony Benn was, 'Tony who?'.

Unlike any previous generation, these children had been brought up in an age when Labour was more often in than out of office, and the Party had developed an essentially pragmatic conception of socialism, first under Wilson and then under Callaghan. Previously it may have been possible to maintain a belief that when Labour came to power things would be radically different, but for the generation of adolescents we studied, this forward-looking, optimistic view of socialism was not present (Billig and Cochrane 1982a).

Some effects of this could be seen in the comments of those youngsters who still supported Labour. Even the standard, uncompromising rejection of Thatcher and the Conservatives was often not accompanied by any optimistic radicalism. Abusive references to the Prime Minister were common, but amongst those who supported the Labour party the mood of anger was contained within the pragmatic conception already referred to and which is summed up in the comment, 'things weren't so bad under the Labour government'.

Many of the residual Labour supporters had this kind of nostalgic view of the party but rejected the traditional ideals of socialism. Indeed they saw the Labour party as essentially conservative. Perhaps the most dramatic example of this was provided by a girl who wanted to be a social worker but who was leaving school with no qualifications and no job. She rejected Mrs Thatcher because she was allowing immigrants to 'pour in' and pointed out that a row of shops, which were now all owned by Pakistanis had all been owned by 'English people' when Labour was in power.

This is illustrative of the view already referred to and held by many of the white youngsters in our sample that the problem of unemployment could be solved, at a stroke, by the expulsion of non-whites. We found, as other investigators of contemporary racist discourse have found (van Dijk 1984; Reeves 1983), that the racist themes were interspersed with declarations of tolerance. As well as vehemently denying that they were prejudiced, and pointing out that they had black and brown friends in school, the young people who voiced racist sentiments were also quite clear that 'we are all the same really', and that black youngsters had a much harder time getting a job than did a white school leaver. A rejection of discrimination and prejudice coexisted with the view that 'they should be sent back to where they came from' and the tendency to laugh at crude racist jokes. These kinds of beliefs were widely diffused even amongst those adolescents who tried to distance themselves from blatant bigotry. On many occasions we encountered a reluctant endorsement of a point of view which was recognized as inhumane, but which was seen as the only way out of a crisis. Lacking any clearly defined alternatives, these youngsters found themselves drifting towards accepting an idea which symbolized a quick solution to intractable economic problems. They often prefaced their comments with phrases such as, 'I'm not National Front, myself, but . . .' (Cochrane and Billig 1984; Billig 1986e; for a rhetorical analysis of this strategy, see Billig 1986b and Billig et al. 1988).

There were other aspects of support for the Labour party which do not square with traditional views of political socialization. Just as the Labour party appeared to be attracting support from those who expressed non-socialist attitudes, so conversely it was being rejected by a significant number of those who did have left-wing attitudes. From the questionnaire data, it was possible to construct a crude measure of 'socialist attitudes', based on responses to questions on nationalization, trade union power, the redistribution of wealth, and other such topics. About 50 per cent of those with high scores on this index said that they would not support the Labour party. Nor were they turning further to the left than Labour, for the numbers supporting the Communist party, or other Marxist groups were minuscule and static. Instead, these people either rejected the whole idea of politics, or gave their support to the SDP, National Front, or British Movement.

A clear example of this was the girl who thought that the main problems of the country arose from 'low wages' and the 'stupidity by some people in high places'; there were 'too many Big Bosses closing down firms for their own good' and wealth should be redistributed so that 'everyone should have roughly the same'. Unusually, this girl did have an image of a future society where, she said, 'everyone contributes to society and everyone gets listened to' and where politicians would 'take note of what ordinary people want, instead of working against less well-off people'. Far from this girl seeing her utopian and egalitarian hopes expressed within the Labour movement, she condemned all politicians equally, and despite a strong interest in politics, she declared that it was a waste of time to vote.

In many ways the most consistent views were expressed by the young people who said they would support the National Front or British Movement, but even here there were some paradoxes. One could be forgiven for thinking that as political forces in Britain, the fascist parties were dead. This was evidenced, for example, by their pathetic showing in elections since 1979 and the fragmentation of the National Front and British Movement into squabbling factions. However, figures indicating how many people vote for fascist parties tell only half the story. Clearly the number of 15 and 16-year-olds endorsing the NF or BM (14.2 per cent) was far greater than the number of adults willing to vote for them, but further sympathy for fascism was revealed when we asked which party the white children would support if they could not support their first choice. A further 16 per cent gave a fascist party as second choice to produce a total of slightly over 30 per cent of all respondents in 1982 in these particular schools who expressed some support for fascist parties. Thus we found that at the very time when fascist politics seemed to be in decline, support at school level was dramatically increasing.

The support received by these parties had little to do with the actions of the fascist leaders themselves. Apart from a tiny minority of instances, these youngsters had had no actual contact with the fascist parties, and this in itself implied a difference from mainstream political support. Whereas supporters of the main parties may have had some sort of vicarious contact with the party of their choice by, for example, seeing their party leaders on television, and recognizing their names if not their faces, the supporters of the fascist parties were ignorant about their chosen parties and their leaders.

This is a complete reversal of the situation which is often suggested to exist. Theoretically, those who support extreme parties (especially extreme right-wing parties) do so on the basis of identifying with the charismatic leaders, while support for mainstream parties is based on policies (Cochrane and Billig 1982; Fromm 1941; Willner 1984). Whereas almost everyone knew Thatcher and Foot or Healey, virtually no one knew the name of a single leader of any of the fascist parties. Support for such parties could be seen as a form of symbolic politics and above all, this symbol represented to these youngsters the policy of expelling non-whites from Britain. Although little else was known about the fascist parties, the association of fascist parties with the policy of expulsion was immediately recognized by supporters and non-supporters alike. Moreover, with regard to supporters at least, this policy was itself seen as a symbol for a quick, simple and, to them, desirable solution to complex economic problems. In other words, with the growth of unemployment the symbol of expulsion became, for these white teenagers, the symbol of an easy means of providing jobs.

What was frightening was that the expulsion policy of the fascist parties was better known than any other single policy of any other political party. Most fifth formers were at a loss to say what the Labour or Conservative parties stood for with the same immediacy and regularity that they could identify the National Front and the British Movement with the expulsion of non-whites. As far as specific policies were concerned, the fascist policy of expulsion stood out as a vivid symbol against an otherwise completely hazy and poorly distinguished background.

At the beginning of our study the supporters of the fascist parties were fairly easily identifiable as a group in each school although they came from a variety of family backgrounds. They were almost all boys, often skin-heads—the kind of pupil who sits at the back of the class passing comments and making rude noises. These hard-core fascist sympathizers rejoiced in their prejudices and openly boasted of their real or imagined assaults on immigrants. Over the three years of the study, however, the louts were joined in their support for the NF by a more 'respectable' type of pupil, a trend which reflected the growing despair with conventional politics and its inability to ever regain control of the economic and social situation. These new NF supporters shared with the SDP supporters the belief that 'Thatcher does not give a damn about us or anyone else and this goes for all parties', and that politicians were just 'rich snobs' (Cochrane and Billig 1982).

Obviously, the support for the fascist parties and their ideology was almost totally divorced from actual political involvement. Indeed, had the fascist parties been stronger, the grubby reality of their politics and leaders might well have worked to the detriment of this symbolic attachment. It would, however, be dangerous to dismiss this support as 'only' symbolic. A potential reservoir of support existed among many who currently rejected the extreme parties; it was there ready to be exploited by unscrupulous politicians, and parties, who might have wished to gain some short-term advantage if they found themselves facing otherwise certain electoral defeat.

In closing this description of some social and political beliefs of adolescents, it is recognized that it is possible to overstate the significance of the political views of 15 and 16-year-olds as indicators of future voting intentions or other forms of adult political activity. Indeed, the traditional view has been that, while at school, political opinions are unrestrained by reality and therefore tend towards the fantastic. The schoolboy or girl is, therefore, able to show off his or her daring, shocking, or extreme views. When, however, the young person is exposed to the reality of the workplace then harder economic influences take over and the vast majority of people become socialized into accepting one of the (up until 1981) two main parties. In our largely working-class samples, this socialization would often naturally occur via trade unions and would lead to support for the Labour party. The middle-class minority who went into family businesses or white-collar jobs would encounter similar pressures towards voting Conservative. There are two points to be made about these assumptions.

First, it is significant that, within the white youth culture that we studied, if showing off was evident it practically always took the form of racial bigotry. It was not merely that young people could find some peer status in boasting extreme views, for there were no self styled 'Communists', 'Marxists', or 'Trotskyites'. We are convinced that racism was endemic in our sample and that many people would retain an inclination towards supporting a policy of forced expulsion of non-whites if it were ever offered by a 'respectable' political party in the context of simultaneous expressions of human rights, dignity, and freedom.

Second, the traditional, dismissive view of adolescent politics is based on the assumption that school leavers will get jobs. This assumption is clearly no longer viable in many areas. Up to 80 per cent of some of the classes we looked at left school with no jobs, and no immediate prospects of finding any. For them, the foreseeable future was to drift from training courses to

Youth Opportunity Programmes to the dole. Our respondents are now voters but some have never had a job; perhaps some of them will reach 35 years of age without ever having had a job. If, because of this, they escape countervailing socialization pressures, then the frightening prospect emerges of their symbolic politics becoming political practice.

A rhetorical analysis of political beliefs

The remainder of this chapter will be spent examining the political attitudes of adolescents from a rhetorical perspective. Before embarking on this, it is necessary to make a few remarks about rhetoric and its relation to social psychology, especially as the present approach is not derived from the usual interpretation of rhetoric. Certainly rhetorical approaches have not been unknown in social psychology and the last few years have seen a definite reawakening of interest in a rhetorical approach to social psychology, whether on a general meta-theoretical level or in order to understand specific issues (e.g. Shotter 1986a and 1986b; Antaki 1985; Murray 1984; Weinreich-Haste 1984). Typically, the call for social psychologists to adopt a 'rhetorical approach' serves as a plea for recognizing the expressive and symbolic aspects of human communication. For instance, such a plea is uppermost in Harré's (1980, 1981) arguments that social psychologists should take as their basic model 'Man the rhetorician'. This sort of plea would seem to be particularly apposite when political behaviour is being studied, for as already suggested, the symbolic and expressive elements of political communication are immensely important and subtle in their consequences (Edelman 1964, 1977). For example, in our study we were interested in the support expressed for the National Front, but not just in quantitative terms. So not only did we look at the proportion of young people supporting the National Front and the class backgrounds from which they came (Cochrane and Billig 1982), but also at the way supporters talked about their political views. Over and above this we were interested in the use of the National Front as a political symbol in the context of political arguments (Cochrane and Billig 1984).

Nevertheless, the present 'rhetorical approach' involves more than a call for the study of symbols, and it is not specifically tied to an argumentative approach to rhetoric. All too often the rhetorical aspects of communication have been viewed as those concerned with the adornment and presentation of messages, and, in consequence, with the forms of persuasion (Billig 1985b). However, there has always been a further dimension to rhetoric, which is concerned with the processes of argumentation, and it is this aspect of rhetoric which is emphasized here. Billig (1985a, 1985b, 1986a, and 1986c) has been attempting to revive some of the ancient traditions of argumentative rhetoric, in order to produce a social psychological approach, which stresses the integral connections between human thought and argumentation. It will be suggested that the assumptions of this rhetorical, or argumentative, analysis are particularly well-suited to the study of political beliefs, for they point to dimensions of widespread social beliefs involving dilemmas and ambivalences, which are frequently overlooked by non-rhetorical perspectives, especially those involving the notion of political socialization (Billig *et al.* 1988).

One of the key assumptions of the rhetorical approach proposed by Billig (1985*a*, 1986*a*, and 1986*b*) is that argumentation plays a central role in human thinking. What William James called 'deliberative thought' is modelled upon publically observable argumentation. In this way deliberation is an inherently social psychological process, rather than one locked mysteriously into the inner recesses of the individual cortex. It is also assumed that people do not merely react unthinkingly in their social world, as if they had been fully programmed with all the necessary instructions for navigating themselves through the channels of everyday life. Instead, it is assumed that people think and argue about themselves, their acquaintances, and their society. In particular, modern society, with its constantly changing complexity, is particularly puzzling to its members and constantly poses dilemmas for deliberation (Billig *et al.* 1988).

In order to be puzzled about a social issue, or to have an internal argument, it is necessary to possess contrary mental structures and contrary themes, particularly of a commonsensical nature (Billig 1985*a*). The act of deliberation typically involves the juggling of contrary themes, or commonplaces, to use the terminology of traditional rhetoric. Thus, the image of the thinker that emerges from a rhetorical approach is of an individual whose thinking is characterized by contrary tendencies. This image is very different from that which is dominant in most contemporary social psychological approaches, where there is frequently an assumption of inner mental unity (Billig 1982; Billig *et al.* 1988).

Certainly it was apparent in our study that most of the young people had no consistent ideology or even detailed political knowledge. Yet despite this lack of sophistication, they were quite able to join in debates about political controversies. Moreover, the controversies themselves, as revealed in the discussion groups, did not have a clear-cut form, in the sense of some youngsters arguing consistently for a point of view with others arguing against it. Instead, the young people were often able to contribute arguments on both sides of an issue. In order to do this without political sophistication, it is necessary to base one's discourse on cultural maxims, or commonplaces. This was particularly clear in the discussions revolving around the issue of race, where typically the commonplaces of tolerance and those of racism could be, and would be, expressed by all except, perhaps, those self-consciously adopting the fascist stance.

For this to occur, people must possess contrary themes in their linguistic repertoires, and these contrary themes will both be 'reasonable' in that they are supported by contrary arguments and justifications. Since such contrary themes will typically be drawn from the 'common-sense' of the society, then there will be contrary themes, enthymemically expressed, in such 'common-sense'. Thus the contents of 'common-sense', far from being internally consistent and systematized, will be contrary. These contradictions will tend to be reproduced in the minds of the average members of the society, for they will have internalized as 'common-sense' the contrary values of their group's *loci communes*. In consequence, the rhetorical analyst of widespread beliefs should specifically search for that aspect of attitudes which social psychologists have tended to ignore: their contrary tendencies.

From a rhetorical point of view, an attitude is not to be treated merely as the personal expression of some conative leaning. What social psychologists have termed 'attitudes' are expressions which are located within a public controversy; see Billig 1986*a* and 1986*b* for further details of this position. Thus, if people can be said to possess attitudes, this describes their willingness to locate themselves within a public argument. The argumentative, and thereby social, aspects of attitudes are not bits and pieces tacked onto a basic affective core, but they are central to the meaning of 'attitude'. This argumentative aspect of attitudes is a dimension which is frequently overlooked by social psychologists, for whom the rhetorical features of everyday life are not of prime concern.

If the rhetorical dimension is a basic component of political attitudes, then the expression of attitudes will be linked to rhetorical contexts. At present, social psychologists have not investigated in great detail the effects of argumentative context upon the expression of communication. However, it is clear that the issues involved are complex and that a number of social psychological effects, established in laboratory conditions, have important rhetorical dimensions. For example, Billig (1986*b*) suggests that the phenomenon of 'reactance' represents a reversal of expressed position to meet changed rhetorical circumstances. As such, 'reactance' is an example of the more general rhetorical switching of positions in which people take the side of the other. What this suggests is that people do not have one way of entering into attitudinal controversies, expressing themselves with monotonous consistency. Instead, people can react to changes in the rhetorical, or controversial, context and, consequently express themselves in differing, and sometimes seemingly contradictory, ways.

Thus, in our studies of the political attitudes of adolescents we have sought to uncover the contrary dimensions of thought. We have not treated internal contradictions as signs of inadequate 'socialization'. We do not assume that with a slightly more efficient enculturation the contrary elements will disappear. Rather, the assumption is that the young adults are being socialized into a society which is fundamentally contradictory and which poses outward dilemmas for its members. Thus the lack of consistency is not a preliminary stage on some sort of long march towards psychological and social consistency. Instead, we suggest the contrary elements have to be mastered by anyone who is to be an expert in the arguments of common-sense; see Billig 1986a and 1986b for an extended discussion of the rhetorical and social psychological significance of the Protagorean Principle.

There is a methodological implication which follows from this theoretical perspective. Since the rhetorical perspective assumes the social psychological significance of argumentation in human cognition, then argumentation itself can be used as a methodological resource. In fact the expression of attitudes in the context of argumentation could be said to be more natural than to be asked to respond to a stranger's request for a location of self upon some precisely graded scales. We have not used discussion groups in order that individuals' 'real' attitudes will be revealed, as if it is possible to divorce the expression of views from the rhetorical context. Nor have we assumed that discussions and arguments always pit against each other people who cling monolithically to opposing positions. In fact, if there are contradictions in common-sense, and the discussions concern the matters of controversy, then it is likely that the discussions will be contexts for airing social dilemmas, rather than resolving them. Under these circumstances one might not expect agonistic division into clearly demarcated opposing camps, but a pooling of shared contrary themes. When this occurs, apparent contradictions between discussants reflect the contradictions and perplexities of the discussants themselves, and their unsystematized but continuing potentiality for inner argument.

References

Althusser, L. (1971). *Lenin and philosophy and other essays*. New Left Books, London.

Antaki, C. (1985). Ordinary explanations in conversation: causal structures and their defence. *European Journal of Social Psychology*, **15**, 213–30.

Billig, M. (1982). *Ideology and social psychology*. Basil Blackwell, Oxford.

Billig, M. (1985a). Prejudice, categorization and particularization: from a perceptual to a rhetorical account. *European Journal of Social Psychology*, **15**, 79–103.

Billig, M. (1985b). Rhetoric and the science of persuasion. Paper given at Madingley Conference on Social Beliefs, Cambridge.

Billig, M. (1986a). *Thinking and arguing*. Loughborough University.

Billig, M. (1986b). *Arguing and thinking: a rhetorical approach to social psychology*. Cambridge University Press.

Billig, M. (1986c). Political psychology and social psychological theory. In *Political psychology in the Netherlands* (ed. M. Brouwer, J.V. Ginneken, L. Hagendoorn, and J. Meloeu). Mola Russa, Amsterdam.

Billig, M. (1986d). Consistency and ideology: group and intergroup aspects. Paper given at Conference on Social Justice in Human Relations, Leiden.

Billig, M. (1986e). Very ordinary life and the young conservatives. In *Getting into life* (ed. H. Beloff). Methuen, London.

Billig, M. and Cochrane, R. (1981). The National Front and youth. *Patterns of Prejudice*, **15**, 3–16.

Billig, M. and Cochrane, R. (1982a). Youth against Labour? *New Socialist*, **4**, 38–41.

Billig, M. and Cochrane, R. (1982b). Extremism of the centre: the SDP's young followers. *New Society*, **60**, 291–2.

Billig, M., Condor, S., Edwards, D., Gane, M., Middleton, D., and Radley, A.R. (1988). *Ideological dilemmas of everyday thinking*. Sage, London.

Braungart, R.G. and Braungart, M.M. (1986). Life-course and generational politics. *Annual Review of Sociology*, **12**, 205–31.

Butler, D. and Stokes, D. (1974). *Political change in Britain*. Macmillan, London.

Cochrane, R. and Billig, M. (1982). Adolescent support for the National Front: a test of three models of political extremism. *New Community*, **10**, 86–94.

Cochrane, R. and Billig, M. (1984). 'I'm not National Front, myself, but . . .' *New Society*, **68**, 255–8.

Coffield, F., Borrill, C., and Marshall, S. (1986). 'Shit jobs, govvy schemes or the dole': occupational choice for young adults in the north-east of England. In *Getting into life* (ed. H. Beloff). Methuen, London.

Conover, P. and Feldman, S. (1984). How people organize the political world: a schematic model. *American Journal of Political Science*, **28**, 95–126.

Crewe, I., Sarlvik, B., and Alt, J. (1977). Partisan realignment in Britain, 1964–1974. *British Journal of Political Science*, **7**, 129–90.

Van Dijk, T.V. (1984). *Prejudice in discourse*. Benjamins, Amsterdam.

Edelman, M. (1964). *The symbolic uses of politics*. University of Illinois Press, Urbana.

Edelman, M. (1977). *Political language: words that succeed and policies that fail*. Academic Press, New York.

Fromm, E. (1941). *Escape from freedom*. Holt, Rinehart and Winston, New York.

Furnham, A. (1985). Adolescents' sociopolitical attitudes: a study of sex and national differences. *Political Psychology*, **6**, 621–36.

Hagendoorn, L. and Janssen, J. (1986). Right-wing beliefs among Dutch secondary school pupils. *Sociologia Neerlandica*, **22**, 87–96.

Hamill, R., Lodge, M., and Blalle, F. (1985). The breadth, depth and utility of class, partisan and ideological schemata. *American Journal of Political Science*, **29**, 850–70.

Harré, R. (1980). Man as rhetorician. In *Models of man*. (ed. A.J. Chapman and D.M. Jones). British Psychological Society, Leicester.

Harré, R. (1981). Rituals, rhetoric and social cognition. In *Social cognition* (ed. J.P. Forgas). Academic Press, London.

Himmelweit, H.T., Humphreys, P., and Jaeger, M. (1985). *How voters decide*. Open University Press, Milton Keynes.

Inglehart, R. (1977). *The silent revolution: changing values and political styles among Western publics*. Princeton University Press.

Jennings, K.M. and Niemi, R.G. (1971). The division of political labour between fathers and mothers. *American Political Science Review*, **65**, 64–82.

Jennings, K.M. and Niemi, R.G. (1981). *Generations and politics: a panel study of young adults and their parents*. Princeton University Press.

Lipset, S.M. (1960). *Political man*. Doubleday, New Jersey.

Litton, I. and Potter, J. (1985). Social representations in the ordinary explanation of a 'riot'. *European Journal of Social Psychology*, **15**, 371–88.

Marx, K. and Engels, F. (1968). *Selected works*. Lawrence and Wishart, London.

Moscovici, S. (1981). On social representations. In *Social cognition: perspectives on everyday understanding* (ed. J. Forgas). Academic Press, London.

Murray, E.L. (1984). The significance of rhetoric in human science research. *Journal of Phenomenological Psychology*, **15**, 169–75.

Potter, J. and Litton, I. (1985). Some problems underlying the theory of social representations. *British Journal of Social Psychology*, **24**, 81–90.

Reeves, F. (1983). *British racial discourse*. Cambridge University Press.

Sharp, C. and Lodge, M. (1985). Partisan and ideological belief systems: do they differ? *Political Behaviour*, **7**, 147–66.

Shotter, J. (1986*a*). The rhetoric of theory in psychology. In *Proceedings of the Founding Conference in the International Society for Theoretical Psychology* (ed. J.F.H. van Rappard *et al.*). North Holland Publishing Co., Amsterdam.

Shotter, J. (1986*b*). Warranting accounts, justifying privileged forms of speech. Paper given at Conference of British Psychological Society, Social Psychology Section, University of Sussex.

Sidanius, J. and Ekehammar, B. (1979). Political socialization: a multivariate analysis of Swedish political attitude and preference data. *European Journal of Social Psychology*, **9**, 265–79.

Sidanius, J., Ekehammar, B., and Brewer, R.M. (1986). Political socialization determinants of higher order sociopolitical space: a Swedish example. *Journal of Social Psychology*, **126**, 7–22.

Tajfel, H. (1982). Intergroup relations, social myths and social justice in social psychology. In *The social dimension* (ed. H. Tajfel). Cambridge University Press.

Weinreich-Haste, H. (1984). Morality, social meaning and rhetoric: the social context of moral reasoning. In *Morality, moral behaviour and moral development* (ed. W.M. Kurtines and J.L. Gewirtz). John Wiley, New York.

Willner, A.R. (1984). *The spellbinders: charismatic political leadership*. Yale University Press, New Haven.

10 The social dimension in relative deprivation

Patten Smith and George Gaskell

Introduction

It is now commonly accepted that in the past social psychologists have been naïve in assuming that generalizations arising from research on individuals' psychological processes may be used to explain, without difficulty, social behaviour in social contexts. Recent developments, particularly in Europe, have emphasized the importance of analysing social psychological phenomena in ways which respect their *social* nature (e.g. Tajfel 1984). This chapter takes relative deprivation theory as a case in point, comparing 'individualistic' with 'social' approaches in two rather different respects. The first involves the obvious comparison between individualistic measures and apparently social measures of relative deprivation, that is egoistic and fraternalistic relative deprivation respectively. The second entails the more radical argument that relative deprivation theory will only achieve really substantial predictive and explanatory power when it succeeds in moving towards a genuinely social perspective such as one incorporating assessments of widespread and shared beliefs in the populations in question.

The central idea in relative deprivation is that militant collective behaviour is better explained by reference to people's sense or feelings of deprivation rather than by their absolute level of deprivation. Historians and political scientists have employed the concept to account for a variety of episodes of collective action from the French Revolution to the urban riots in America in the 1960s, having found that purely economic accounts were insufficient. Over and above such considerations people's feelings of despair, discontent, and frustration arising from changed economic circumstances, comparisons with others or the perceptions of intolerable discrepancies between what they had and what they wanted, had to be recognized. This development is an acceptance of the fact that a satisfactory explanation must include a psychological dimension. So Hobsbawm and Rudé (1970) wrote about the Captain Swing riots in Britain in the nineteenth century:

'We have seen plenty of causes of labourers' unrest and it is difficult to see how they could not have revolted. But causes are not the same as acts. Human beings do not react to the goad of hunger and oppression by some automatic and standard response of revolt. What they do or fail to do depends on their situation among other human beings, on their environment, culture, tradition and experience.'

This quotation, giving centre stage to the social context and furthermore to beliefs centred in the group rather than isolated individuals, anticipates many of the shortcomings of some of the narrowly focused social psychological approaches to relative deprivation.

Relative deprivation referring to a person's *sense* of deprivation relative to a standard of comparison was introduced by Stouffer *et al.* (1949) in their study of the American soldier in order to provide plausible *ex post facto* explanations of occasions where perceptions of deprivation were not related to objective conditions in straightforward ways.

The first major development of the theory arose in Runciman's (1966) study of the relationship between people's positions in class, status and power hierarchies, and feelings of deprivation. Runciman proposed that a person is relatively deprived of any valued object when four necessary and, together sufficient, conditions are present:

(1) the person does not have it;
(2) the person sees other person(s) as having it (the other can include self in the past or at an expected time, or an abstract idea);
(3) the person wants it;
(4) the person sees it as feasible that he/she should have it.

He proposed that relative deprivation should be understood as a *sense* of deprivation which can vary for a person on two dimensions: on *magnitude*, which is the subjective extent of the difference between the desired situation and the position of the person desiring it; on *degree* which is the emotional intensity with which relative deprivation is felt. In addition it varies across social groups in *frequency* which is the proportion of the group feeling it. This criterion of frequency, generally ignored in the research literature, may be one of the keys to developments in the theory.

Egoistic and fraternalistic relative deprivation

Central to the present discussion was Runciman's distinction between social and individualistic definitions of relative deprivation. He termed the former *fraternalistic* relative deprivation, where the individual feels that his/her membership group as a whole is deprived with respect to another group, and the latter *egoistic* relative deprivation where the individual feels deprived relative to a reference other or group. Runciman argued that only the fraternalistic variety with its related feeling of social injustice could instigate social action. It would be a feature of groups with strong solidarity, for example, the working class, religious, or ethnic minorities; their perceptions of a collective relative deprivation would play a part in the transformation of existing social inequalities. On the other hand, egoistic relative deprivation, he thought, would be typical of 'strivers', dissatisfied with their present situation but without common cause with others.

Notwithstanding Runciman's distinction, most subsequent theory and research has been firmly based on the egoistic definitions (Gurr 1970; Crosby 1976). Although these models of egoistic relative deprivation are quite complex, empirical studies have generally tested for simple relationships between hostile or militant social attitudes or behaviours, and measures of relative deprivation. A considerable number of studies have found at least some support for the hypothesis that egoistic relative deprivation predicts hostile social attitudes and behaviours (Abeles 1976; Bowen et al. 1968; Crawford and Naditch 1970; Muller 1972; Grofman and Muller 1973; Morrison and Steeves 1967; Sears and McConahay 1970; Isaac et al. 1980; Gaskell and Smith 1984). However, in these studies coefficients of association have tended to be small (cf. McPhail 1971), and some negative findings have been obtained (Portes 1971; Geschwender and Geschwender 1973; Newton et al. 1980; Taylor 1982). Overall, hypotheses linking egoistic relative deprivation to negative social attitudes and behaviours have received only moderate support.

Following Runciman, other writers have argued that fraternalistic relative deprivation is a theoretically more appropriate predictor of shared attitudes and collective behaviours than egoistic relative deprivation (Vanneman and Pettigrew 1972; Williams 1975; Tajfel 1978; Walker and Pettigrew 1984; Dion 1986). Walker and Pettigrew (1984) in particular develop a conceptual rationale for the shift in emphasis towards fraternalistic relative deprivation, a shift which would enable progress towards a synthesis between the theory and Tajfel's ideas on categorization-identity comparison.

Tajfel, and the subsequent research from the 'Bristol School', gives theoretical support to Runciman's distinction between egoistical and fraternalistic relative deprivation (RD). For Tajfel all social behaviour can be characterized on a continuum between the extremes of interpersonal and intergroup behaviours. At the interpersonal pole, interactions are the product of the characteristics of the individuals themselves, their personal identities, self concepts, or self images.

At the intergroup pole, behaviour tends to be determined by the person's social group membership, a categorization used to define the person's place in society and giving the individual a social identity. Like the self concept, people strive for a positive social identity, which requires a definition of their membership groups in terms of favourable comparisons with respect to relevant out-groups. However, if the in-group is evaluated unfavourably, a number of reactions are possible: individual mobility—joining the higher status group; social creativity—changing the criteria of comparison or changing the comparison group; and finally social competition. Here, and relevant to relative deprivation, unfavourable comparisons may lead to an attempt to change the positions of the in- and out-groups, a change which may imply social conflict.

Thus one can conclude from Tajfel that social conflict will not be the product of personal discontent since this will be located at the interpersonal pole of the behavioural continuum. Only when a person is thinking in terms of his/her social identity, that is, membership of some social category, will relevant out-groups be considered. And only when these comparisons are unfavourable will a person, and by implication the social category in general, feel fraternally deprived and be inclined to resort to collective actions to improve their position.

Empirical evidence also supports this emphasis of fraternalistic relative deprivation. Vanneman and Pettigrew (1972) found that fraternalistic relative deprivation was a better predictor of black unrest in the 1960s than was egoistical relative deprivation, and that reluctance to support black candidates was greatest among fraternally deprived whites. Caplan and Paige (1968) found that self-reported black 'rioters' were likely to think that the income gap between better-off and poorer blacks was increasing, but no more likely to think that the gap between blacks and whites was increasing. Geschwender and Geschwender (1973) found that perceived distance from achieving aspirations for blacks as a group predicted self-reported 'combattive' involvement in civil rights activities by black respondents, while differences between blacks and whites on how close they were to achieving aspirations (egoistic relative deprivation) did not predict civil rights activities. Abeles (1976) found that when 'well-educated blacks' were used as a reference group and compared with 'whites', 'white-collar workers', 'blue-collar workers', and 'professionals', the highest associations between these fraternalistic comparisons and militant attitudes amongst blacks were obtained. He argues that the position of well-educated blacks may be a litmus test for other blacks. 'If they, who have played by the rules were not succeeding, the respondents were likely to become more militant upon concluding that the level of racial justice was intolerable'. Guimond and Dube (1983) found that fraternal relative deprivation measured by the extent of frustration about the way in which salaries were distributed between Francophones and Anglophones predicted nationalist attitudes amongst Francophones in Quebec better than egoistic relative deprivation. In a more recent review, Dube and Guimond (1986) conclude that group discontent, and not personal discontent, is a major variable in explaining protest movements, a finding supported in a study of unemployed people in Australia (Walker and Mann 1987).

An empirical comparison of egoistic and fraternalistic approaches to relative deprivation

The research reported in this section directly compares fraternalistic and egoistic approaches to relative deprivation among samples of young black and young white males in London. Before outlining how this was done, however, three important issues will be briefly discussed. First, there is a problem concerning the kind of dependent variable to be examined. Measures of political militancy (e.g. Abeles 1976) or of discontent (e.g. Crosby 1982) have been commonly used in the past, but as we have argued elsewhere, if relative deprivation is to be transformed into militant attitudes or behaviours it is plausible that discontent will be first focused upon the social institutions and groups seen to cause that deprivation (Gaskell and Smith 1984; Smith 1984). If this is accepted, it implies that relative deprivation should be associated with negative attitudes to a number of social institutions as well as with direct indices of militancy.

Secondly, there is a problem concerning which group should be treated as the respondent's 'membership' group and which as the comparative reference group in measuring fraternalistic relative deprivation. So far there are no theoretical propositions on this key issue, and previous research has used 'obvious' social categories like black and white, or white-collar and blue-collar workers, without assessing their subjective importance to respondents. As there are no good *a priori* reasons for choosing one social category rather than another we feel that research should attempt to elicit from respondents those groups which they themselves feel to be important.

Thirdly, there is some evidence that blacks and whites might react differently to relative deprivation (Isaac *et al.* 1980; Gaskell and Smith 1984). If this is so, it suggests that relative deprivation may not have the universal effects implied in the theoretical literature, but instead have effects dependent upon cultural factors. This suggests that cultural differences in responses to relative deprivation are worthy of study.

In what follows, we empirically compare the effects of egoistic and fraternalistic relative deprivation on a range of dependent measures, using both researcher-defined and respondent-defined 'membership' groups to operationalize fraternalistic relative deprivation, for both black and white respondents. Full details of the study will be available elsewhere (Gaskell and Smith, forthcoming). Here only a synopsis of the research is presented to give a rationale to our conclusions.

The study was based on face-to-face interviews with a random sample of school leavers in one London borough. From the population of male school leavers of two years previously, a sample of 106 white and 98 blacks was achieved. The key indices covered in the interviews were as follows:

Relative deprivation

1. Egoistic relative deprivation was assessed by Cantril's self anchoring scale (Cantril 1965), a procedure which has been widely used by other researchers (Bowen *et al.* 1968; Muller 1972; Geschwender and Geschwender 1973; and Gaskell and Smith 1984).

2. Fraternalistic relative deprivation was measured using a procedure derived from Abeles (1976). Here, however, we included two varieties of the concept. The first was based on *a priori* membership and comparison groups. Comparison groups included, for example, young black people in Britain and young white people in Britain, educated whites and educated blacks. The membership groups were assumed to be young blacks and young whites for the black and white respondents respectively. The second approach allowed respondents to select their own membership group via procedures described in detail in a paper on social identity theory (Gaskell and Smith 1986). Own membership group was then contrasted with the four possible comparison groups described in the last paragraph. Respondents placed each group on a ladder depicting the 'different ranks in British society' and from this a set of seven plausible indices of fraternalistic relative deprivation was computed.

Social attitudes

Twelve selected institutions in Britain were assessed on a five-point rating scale ranging from very good to very bad. Of the twelve, attitude to the *police* was treated separately because of its particular relevance to young men in general (Hough and Mayhew 1983) and to young blacks in particular (Smith 1983; Small 1983). The rest were factor analysed to provide more general indices of social attitudes. The four factors which emerged were labelled as follows:

- Traditional authority: armed forces—royal family
- Political: the Conservative party—the current party in power in Britain
- Democratic institutions: parliament, local councils, law courts
- Educational institutions: school, further education colleges, and youth opportunity programmes (YOPs)

Orientation to militancy

Two measures were used. The first covered attitudes to violence as a means of political change, the second comprised attitudes to the urban riots that had occurred in Britain in 1981.

The analysis used multiple regression procedures. Social attitudes and orientation to militancy were regressed on the various indices of relative deprivation as well as two objective characteristics: whether the person was employed or unemployed, and whether the person had some or no qualifications.

Taking the total sample, that is both blacks and whites, relative deprivation was a better predictor of social attitudes than the measures of objective deprivation. Neither unemployment nor lack of qualifications, as indicators of objective deprivation, were significantly associated with social attitudes. For both egoistical and fraternalistic relative deprivation, the more deprived the person felt the more hostile they were to the police and to what we have termed democratic institutions. That said, no single measure of relative deprivation performed remarkably better than any other, and while most gave significant regression coefficients these were typically of the order of -0.15. At the same time some attitudinal objects for which significant associations with relative deprivation might be assumed, e.g. orientation to militancy, were not found. For the whole sample therefore the models linking egoistic or fraternalistic relative deprivation to attitudes towards social institutions and to militancy gain only modest support with no reason to favour one variety of relative deprivation above the other.

Because blacks have been so frequently used in tests of relative deprivation (Abeles 1976; Caplan and Paige 1968), a similar set of regressions were run for them alone. In contrast to the previous analyses on the whole sample, the results for blacks provide considerably stronger support for relative deprivation theory. The statistically significant findings are shown in Table 3.

The general findings from Table 3 can be summarized as follows. Any type of relative deprivation, either egoistic or fraternalistic is associated with hostile attitudes to the police. However, while variants of fraternalistic relative deprivation are associated with social attitudes, in no case was egoistic relative deprivation found to predict attitudes to social institutions that might be thought of as contributors to the person's felt deprivation.

The various indices of fraternalistic relative deprivation perform quite well in predicting attitudes to the riots in 1981, 'traditional authority' and to 'democratic' and 'educational institutions'. Of the measures of fraternalistic relative deprivation, two look rather more promising than others. The perceived gap between educated whites and young blacks, perhaps a comparison between the white middle class and blacks, is associated with attitudes to the police, 'democratic' and 'educational institutions'. As this form of fraternalistic relative deprivation increases, so does hostility to these institutions, which may be thought of by the blacks as serving to protect middle-class interests and prejudice against blacks.

Secondly, and in line with Abeles (1968), comparisons between educated whites and educated blacks are associated with attitudes to the police, riots,

Table 3 Regressions of attitudinal variables on relative deprivation for blacks only (standardized regression coefficient). ERD: Egoistic Relative Deprivation; FRD: Fraternalistic Relative Deprivation; educ: educated

Dependent variable Attitude to:		Index of relative deprivation scores derived from ladder positions of:	
Police	ERD	self	− .303**
Police	FRD	own membership group	− .316**
Police	FRD	young blacks	− .212*
Police	FRD	educ. whites—own group	− .365***
Police	FRD	educ. whites—young blacks	− .242*
Police	FRD	educ. whites—educ. blacks	− .245*
Riots of 1981	FRD	educ. whites—educ. blacks	− .203*
Traditional authority	FRD	educ. whites—educ. blacks	− .280*
Democratic institutions	FRD	young whites—young blacks	− .315**
Democratic institutions	FRD	young blacks	− .274*
Democratic institutions	FRD	educ. whites—young blacks	− .263*
Educational institutions	FRD	educ. whites—young blacks	− .241*

* Sign at 0.05
** Sign at 0.01
*** Sign at 0.001

and traditional authority. Perhaps our respondents are thinking that 'If even educated blacks can't make it in British society, what hope is there for me?'.

On the whole, therefore, for the blacks in our sample the fraternalistic varieties of relative deprivation perform better than the standard egoistic measure producing associations of a magnitude rather similar to those obtained by Abeles (1968) and Dube and Guimond (1986). In general, the use of own membership group rather than young blacks does not appear to improve the quality of the results.

Taking the results as a whole, fraternalistic relative deprivation receives more support than egoistic relative deprivation. Two indices of fraternalistic relative deprivation which use educated whites as a comparative reference group (cf. Kelley 1947) performed somewhat better than the others for blacks. But in general McPhail's (1971) point that relative deprivation theory receives only low grade empirical support still stands, whatever operationalizations are used, whether fraternalistic or egoistic, and whether based on subjective membership groups or 'objective' ones.

Individualistic and social explanations

While fraternalistic relative deprivation is a better predictor of social attitudes and militancy than egoistic relative deprivation, the results for the former social variety are hardly strong enough to lay a claim to a substantial empirical corroboration. Does this imply that, at least for these phenomena, analyses using constructs based on a 'social' level of analysis are hardly better than ones based on an 'individualistic' level of analysis? We believe that this is not the case, but rather than the theory of fraternalistic relative deprivation performs poorly because in one important way it is not social enough.

The term 'social' carries a number of meanings which are not always treated as analytically distinct. Here we note three ways in which a psychological theory or concept might claim to be social (see Hewstone and Jaspars 1984, for a similar analysis):

(1) if it refers to cognitions, affects, or behaviours which pertain to social *objects* or processes (e.g. attitudes to Asians, beliefs about unemployment);

(2) if it refers to cognitions, affects, or behaviours which are social in *origin* (it is difficult to give examples because so much of what we think, feel, or do is social in origin);

(3) if it refers to cognitions, affects, or behaviours which are *shared* (e.g. religious beliefs shared by a sect).

The important point to arise from these distinctions in this context is that a concept can be social in sense (1) but entirely asocial in sense (3). Thus a theory can posit individualistic explanations (i.e. treating individual as isolated units of analysis) of beliefs, attitudes, or behaviours which concern social objects.

Egoistic relative deprivation concerns an individual's belief about his/her position relative to some standard, and is thus asocial in sense (1). Fraternalistic relative deprivation concerns an individual's belief about his/her membership group and is thus social in sense (1). However, because relative deprivation is usually analysed as an *individual* psychological state, both fraternalistic and egoistic measures are *de facto a*social in sense (3). We believe that explanation of a socially significant attitude such as attitude to the police or to militancy, requires us to posit theories which acknowledge the fact that whole groups evolve beliefs which are shared by their members, and which come to be adopted by new members or would-be members (cf. Kelley 1947; Shibutani 1955) through various socialization processes. The relevance to these kinds of phenomena of theories of *individuals'* psychological processes (such as relative deprivation theory) is by no means clear.

To pursue this line of argument we describe other analyses on the same data set (reported in Gaskell and Smith 1985) which demonstrate the resistance of a shared belief system to individualistic explanation, and we then suggest how these analyses may aid our interpretation of some of the findings reported above. In those analyses we started by regressing attitude to the police on a dummy variable indicating the colour of respondents. We then introduced into the equation three sets of variables which, according to different hypotheses, should account for the black–white attitude differences. The first hypothesis suggested that hostility to the police is symbolic of a more general hostility to British society (Small 1983; Smith 1983). The second hypothesis suggested that differences in attitudes to the police are attributable to differences in frequency of negative contacts with the police. The third hypothesis suggested that the differences are attributable to differential unemployment rates. Inclusion of appropriate variables in a multiple stepwise regression model resulted in 29 per cent of the variance in attitude to the police being explained, and significant coefficients being obtained for the traditional authority, political, and democratic institutions scores, and number of stops by police in last year both on foot and in a car. Most importantly, differences between blacks and whites remained substantial and highly significant. The results seemed to indicate that blacks show hostility to the police which only to a limited extent can be accounted for by other attitudes or by their individual experiences with the police. Further support for this view came from comparisons between blacks and whites who had *not* been stopped or arrested in the last year. Eighty-nine per cent of blacks in this group were able to mention one or more bad points about the police, while only 67 per cent of whites did so. Seventy-six per cent of these blacks, but only 25 per cent of these whites reported that they had ever been really annoyed by the police. Finally these blacks had significantly more negative attitudes to the police than did the whites. We believe that the analyses just reported show that blacks hold a set of beliefs pertaining to the police which are shared, and resistant to purely individualistic explanation. They are the folk history of unpleasant, sometimes frightening, first-hand experiences and often second-hand accounts of experiences with police which have evolved into the collective beliefs of young blacks. Even without direct personal experience, young blacks evoke particular beliefs about the police which both affect contacts they may subsequently experience and give credence to accounts of oppression and harassment. Elements of this folk history probably have solid foundations. The PSI study in 1983 recorded the hostile epithets used for blacks by the police and argued that racialism was almost fashionable in police talk (Smith 1983). Small, a black PSI researcher, graphically described the circumstances surrounding his arrest and detention while working on the project (Small 1983). Over time, the experiences of some members of the in-group become the shared representation of the group as a whole. To this extent these beliefs and attitudes should be seen as social in all three senses outlined above, and perhaps deserve to be accorded the status of a social representation (cf. Farr and Moscovici 1984).

We speculatively suggest that the finding that relative deprivation is associated with attitude to the police for blacks may have more to do with the functioning of social representations of the police than with relative deprivation mechanisms *per se*. It is plausible that many young blacks hold a network of beliefs in which the police play a central role in providing simple and flexible explanations for many of the ills which befall them. What we suggest is that these relative deprivation associations reflect less a *mechanism* in which deprivation *causes* hostile attitudes to the police, and more a *theory* shared by young blacks according to which many of their difficulties are *explained* by the processes of law in Britain today.

Even more speculatively we suggest that shared focal explanatory concepts are pervasive amongst other groups—see, for example, Moscovici's (1984) discussion of left and right-wing causalities—and that for a significant proportion of young whites we might expect 'blacks' or 'Pakis' to fulfil the same function as do the police for blacks (see especially Cochrane and Billig 1984 and their chapter in this volume).

References

Abeles, R.P. (1976). Relative deprivation, rising expectations, and black militancy. *Journal of Social Issues*, **32**, 119–37.

Bowen, D.R., Bowen, E., Gawiser, S., and Masotti, L.H. (1968). Deprivation, mobility, and orientation toward protest of the urban poor. In *Riots and rebellion: civil violence in the urban community* (ed. L.M. Masotti and D.R. Bowen). Sage, Beverley Hills.

Cantril, H. (1965). *The pattern of human concerns*. Rutgers University Press, New Brunswick, NJ.

Caplan, N.S. and Paige, J.M. (1968). A study of ghetto rioters. *Scientific American*, **219**(2), 15–21.

Cochrane, R. and Billig, M. (1984). I'm not in the National Front myself, but . . . *New Society*, **68**, 255–8.

Crawford, T.J. and Naditch, M. (1970). Relative deprivation, powerlessness and militancy: the psychology of social protest. *Psychiatry*, **33**, 208–23.

Crosby, F. (1976). A model of egoistical relative deprivation. *Psychological Review*, **83**, 85–113.

Crosby, F. (1982). *Relative deprivation and working women*. Oxford University Press, New York.

Dion, K.L. (1986). Responses to perceived discrimination and relative deprivation. In *Relative deprivation and social comparison* (ed. J.M. Olson, C.P. Herman, and M.P. Zanna). Lawrence Erlbaum, Hillsdale, NJ.

Dube, L. and Guimond, S. (1986). Relative deprivation and social protest: the personal-group issue. In *Relative deprivation and social comparison* (ed. J.M. Olson, C.P. Herman, and M.P. Zanna). Lawrence Erlbaum, Hillsdale, NJ.

Farr, R.M. and Moscovici, S. (eds) (1984). *Social representations*. Cambridge University Press.

Gaskell, G. and Smith, P.G. (1984). Relative deprivation in black and white youth. *British Journal of Social Psychology*, **23**, 121–31.

Gaskell, G. and Smith, P.G. (1985). Young blacks' hostility to the police: an investigation into its causes. *New Community*, **XII**, 66–74.

Gaskell, G. and Smith, P.G. (1986). Group membership and the social attitudes of youth. An investigation of some implications of social identity theory. *Social Behaviour*, **1**, 67–77.

Geschwender, B.N. and Geschwender, J.A. (1973). Relative deprivation and participation in the Civil Rights movements. *Social Science Quarterly*, **54**, 403–11.

Grofman, B.N. and Muller, E.N. (1973). The strange case of relative gratification and potential for political violence: the V curve hypothesis. *American Political Science Review*, **67**, 514–39.

Guimond, S. and Dube, L. (1983). Relative deprivation theory and the Quebec Nationalist Movement: the cognition–emotion distinction and the personal–group deprivation issue. *Journal of Personality and Social Psychology*, **44**, 526–35.

Gurr, T.R. (1970). *Why men rebel*. Princeton University Press.

Hewstone, M. and Jaspars, J. (1984). Social dimensions of attribution. In *The social dimension* (ed. H. Tajfel). Cambridge University Press.

Hobsbawm, E.J. and Rudé, G. (1970). *Captain Swing*. Penguin, Harmondsworth.

Hough, M. and Mayhew, P. (1983). *The British crime survey: a first report*. Home Office Research Study No. 76. HMSO, London.

Isaac, L., Mutran, E., and Stryker, S. (1980). Political protest orientations among black and white adults. *American Sociological Review*, **45**, 191–213.

Kelley, H.H. (1947). Two functions of reference groups. In *Readings in social psychology* (ed. G.E. Swanson, T.M. Newcomb, and E.L. Hartley). Holt, Rinehart and Winston, New York.

McPhail, C. (1971). Civil disorder participation: a critical examination of recent research. *American Sociological Review*, **36**, 1058–73.

Morrison, D.E. and Steeves, A.D. (1967). Deprivation, discontent, and social movement participation: evidence on a contemporary farmers' movement, the NFO. *Rural Sociology*, **32**, 414–34.

entations (ed. R.M. Farr and S. Moscovici). Cambridge University Press.

Muller, E.N. (1972). A test of a partial theory of potential for political violence. *American Political Science Review*, **66**, 928–59.

Newton, J.W., Mann, L., and Geary, D. (1980). Relative deprivation, dissatisfaction and militancy: a field study in a protest crowd. *Journal of Applied Social Psychology*, **10**, 384–97.

Portes, A. (1971). On the logic of post factum explanations: the hypothesis of lower-class frustration as a cause of leftist radicalism. *Social Forces*, **50**, 26–44.

Runciman, W.G. (1966). *Relative deprivation and social justice*. Routledge & Kegan Paul, London.

Sears, D.O. and McConahay, J.B. (1970). Racial socialization, comparison levels and the Watts riot. *Journal of Social Issues*, **26**, 121–40.

Shibutani, T. (1955). Reference groups as perspectives. *American Journal of Sociology*, **60**, 562–9.

Small, S. (1983). *Police and people in London: a group of young black people*. PSI, London.

Smith, D.J. (1983). *Police and people in London: a survey of Londoners*. PSI, London.

Smith, P.G. (1984). Alienation and relative deprivation in deprived young men: a conceptual and empirical enquiry. Unpublished Ph.D. thesis, University of London.

Stouffer, S.A., Suchman, E.A., De Vinney, L.C., Starr, S.A., and Williams, R.M. (1949). *The American soldier: adjustment during army life*, Vol. 1. Princeton University Press.

Tajfel, H. (1978). *Differentiation between social groups*. Academic Press, London.

Tajfel, H. (1984). *The social dimension*, Vol. 1. Cambridge University Press.

Taylor, M.C. (1982). Improved conditions, rising expectations, and dissatisfaction: a test of the past/present relative deprivation hypothesis. *Social Psychology Quarterly*, **45**, 24–33.

Vanneman, R.D. and Pettigrew, T.F. (1972). Race and relative deprivation in the urban United States. *Race*, **13**(4), 461–86.

Walker, I. and Mann, L. (1987). Unemployment, relative deprivation and social protest. *Personality and Social Psychology Bulletin*, **13**, (2), 275–83.

Walker, I. and Pettigrew, T.F. (1984). Relative deprivation theory: an overview and conceptual critique. *British Journal of Social Psychology*, **23**, 301–10.

Williams, R.M. (1975). Relative deprivation. In *The idea of social structure: papers in honor of Robert K. Merton* (ed. L.A. Coser). Harcourt Brace Jovanovich, New York.

11 Shared economic beliefs

Alan Lewis

Introduction

People have economic beliefs: individuals and families not only organize
their personal finances in terms of the relative merits of spending and saving
and when it is a good time to buy a motor car or put money away in the
bank, but also in terms of macroeconomic policy, such as whether the
government should be doing more to alleviate high unemployment levels
and to reduce inflation. Economists are clearly experts about economics.
And politicians choose between competing economic theories in their
management of the economy. But economists and politicians can only do so
much: in the end the economy is driven by how consumers choose, and how
they choose is in part, and a very important part, influenced by consumers'
economic beliefs.

The present chapter has an ambitious brief. First, shared or widespread
economic beliefs are examined with recourse to attitude survey data. Here it
is revealed, at least as far as contemporary evidence shows, that different
cultures, at least among Western capitalist countries, have economic beliefs
in common. The second section concentrates on differences between cultures, and also within cultures, that is, on the different beliefs of disparate
income groups, social classes, and those sharing varying political affiliations.
Two crucial questions are begged: the first is concerned with the explanation of shared economic beliefs and the levels of such explanations, e.g.
micro or macro, economic, political, or psychological; and the second with
methodology—how are these beliefs elicited and how are they to be
examined?

Survey data: some gross commonalities

Perceived fairness: costs, prices, and profit

In the general economic theory of action people are portrayed as utility
maximizers driven by the motivation of self interest. Similarly firms
maximize their profits and minimize their losses. Of course, no markets are
perfect; there are inefficiencies, interventions, and constraints. What is
clear is that firms, and indeed individuals, do not maximize their utilities
in the macro-economic sense; rather firms may choose a stratagem of

'satisficing', as Herbert Simon (1957) has described it, where the 'best' economic alternative is not struggled for, but a 'good' option is acceptable. The risks may be lower and the owners may feel the firm has already reached a satisfactory size and market share. Such notions as Simon's have led to the development of a new transdisciplinary field called 'economic psychology' (Lewis 1982; Furnham and Lewis 1986; Lea *et al.* 1987; MacFadyen and MacFadyen 1986; Earl 1987), among the basic premises of which are that people's perceptions, attitudes, values, and expectations— the staples of social psychology—have economic consequences, and possibly economic antecedents. Within economic psychology, lack of apparent utility maximization is explained not by recourse to economic constraints and inefficiencies but to the ways in which individuals and groups choose to act because of their psychological, rather than economic, nature. What is plain is that many of the things that so-called rational economic man, or woman, is expected to do are repugnant and indeed there appear to be widespread beliefs about what is fair and appropriate in particular economic circumstances. Kahneman *et al.* (1986), in a timely article, have investigated precisely this—shared economic beliefs about profit seeking. Telephone interviewing was employed in pursuit of participants' views of the acceptability and unacceptability of various economic scenarios, an example of which follows:

Question 2a   'A small photocopying shop has one employee who has worked in the shop for six months and earns $9 per hour. Business continues to be satisfactory, but a factory in the area has closed and unemployment has increased. Other small shops have now hired reliable workers at $7 an hour to perform jobs similar to those done by the photocopy shop employee. The owner of the photocopying shop reduces the employee's wage to $7' (Kahneman *et al.* 1986, p. 780).

Participants in the interview were then asked to indicate whether they thought the owner's reduction in the wage bill was acceptable (fair) or unfair. The results revealed ($N = 98$) that 17 per cent of the sample thought the action was acceptable, while 83 per cent thought it was unfair. These fairness ratings were reversed when the question was slightly altered to read:

Question 2b   'A small photocopying shop has one employee . . . [as in Question 2a] . . . The current employee leaves, and the owner decides to pay a replacement $7 an hour' (p. 730).

In this case, 73 per cent thought the employer's action was acceptable, and 27 per cent that it was unfair ($N = 125$).

The results suggested to the authors that the 'stickiness' of adaptation of wages to changes in macro-economic circumstances, a phenomenon commonly observed, is due in part to participants' shared notions about what is fair and acceptable. To take other examples, Kahneman *et al.* (1986) have shown in what circumstances it is acceptable for a firm to raise prices and the size of these price rises. If, for example, a firm experiences an increase in the cost of materials, these can quite acceptably be passed on to customers. However, if the costs of materials fall there is no symmetrical requirement, in terms of perceived fairness, for the firm to reduce its prices by as much as the reduction in the firm's costs; passing on only a part of these gains to customers is sufficient. It is not acceptable for a firm to increase prices because of shortages of a desired commodity; to quote the authors:

'Conventional economic analyses assume as a matter of course that excess demand for a good creates an opportunity for suppliers to raise prices, and that such increases will indeed occur. The profit seeking adjustments that clear the market are in this view as natural as water finding its level—and as ethically neutral. The lay public does not share this indifference' (Kahneman *et al.* 1986, p. 735).

These findings have major economic consequences, as demand appears not to have a symmetrical relationship to prices and furthermore prices are more responsive to costs than demand and more responsive to cost increases than cost decreases. There is also a lack of symmetry in the public's perception of prices in terms of the loss of discount as opposed to price increases, in that they are viewed differently even though the objective economic consequences are the same: if the demand for a given motor car increases, it is quite acceptable to remove a discount at the point of sale of, say, 10 per cent, but it is not acceptable to 'raise the price' by 10 per cent.

Kahneman and colleagues quite rightly draw attention to the restricted nature of their sample, yet their results are so clear cut and plausible as to suggest that these shared economic beliefs are indeed widespread.

Perceived fairness: income and wealth

There are other noticeable economic beliefs about fairness, this time in terms of income and wealth distribution, which reveal a degree of concordance. Large scale surveys in the USA (cf. National Opinion Research Centre —NORC—1986) and Great Britain (cf. British Social Attitudes Survey, 1984, 1985, 1986), as well as smaller scale studies in the USA (Alves and Rossi 1978) and Belgium (Overlaet and Lagrou 1981) have all shown that people's preferences are for a more compact income distribution, raising the incomes of the poor and reducing the incomes and assets of the wealthy.

Table 4 presents an example of attitudes towards the distribution of wealth, including the appropriate role of government, using survey data collected in the USA, which compares aggregated replies from 1972–82 with 1983, 1984, and 1986 (NORC 1986). The actual question put to respondents was:

'Some people think that the government in Washington ought to reduce the income differences between the rich and the poor, perhaps by raising the taxes of wealthy

Table 4 Attitudes towards distribution of wealth (revised form of Q76, NORC 1986)

		1972–82	1983	1984	1986
Government should do something to reduce income differences between rich and poor		45%*	48%	49%	49%
Mid-point		21%	18%	18%	21%
Government should not concern itself with income differences		34%	35%	33%	30%
	N	2170	1558	1438	1448

* rounded percentages

families or by giving income assistance to the poor. Others think that the government should not concern itself with reducing this income difference between rich and poor.'

Respondents were then asked to place themselves somewhere on a seven-point rating scale anchored at the lower end by the statement, 'Government should do something to reduce income differences between rich and poor' and at the higher end by 'Government should not concern itself with income differences'.

For simplicity of presentation, the first three points on the scale are added as are the last three, the mid-point, a rating of four, is presented separately. While the question asked is hardly a radical one, it is clear that there is remarkably consistent support for at least some, albeit weak, moves towards redistribution.

The public sector

The 'public sector' in this context covers the revenue raised by government (taxes) and the services governments provide, such as social services, health services, and defence. The overall picture has been of antipathy towards taxation, which may be no more newsworthy or surprising than 'dog bites man'. However, this is paralleled with a growing popular support for public expenditure, both in Europe and the USA, especially for health, education, and particular social benefits (cf. Bosanquet 1986; Lewis and Jackson 1985; Edgell and Duke 1982; Taylor-Gooby 1983; NORC 1986). These remarks are generalizations which of course require qualification when looking at differences between countries and groups with varying political allegiances, when interpreting preferences and ideological perspectives, and because of problems in question wording. All of these will be dealt with later. Question wording deserves a specific mention here as it has been repeatedly and internationally shown that when the notions of taxation and public expenditure are linked, thereby making the 'fiscal connection' between the two, preferences are altered: antipathy towards taxation is tempered when it is made clear that taxation pays for much-needed services, such as help for the old and the needy; enthusiasm for the expansion of public expenditure is dampened when it is made clear that this has to be paid for through taxation, in that services have a 'tax price' (Lewis 1982). This said, what might be termed a broad 'collectivism' is apparent in Europe, where governments are held responsible for the delivery of substantial public and social services; in the USA the so-called 'tax backlash' and the popular fiscal conservatism evident in the late 1970s* has softened in more recent years. In British samples, even when the 'fiscal connection' between tax and expenditure is made explicit, the years 1983–85 have shown an increase from 32 per cent to 45 per cent in those prepared to see taxes raised in order to spend more on health, education, and social benefits (Bosanquet 1986).

People are naturally concerned with how public money is spent and while governments are held accountable for many social and economic problems, it is clear that it is not the popular wish that money should be distributed indiscriminately. Taking social security as an example, there is evidence from the USA, Britain, and Europe that a distinction is made in popular consciousness between the 'deserving' and 'undeserving' poor and between different kinds of benefits (Furnham 1983; Coughlin 1980, 1982; Taylor-Gooby 1983). There is general support for benefits often financed in part through insurance principles, as this suggests that receipts are not charity hand-outs but rather one's due. This reverence for prudent behaviour is reflected in the lack of support for 'imprudent' single parents or those who need child-care facilities so that the parent can engage in paid employment. While single-parent families and other 'welfare scroungers' are perceived as the undeserving poor, top of the list for those 'deserving' are invariably the retired, the elderly, the sick, and the disabled.

Inflation and unemployment

The major economic problem faced by many Western nations in the mid-1980s, was what the public perceived as the unacceptably high levels of unemployment. The high levels of inflation in Europe and the USA had passed for the time being; inflation was no longer the pertinent issue in public consciousness. As an example, the British Social Attitudes report for 1985 shows that 69 per cent of the national sample thought that 'keeping

---

* For example, proposition 13 in California, where a two-thirds majority voted in favour of tax and public expenditure cuts.

down unemployment' was the government's top priority; only 26 per cent considered 'keeping down inflation' as the top priority. This is coupled with the view that 81 per cent considered it the government's responsibility to provide a decent standard of living for the unemployed (Goodhardt 1985).

The so-called 'Phillips curve' tracing the inverse relationship between inflation and unemployment has been a popular model in economics, and a reasonably successful one, until the 'stagflation' periods of the early 1970s when both unemployment and inflation rose substantially. Popular opinion as described by national opinion polls generally mirrored these relative changes in the trade-off between inflation and unemployment as did the 'agenda setting' of newspapers and the rest of the media (Mosley 1983). It has further been claimed that the perceived economic preferences of the public, in conjunction with political factors, can produce cyclical rhythms in inflation and unemployment levels (cf. Tufte 1978; Nordhaus 1975).

Economic problems: causes and cures

So far it has been shown that there is evidence, usually in the form of replies to social survey questions, that there are shared beliefs about economic fairness, income distribution, taxation, public expenditure, unemployment, and inflation. For some, these results will seem glib: the respondent after all has done little more than agree or disagree with a ready-made statement. More interesting perhaps is the examination of shared economic 'theories' and explanations of, say, the causes of unemployment and poverty and how such economic problems can be assuaged. Explorations of 'lay' accounts have taken a similar form to the research already reviewed, with, however, respondents being given more freedom of expression by being presented with a range of alternative economic explanations, or, in some cases, given comparatively free range with open-ended questions.

It would seem probable that a coherent account of an economic phenomenon, for example poverty, would include a perceptual component, e.g. is there any poverty? Where is it? What is it? Poverty has to be seen to exist, it has to be salient, it has to be 'a problem' requiring explanation for an examination of lay explanations to have any value. It follows that these perceptions would be linked to accounts of causes and also to the likely efficacy of cures. For example, one group of explanations may have as their starting point a notion of 'absolute' poverty, a belief that such poverty is rare and where it is evident is caused by the failings and weaknesses of the poor themselves given the ample opportunities for improvement and the financial support given by governments; it may follow from such beliefs that poverty was in some sense inevitable and there was little governments could do to help.

Other scenarios than the one outlined above are of course plausible, and indeed the most common, in Europe at least, is the view in which poverty is perceived as a mixture of 'relative' and 'absolute' poverty, where economic organization and the structure of society is attributed as its major cause, and where government intervention is broadly welcomed as an appropriate method for its alleviation (cf. Commission of the European Communities 1977; Furnham 1982a; Feather 1974).

Furnham, in a series of factor analytic studies of explanations for poverty and unemployment in Britain, has refined research a little further by identifying three major types of explanation, namely 'individualistic', 'societal', and 'fatalistic' causes. In the case of unemployment, individualistic causes lay the blame for unemployment squarely on the unemployed themselves, 'societal' explanations are couched in terms of the structure of society and inequities of opportunity, and 'fatalistic' explanations stress the inevitability of unemployment (Furnham 1982b). For both unemployment and poverty, 'societal' explanations are by far the most commonly called upon by respondents (Lewis et al. 1987; for a full review of this type of research see Furnham and Lewis 1986).

The 1986 British Social Attitudes report records some popular reactions to possible remedies for unemployment (Mann 1986). In this survey, 83 per cent of respondents supported lowering the retirement age, 64 per cent supported restricting overtime, 45 per cent supported job sharing, but only 25 per cent supported shortening the working week and reducing wages. Mann concludes that the results suggest that people are generally against a market forces ideology when it comes to solving social problems like unemployment. While this conclusion is a big step from the evidence provided, in another smaller questionnaire study of 448 respondents, over 66 per cent of the sample thought the government should spend more money in order to reduce unemployment (Lewis and Furnham 1986). Lewis and Furnham (1986) also gave people the opportunity to provide answers of their own, without pre-coding, to the question 'How do you think unemployment in Britain could be reduced?'. A content analysis of the numerous suggestions reduced the information to thirty-one categories, of which the most popular answer (76 responses) in its various forms was 'don't know'! However the three next most common answers suggest that the conclusions reported by Mann (1986) from closed questions, did not do the views of respondents too much injustice. Unprompted, 38 replies were for lowering the retirement age, 38 for increasing public spending on services and 36 for increasing job creation schemes. Closed questions may inflate the apparent popularity of certain proposals. It is very important to know how many people have nothing to say, but there is an inhibition to such a response in the 'forced choice' procedure. There is always a danger of putting words into people's mouths from which considerable political capital can be made. In free responses, only 20 mentions were made of reducing immigration and only 8 suggesting that women should relinquish paid employment or work part-time rather than full-time, yet in the forced choice procedure a third of the sample agreed that 'women with husbands in full-time employment should give up their jobs in order to reduce unemployment amongst men' and more spectacularly, nearly 58 per cent agreed that 'immigration should be restricted further' (Lewis and Furnham 1986).

Some gross differences and sectional commonalities

Countries

So far, shared or widespread economic beliefs have been portrayed in an unrefined way; it is as though all cultures share the same economic beliefs and within a given culture there are no important differences between people with different political persuasions and varying socio-economic backgrounds; clearly this is a false picture. Given the enormous investment required in staging international social surveys, opportunities to examine replies to matched questions are comparatively rare. Where they do occur, there are the unenviable and perhaps insurmountable problems of translation and interpretation in different cultures. Without the luxury of such matched questions, Richard Coughlin has made a brave and scholarly attempt to integrate social survey research on attitudes towards taxes and spending in USA, UK, West Germany, France, Sweden, Denmark, Canada, and Australia (Coughlin 1980), and although these countries do not include Third World or socialist countries it may none the less be a surprise to some that there is a degree of concordance of economic preferences across these Western industrialized nations for what could be termed a broad 'collectivism'. However, whether or not this 'collectivism' is an 'ideological' rather than an 'operational' collectivism will be discussed in a later section. Predictable differences emerge between the countries surveyed in that, generally, support for interventionist policies and the Welfare State are more prevalent in nations with a long history of such policy implementations and with a proportionately large public sector, for example, Sweden compared to the USA. Beliefs or opinions assessed from national social surveys are rarely radical and when looking at the most common preferences as an access to an understanding of shared beliefs one is almost inevitably faced with a reiteration of the status quo.

There are noticeable exceptions to this rule: the broadly monetarist philosophy of the present government in Britain appears to be at odds with popular economic preferences and beliefs (cf. Taylor-Gooby 1983; Bosanquet 1986; Lewis and Jackson 1985). This too could be explained, however, if one were to recall that the political status quo in Britain since 1945 has been interventionist and also if one were to describe President Reagan and Mrs Thatcher's rejection of Keynesianism as a 'radical' shift in economic policy. It is also plausible, precisely because of the degree and length of

government intervention in social policy, that poverty, should it arise, may
be perceived by a sizeable minority to be the fault of the poor themselves.
In a study, *'The perception of poverty in Europe'*, which used matched
questions in national samples of the then nine member countries of the
European Economic Community (EEC), respondents were invited to give
their views on the causes of poverty, choosing from four main options:
injustice in society; laziness and lack of will-power; misfortune; and the
inevitability of poverty as a part of progress in the modern world. Across
countries the most common explanation was social injustice (26 per cent)
and there were particularly large differences when considering 'laziness' as
an explanation: only 11 per cent of the Danes and 12 per cent of the Dutch
chose this while, in marked contrast, it was far and away the most favoured
attribution among respondents from the UK where 43 per cent chose it.
Overall across the community, 54 per cent thought the authorities, i.e. the
government, were doing too little to combat poverty and only 7 per cent too
much; however the figures for the UK sample were 36 per cent and 20 per
cent respectively (Commission of the European Communities 1977). These
results are indeed perplexing, as the explanation of this result in terms of a
social history of the Welfare State may fit for Britain but will not do for
other countries when one realizes that similar results to the UK sample have
been recorded among respondents in the USA (see Coughlin 1980, p. 112).

Sectional interests

There are very many examples in the growing literature on economic
psychology of consistent and predictable differences in economic beliefs
between identifiable demographic groups, a flavour of which can be given by
results showing the following: the tendency to attribute causes of poverty to
individualistic reasons is associated with voting Conservative, identification
with the 'protestant work ethic', and lack of allegiance to post-materialist
values (Furnham 1982c; Feather 1974; Commission of the European Community 1977); Conservative voters and those in employment are more likely
to favour individualistic explanations for unemployment than Labour
voters and the unemployed (Furnham 1982b, 1982c); Conservative voters
and those who associate themselves with the protestant work ethic are more
antipathetic towards taxation, feel the tax system is unfair, believe government intervention is unwarranted, and are more likely to condone tax
avoidance schemes (Furnham 1984); Conservative voters favour a reduction
in government spending overall, an option not favoured by Liberal/SDP
voters, and especially Labour voters who support an increase in government
expenditure; Conservative voters advocate substantial reductions in social
security spending and substantial increases in defence expenditure (Lewis
1980; Lewis and Jackson 1985).

What is striking about these and many other sectional differences in economic beliefs is that they make sense. The next section addresses the question 'in what sense do they make sense?'.

Explaining sectional differences and similarities

Ideology

The most reliable and consistent discriminator of economic beliefs is reported voting pattern and party political preference. It is tempting, then, to suggest that shared economic beliefs are indeed shared ideological beliefs. But such a suggestion requires qualification: what is meant by ideology? What is the relationship between voting preferences and ideology?

As Elinor Scarbrough has documented in Chapter 6, ideology has been frequently defined and in many different ways. For the purpose of the present chapter, ideology will be considered to be fundamental and broad belief systems used by social groups to interpret their social world. Ideological systems are normally political belief systems, e.g. ideological 'conservatism' or ideological 'liberalism', but it does not follow that an ideological conservative will necessarily vote for the Conservative or Republican party or that an ideological liberal will vote for the Liberal or the Democratic party. Certainly there is a burgeoning literature which has pointed towards the lack of correspondence between political and economic values and voting choice where the explanatory variables of social class, education, and income take the upper hand (Butler and Stokes 1971). No less convincing has been the wealth of publications pointing to the lack of political knowledge and awareness of the electorate (Converse 1975). However more recent studies have shown that the awareness of economic issues is growing, that social class carries less weight in voting choice than before, and voters are becoming more issue-conscious (Sarlvik and Crewe 1983). This is substantiated by studies conducted in Britain which have shown fiscal preferences closely allied to the political programmes of the political parties to which respondents show allegiance (Edgell and Duke 1982; Lewis and Jackson 1985). This may prove a surprise to many, especially as these predictable preferences are apparent among undergraduates with little or no experience of paying tax, and even among school children (Lewis 1983; Furnham 1987). There are good grounds for supposing that economic and political socialization are allied (Lewis and Cullis 1988).

Political rhetoric and direct experience of the recession have both played their part in raising ideological consciousness. The Reagan administration, and even more so, the Thatcher administration have challenged the political wisdom of the last 40 years. The ideology of individualism, and the values of private enterprise and self-interest are 'in'; collectivism, altruism, and the notion of a benevolent state are 'out'. Furthermore, more and more people have experienced the traumas of unemployment both directly and through

the experiences of relatives, friends, and neighbours. Cuts in public expenditure have sharpened the fiscal, economic, and political consciousness of
public sector workers from dustmen and public health inspectors to medical
consultants and university professors. The discussion of economic issues is
pervasive in the media; it is hardly surprising that some of this rubs off.

It has been argued that voting preferences are not a direct reflection of
ideology but that the correspondence between ideological beliefs and voting
behaviour may well be increasing. Voting preferences not only discriminate
between ideological perspectives, they also reflect social class and income
differences which give added emphasis to the discriminatory power of this
simple measure.

Self-interest

Economic beliefs are shared in the grandest sense just as one shares a
culture and a history. At a slightly lower level it has been speculated that
particular combinations of economic beliefs are shared by those who also
share a political ideology, or, more accurately, have shared voting preferences. The explanation for these shared economic beliefs would, in turn,
make sense to anthropologists, historians, political scientists, and sociologists: the next logical step is to examine how economic beliefs might be
interpreted by an economist, i.e. how economic beliefs reflect self-interest.

Rational economic men, and presumably women, seek to maximize their
utilities, given certain constraints. Extending this notion we can see that a
wealthy person is hardly likely to support extra taxes on the wealthy and an
unemployed one, cuts in unemployment benefit. This interpretation of
shared economic beliefs has intuitive appeal; the cohesiveness of social
groups may be enhanced by shared economic beliefs which not only explain
people's position in society but also do so favourably: wealthy people and
their wealthy friends and colleagues praise the free enterprise system and the
rules of the race in which they are the winners.

The concepts of 'self interest' and 'rationality', and the difficulties
thereof have been discussed at length in the literature, and interested readers
are directed elsewhere (e.g. Hollis and Nell 1975; Caldwell 1984; Marr and
Raj 1983). Self-interest is in effect tautological: if an action appears to be
contrary to an actor's best interests this does not negate the view that the
action was self-interested; and what is in the interests of the actor is for
the actor to decide, it need not make sense to others. For the purposes of the
present chapter it will be assumed that the notion of self-interest will be
used in an external and predictive way: it is in this sense that all the sectional
differences in economic beliefs that have been mentioned in the previous
section make sense.

The self-interest interpretation is a very consistent one but there are
notable exceptions. Evidence presented by Cullis and Lewis (1985) and

Lewis (1982) both show that people in professional occupations, with higher than average incomes, are less fiscally conservative than one would predict from a straightforward self-interest interpretation alone. The preferences of this group regularly reveal at least some support for raising taxes, at a cost to themselves, in order to improve welfare benefits, of which they will be extremely unlikely to ever be a beneficiary. The self-interest explanation is saved with recourse to the 'social control' hypothesis.

'This hypothesis in the commonest form usually states that social security spending or welfare state programmes facilitate the social, political and economic control exercised by political elites: elites that are threatened by the masses, or organized protest and reform movements, or political violence, institute social security spending programmes, or increase the level of spending on extant programmes, in order to quell social unrest or the threat of such unrest' (Coughlin and Armour 1981, p. 1).

This is not an argument a mainstream economist would use, and is more familiar to sociologists and political scientists, but it serves as an example of the ubiquitous nature of the self-interest explanation. Even a Marxist analysis has recourse to it: the reason a working-class voter may vote Conservative and support the status quo is because of 'false consciousness': the capitalist class have sold to the workers ideas which the workers think are in their best interests but which really are in the interests of the capitalists.

While economic texts generally make great play of the 'neutrality' of self-interest assumptions and hypotheses, for many non-economists the self-interest assumptions imply a kind of cynicism, which diminishes people, stripping them of moral judgements, religious and other beliefs and values. The position that the present author takes is similar to that of Taylor-Gooby who, in his studies of welfare attitudes and their interpretation, propounds a mixture of self-interest, ideological, and moral influences (Taylor-Gooby 1983).

Contradictions and confusions

For shared beliefs to have meaning, it is not sufficient, at least when considering social representations, for this sharing, as we have said, to be merely popular or numerical. It is required instead that these beliefs should have a coherent and common structure at some level, for example, within cultures or within identifiable demographic and/or social groups. When considering ideology this shared structure may lie not in consistency but in common contradictions. This turns much of social psychological research of the 1960s and 1970, confirming consistency, congruity, and dissonance theories, upside-down. This is also partly a methodological point: survey questions and purely numerical analyses, including factor analysis, may depict a consistency and structure which simply is not there. When, instead of asking questions on a questionnaire, one listens to people talking, contradictions abound which neither the speaker, nor the audience, feels a need to 'correct', *because the 'contradictions' themselves are the things that are shared*. (See also Chapter 9, this volume by Cochrane and Billig.)

This is not to say that social survey methodology cannot be extremely useful. It *is* possible to highlight the contradictions between answers to differing questions. But in the researcher's 'effort after meaning' in terms of 'consistent' patterning of replies, this is often lost.

When reviewing the social survey data on attitudes towards the public sector there is ample evidence of support for favoured public expenditure programmes, even the possibility of the influence of an ideological 'collectivism'. Such 'collectivism' must be viewed in the very weakest sense when considering the United States of America, where there is massive public support for the 'free enterprise' system and where there is an absence of any noticeable socialist or Marxist political tradition. In their view of the major social surveys and polls in the United States, Lipset and Schneider (1983) point out other 'contradictions':

'Americans hold their political and economic institutions in high esteem and realize that it is the exercise of competitive self interest that makes those institutions work. But at the same time, they do not admire self interested behaviour and look with suspicion at anyone who has succeeded in acquiring political and economic power' (Lipset and Schneider 1983, pp. 5–6).

People also make a powerful distinction between the plight of the nation and personal circumstances, which suggests that shared economic beliefs could be on two very different levels; the first being a relatively apolitical judgement of personal circumstances and domestic management, and the second being beliefs about national economy and economic priorities which are heavily influenced by political factors. Goodhardt (1985) in a summary of British attitude data has shown that while 69 per cent of a national sample considered that 'keeping down unemployment' was the government's top priority, compared with 26 per cent citing 'keeping down inflation', when the question was altered so that it addressed the economic issue of most concern to 'you and your family', the priorities were reversed, 44 per cent mentioning unemployment and 52 per cent inflation.

Free and Cantril (1968) have also recognized two broad levels of political and economic beliefs applicable to North American samples, which they term 'ideological' and 'operational': the former referring to broad abstract notions and the latter to agreement or disagreement about specific issues where there are no abstract rationalizations to back them up. Such a distinction explains why, in samples from the United States, respondents frequently reveal an ideological conservatism, yet appear 'liberal' when asked about specific welfare programmes. It is one of the problems of social survey methods, say Free and Cantril (1968), that almost all questions are of the operational type, which makes the exploration, in the present context, of genuinely shared economic beliefs, and their structure, problematic.

An alternative way to proceed, more common in the sociological rather than the social psychological literature, is the use of small-scale qualitative studies, where participants are given an opportunity to talk and explain themselves. An example of such a study is *Workers divided* by Nichols and Armstrong (1976). In part of the book, ten foremen at a chemical factory were interviewed about their notions of industrial relations. The foremen were all middle-aged, of comparable socio-economic backgrounds, and life-long voters for the Labour party in Britain. The authors concluded that although these people were Labour supporters they did not exhibit a socialist ideology, and many of their judgements and beliefs stemmed directly from their early working experiences in the industrial north of England and from their notions of 'the real working class' of earlier times. There was a revulsion against the 'strike happy' and 'greedy' workers of today. For the foremen, most battles of labour had been won. They generally supported the structure of society and did not envisage it changing much.

From these and other interviews the authors describe the political and economic attitudes exhibited as 'conflicting' and 'inchoate'. Conflicting because what the authors describe as the 'dominant ideology' constructs a reality which is difficult to challenge coherently without rejecting the whole 'common-sense' world of conventional wisdom. This common-sense world is:

'One which not only denies the necessity or possibility of radical change in society and which essentially denies the very existence of antagonistic class relations, but which, in making political economy a mystery, mystifies; and which just for good measure, separates 'politics' (the realm of 'democracy') and 'economics' (which is taken to constitute something natural and immutable—'the facts of life')' (Nichols and Armstrong 1976, p. 127).

The work of the psychologist Dickinson (1984) on the development of economic common-sense is of relevance here. In a series of studies employing semi-structured interviews, Dickinson investigated perceptions and attributions of pay inequalities among groups of state and privately educated children in Scotland with mean ages ranging from 11 to 15. Explanations for different rates of pay in different jobs were classified as: 'status descriptive'—e.g. 'because he is just a roadsweeper'; or 'individual' —'because he has qualifications'; or 'social'—'higher demand for his skills'. The majority of explanations were 'individual', and the next most common 'status descriptive'; 'social' explanations were comparatively rare, although more common among middle-class than working-class children. Overall, working-class children give more 'descriptive' explanations.

'Individual' and 'social' explanations increase with age but it is the dis-aggregation by class which may be more informative. Descriptive explana-tions are in a sense tautological and may indicate that differences in income are the outcome of a natural and inexplicable state of affairs. It will be remembered that middle-class children are keener on 'individualistic' and 'social explanations' which leads Dickinson to write:

'It is tempting to think that those who stand to benefit most from the system of income inequalities are the ones who are best equipped with the means of justifying that system' (Dickinson 1984, pp. 26–27).

This fits neatly with Huber and Form's (1973) concept of ideology as a belief system for explaining and justifying social institutions and inequal-ities. And Dickinson's research stresses the importance of conducting more research into the development of social beliefs and the functions they may serve.

Conclusions

From the psychological point of view it is natural that much of the interest in social representations and shared beliefs should be in examining processes whereby, for example, reified economics is transformed into consensual economics, using Moscovici's (1981) terms. The study of shared economic beliefs is of necessity interdisciplinary and stresses not just how these trans-formations take place but why the representations take the form that they do, given sectional and personal influences. Consequently social beliefs are not solely about cognitive processes; such cognitive processes are clearly the domain of psychologists, but psychologists should not lose sight of the sociological and political implications of such transformations. It follows from the comments made in the previous section that the construction and maintenance of common-sense can be a political tool which serves to preserve the status quo. And two methodological points follow which are of prime importance for future research. The first is that one should not only be concerned with the social representations and beliefs of ordinary indi-viduals but also with predominant values of political and economic élites. Similarly it would be productive to examine the development of economic beliefs by tracing the presentation of economic news in newspapers, tele-vision, and radio. The second methodological issue points to the need for ethnographic and qualitative research. For far too long 'contradictions' and 'confusions' have been ignored; people have not been allowed to express themselves *in situ* and in their own language. It is time to grasp the nettle, long debated by anthropologists and sociologists, of attempting to compre-hend the frames of meaning and social representations of social groups as they themselves understand them.

Acknowledgements

The author wishes to thank Lindsay Brook, Graham Cox, and Paul Webley for their assistance in the preparation of this chapter.

References

Alves, W. and Rossi, P. (1978). Who should get what? Fairness judgements of the distribution of earnings. *American Journal of Sociology*, **84**(3), 541–64.

Bosanquet, N. (1986). Public spending in the welfare state. In *British social attitudes* (ed. R. Jowell, S. Witherspoon, and L. Brook). Gower, Aldershot.

British Social Attitudes (1984). Ed. R. Jowell and C. Airey. Gower, Aldershot.

British Social Attitudes (1985). Ed. R. Jowell and S. Witherspoon. Gower, Aldershot.

British Social Attitudes (1986). Ed. R. Jowell, S. Witherspoon, and L. Brook. Gower, Aldershot.

Butler, D. and Stokes, D. (1971). *Political change in Britain*. Penguin, Harmondsworth.

Caldwell, B. (ed.) (1984). *Appraisal and criticism in economics*. Allen & Unwin, Boston, MA.

Commission of the European Communities (CEC) (1977). *The perception of poverty in Europe*. CEC, Brussels.

Converse, P. (1975). Public opinion and voting behaviour. In *Handbook of political science* Vol. 2 (ed. N. Polsby and F. Greenstein). Addison-Wesley, Boston.

Coughlin, R. (1980). *Ideology, public opinion and welfare policy*. Institute of International Studies, University of California, Berkeley, CA.

Coughlin, R. (1982). Payroll taxes for social security, in the United States: the future of fiscal and social policy illusions. *Journal of Economic Psychology*, **2**, 165–85.

Coughlin, R. and Armour, T. (1981). The political control functions of welfare spending. Paper presented to Political Sociology Section, Southwestern Social Sciences Association, Dallas, Texas.

Cullis, J. and Lewis, A. (1985). Some evidence on tax knowledge and preferences. *Journal of Economic Psychology*, **6**, 271–87.

Dickinson, J. (1984). Social representations of socio-economic structure. Paper presented at the British Psychological Society London Conference.

Earl, P. (1987). *Psychological economics: development, tensions, prospects*. Kluwer, New York.

Edgell, S. and Duke, V. (1982). Reactions to public expenditure cuts: occupational class and party realignment. *Sociology*, **16**, 431–9.

Feather, N. (1974). Explanations for poverty in Australian and American samples: the person, society and fate. *Australian Journal of Psychology*, **26**, 199–216.

Free, L. and Cantril, H. (1968). *The political beliefs of Americans*. Simon & Schuster, New York.

Furnham, A. (1982*a*). Why are the poor always with us? Explanations for poverty in Britain? *British Journal of Social Psychology*, **20**, 311–22.

Furnham, A. (1982*b*). Explanations for unemployment in Britain. *European Journal of Social Psychology*, **12**, 335–52.

Furnham, A. (1982*c*). The protestant work ethic and attitudes towards unemployment. *Journal of Occupational Psychology*, **55**, 277–86.

Furnham, A. (1983). Attitudes towards the unemployed receiving social security benefits. *Human Relations*, **36**, 135–50.

Furnham, A. (1984). Determinants of attitudes towards taxation in Britain. *Human Relations*, **37**, 535–46.

Furnham, A. (1987). The determinants and structure of adolescents' beliefs about the economy. *Journal of Adolescence*, **10**, 353–71.

Furnham, A. and Lewis, A. (1986). *The economic mind: the social psychology of economic behaviour*. Wheatsheaf, Brighton.

Goodhardt, G. (1985). Prices, income and consumer issues. In *British social attitudes* (ed. R. Jowell and S. Witherspoon). Gower, Aldershot.

Hollis, M. and Nell, E. (1975). *Rational economic man*. Cambridge University Press.

Huber, J. and Form, W. (1973). *Income and ideology*. Free Press, New York.

Kahneman, D., Knetsch, J., and Thaler, R. (1986). Fairness as a constraint on profit seeking: entitlements in the market. *American Economic Review*, **76**, 728–41.

Lea, S., Tarpy, R., and Webley, P. (1987). *The individual and the economy*. Cambridge University Press.

Lewis, A. (1980). Attitudes to public expenditure and their relationship to voting preferences. *Political Studies*, **28**, 284–92.

Lewis, A. (1981). Attributions and politics. *Personality and Individual Differences*, **2**, 1–4.

Lewis, A. (1982). *The psychology of taxation*. Martin Robertson, Oxford.

Lewis, A. (1983). Public expenditure: perceptions and preferences. *Journal of Economic Psychology*, **3**, 159–67.

Lewis, A. and Cullis, J. (1988). Preferences, economics and psychology and the economic psychology of public sector preference formation. *Journal of Behavioural Economics*, **17**, 19–33.

Lewis, A. and Furnham, A. (1986). Reducing unemployment: lay beliefs about how to reduce current unemployment. *Journal of Economic Psychology*, **7**, 75–85.

Lewis, A. and Jackson, D. (1985). Voting preferences and attitudes to public expenditure. *Political Studies*, **XXXIII**, 457–66.

Lewis, A., Furnham, A., and Snell, M. (1987). Lay explanations for the causes of unemployment in Britain: economic, individualistic, societal or fatalistic? *Political Psychology*, **8**, 427–39.

Lipset, S. and Schneider, W. (1983). *The confidence gap: business, labour and government in the public mind*. Free Press, New York.

MacFadyen, A. and MacFadyen, H. (ed.) (1986). *Economic psychology*. Elsevier, Amsterdam.

Mann, M. (1986). Work and the work ethic. In *British social attitudes* (ed. R. Jowell, S. Witherspoon, and L. Brook). Gower, Aldershot.

Marr, W. and Raj, B. (eds) (1983). *How economists explain*. University Press of America, Lanham.

Moscovici, S. (1981). On social representation. In *Social cognition: perspectives on everyday understanding* (ed. J. Forgas). Academic Press, London.

Mosley, P. (1983). Popularity function and the role of the media: a pilot study of the popular press. *British Journal of Political Science*, **14**, 117–33.

National Opinion Research Centre (NORC) (1986). General Social Surveys, 1972–86: Cumulative Codebook. University of Chicago Press.

Nichols, T. and Armstrong, P. (1976). *Workers divided*. Penguin, Harmondsworth.

Nordhaus, W. (1975). The political business cycle. *Review of Economic Studies*, **42**, 169–90.

Overlaet, B. and Lagrou, L. (1981). Attitude towards the redistribution of income. *Journal of Economic Psychology*, **1**, 197–215.

Sarlvik, B. and Crewe, I. (1983). *Decade of dealignment*. Cambridge University Press.

Simon, H. (1957). *Models of man*. Wiley, New York.

Taylor-Gooby, P. (1983). Moralism, self interest and attitudes to welfare. *Policy and Politics*, **11**, 145–60.

Tufte, E. (1978). *Political control of the economy*. Princeton University Press.

12 Social beliefs about gender differences

Glynis M. Breakwell

The nature of social beliefs

The notion of 'social beliefs' is fraught with ambiguity. It has a siren quality which lures the brave into efforts after definition and comparisons with other problematic concepts such as attitudes, public opinion, social cognitions, social representations, conceptual schemata, or ideology.

Suffice it to say that for the purpose of this paper it is assumed that social beliefs are commonly held interpretations of socially important phenomena. They are what some others in this volume have termed 'widespread beliefs'.

Any socially important phenomenon will have more than one set of social beliefs encircling it, since more than one group of interests will attach to it. Social beliefs are created within an intergroup context. They come into being because a group wishes to delineate the meaning or establish the 'facts' about a phenomenon. This erection of meaning and interpretation is self-serving, it will suit the interests and purposes of the group concerned. Each group has its own set of social beliefs organized into systems which justify its action, specify its identity, and serve its interests. Consequently, the greater the number of groups for whom a social phenomenon is relevant, the greater will be the variety and complexity of the social beliefs surrounding it. This becomes patently obvious in examining social beliefs about gender differences.

Framing social beliefs in their intergroup background indicates that they should not be seen as value free. Social beliefs have an emotional charge. The social beliefs of one's group are deemed good and are positively valued. Failure to accept a social belief important to the group can be a heinous offence. The idea that social beliefs operate in the cognitive rather than motivational domain is naïve; they have a life in both simultaneously. This can result in a situation where a social belief can itself be the target of a positive or negative attitude while in turn inciting a positive or negative attitude towards the object about which it makes statements. Rejection of the social belief itself will clearly modify its power to influence both attitudes and action. In understanding the role of social beliefs, an appreciation of the rules of acceptance or rejection by the individual of the group's proffered social belief seems vital.

The concept of gender differences

It is necessary to distinguish sex differences from gender differences (Deaux 1985). Since the advent of the feminist critique of the social sciences in the 1960s (critically reviewed by Eichler 1980), 'sex differences' is a label which has come to be used to refer to strictly biological differences between men and women. 'Gender differences' refer to distinctions attributed by society (Archer and Lloyd 1982).

This is really a case where matters of terminology plunge immediately into matters of beliefs and ideology. The labels 'sex' and 'gender' differences are infused with particular types of explanatory assumptions (Sayers 1982). Those who use the phrase 'gender differences' offer an explanation for the differences between men and women primarily in terms of societal processes and socialization pressures. Those who refer to sex differences propose a biological, even socio-biological, explanation. Moreover, the labels carry undercurrents of implications for action which might bring about changes in the differences between men and women. The 'gender difference' is ultimately malleable, open to large-scale eradication. The 'sex difference' is a biological imperative, irreversible and, what is more, its reversal would be considered undesirable.

Choosing a label for the differences between men and women is not easy, if you wish to avoid all this baggage of connotation. The reality of the matter is, of course, that most end-state differences between the sexes are inevitably a product of both society and biology, especially in the realm of psychological characteristics. Even the so-called 'pure' biological differences (e.g. genitalia, facial hair growth, etc.) gather their significance only within a specific context.

I shall use the label 'gender differences' but these cautionary remarks about the implications of the term should be considered seriously. The label is used here denuded of its explanatory and policy overtones. Biological differences between the sexes will not be discussed except in so far as they impinge upon social beliefs about gender differences. For instance, men and women differ in their biological abilities to become pregnant but this would be discussed only in so far as it might be treated as central in a social belief about the relative role of men and women in the labour force.

Social beliefs about the differences between men and women

Social beliefs about the differences between men and women cover two distinct areas:

(1)   they specify what the differences are;

(2)   they say why those differences exist.

In a sense, social beliefs establish both social facts and social explanations. The social beliefs about gender differences state what they are and then offer acceptable explanations for the 'truth' they create. The process is one of social attribution (Hewstone *et al.* 1982). Social beliefs serve a group's interests, social attribution does likewise. Social beliefs which erect such explanations short-circuit the need for the individual to make any of the probabilistic calculations required under the dictates of Kelley's (1967) original attribution theory. Social attributions remove the individual's responsibility for making decisions about causation. Once the individual assimilates a certain social belief which encompasses the explanation of gender differences, the individual no longer has to deduce rationally, on the basis of information given, the reasons for differences between the sexes because the reason is already there within the social belief, ready to be taken off the peg and worn.

Social beliefs contain shifts between the description and explanation of gender differences with consummate ease. What is a description of differ-ence at one level becomes an explanation of differences at the next. This can be seen most clearly in the distinction that can be drawn between differences at the psychological and the social role levels. So-called psychological differences between the sexes are frequently used to explain why there should then be differences in social role. For instance, men are more ag-gressive and competitive it is claimed; subsequently, it is claimed that this explains why men dominate in social roles which have power or social standing. Or, for example, women are nurturant and that explains their occupancy of roles in the low-paid caring professions. Of course, the causal pathway can be reversed. Some social belief systems insist that social role produces psychological characteristics. Thus this argument goes: the man who is thrust into the role of bread-winner becomes aggressive and inde-pendent; the woman deprived of power becomes passive and dependent. Greenglass (1982) reviews both causal perspectives in terms of the evidence they evince. For the purposes of this discussion of social beliefs, the direc-tion of causality is relatively unimportant, the vital thing is that the social belief *itself* promulgates causal connections. Indeed, very often social beliefs targeted at the psychological level are used to justify social beliefs at the social role level. For instance, if one believes women really are less emo-tionally stable, it is 'justifiable' in certain ideological frameworks to restrict them to social roles without power or responsibility.

Social beliefs about psychological differences between the sexes

Social beliefs about the psychological differences between the sexes have been well-researched. Research on sex stereotypes or gender stereotypes has boomed since the inception of the women's movement with the emphasis upon women's perceptions of women (Fransella and Frost 1977). In mainstream psychology, it typically relies upon asking individuals to ascribe traits to a 'typical man' and a 'typical woman'. The findings of Broverman *et al.* (1972) are representative of a stream of studies. They argued that the descriptions could be arranged around two clusters: the competency–independence and the warmth–expressive clusters. Men are typically seen to embody the competency cluster of traits but not the warmth–expressiveness cluster. Women rate low on competency traits but high on warmth–expressiveness (see Table 5).

The evidence suggests that the stereotypes of the 'traditional man' and 'traditional woman' are both, in essence, one-dimensional. Glennon (1979) suggests that women are archetypically deemed 'expressive' which is meant to connote emotionality and spontaneity without rational calculation in the pursuit of self-interests; the emphasis is upon the woman servicing others because personal relationships are more important than anything else. Men are 'instrumental' in orientation: strength, aggression, and relationships are used as a means to other ends; everything is a move in the great plan to maximize self-gain.

Table 5: Psychological differences

	Women	Men
Competency	Not at all aggressive	Very aggressive
	Not at all independent	Very independent
	Very submissive	Very dominant
	Not at all competitive	Very competitive
	Very passive	Very active
	Has difficulty making decisions	Can make decisions easily
	Not at all ambitious	Very ambitious
Warmth–expressive	Very tactful	Very blunt
	Very quiet	Very loud
	Very aware of feelings of others	Not at all aware of feelings of others
	Very strong need for security	Very little need for security
	Easily expresses tender feelings	Does not express tender feelings at all easily

Few people, male or female, would recognize themselves in these arche-typical portraits. Indeed all the evidence about differences between the sexes supports cynicism with regard to the dominant social beliefs. Psychologists have found no consistent evidence of the proposed differences between the sexes in relation to levels of competitiveness, dominance, nurturance, sug-gestibility, sociability, activity, or desire for achievement (Maccoby and Jacklin 1974). They have found no reliable differences in anxiety levels, cognitive or analytic abilities, or amounts of self-esteem (Wylie 1979). There are small differences in average levels of aggression: men are on average more aggressive but there is tremendous overlap of scores, with many women just as aggressive as men. On tests of verbal ability women on average score better than men but the difference is slight and again there is a wide overlap between the sexes. Men perform marginally better on average on spatial and mathematical tests but again the overlap of scores is marked. The repetition of 'on average' and 'overlap' is not accidental. They emphasize that the sex of a person will not predict their individual abilities. With such a spread of scores, averages say little about individuals.

If attention were paid to the bulk of the evidence, the social beliefs about the psychological differences between men and women would shrivel, if not disappear. Yet they show little sign of doing so. The gender stereotypes prevalent in the United States (Lipshitz 1978) are equally strong in Britain (Williams *et al.* 1977) and are found in children as well as adults (Best et al. 1977).

Presumably the stereotype, which in this case is the fulcrum of the social belief system about gender differences, survives because it is a product of a social structure which continues and in which it serves a valuable purpose (Ashmore *et al.* 1986). Social beliefs about the psychological differences between men and women act to reify the gulf between the sexes. They glorify the dualism of the 'expressive' and the 'instrumental'. But they go further: women are not only different, they are worse than men. The characteristics attributed to women are not as socially valued as those ascribed to men (Broverman *et al.* 1970). The stereotype of womanhood over the centuries can be taken as an exemplar of how a group with power, in this case men, will distinguish itself maximally from those it dominates and will do so in a manner designed to incapacitate them (Deschamps 1982). Women have been characterized through innumerable media of social influence as passive, non-aggressive, dependent, and nurturant (Oakley 1981). If they assimilate this self-image, women are unlikely to unite in attempts to wrest power. Moreover, they can be considered subject to false consciousness: alienated from their true selves by their powerlessness and consequent acceptance of dominant ideologies (Spender 1985).

Of course, the system of attaching value to the stereotype is neither as simple nor as overt as that. There has to be a mechanism which ensures that women do assimilate the self-derogating stereotype. In fact, this lies in the sugar-sweet backdrop to the powerplay tactics. While the female stereotype has low social value, so that women as a social group or category have low status, the individual woman who conforms to it has, traditionally, been given considerable social rewards. The prize goes to the best at being second-best. The result is an all too easy confusion of the value of the stereotype with the value of conforming to it. At a personal level, it is actually in the self-interest of a large number of women to maintain current social beliefs about gender differences.

It is interesting to see how feminists have taken two quite contradictory stances on the stereotype of womanhood. One suggests women should abandon the 'expressive' mould and adopt an 'instrumental' orientation. The other argues that women should deify their 'expressiveness' and work for it to be credited with social value and respect. They claim 'expressive-ness' has great advantages. For instance, Eichenbaum and Orbach (1983) suggest that women are nurturant but not nurtured and can consequently survive crises better than the men they care for and who have hidden de-pendency needs. It should be noted that both feminist responses make the fundamental error of treating the stereotype as if it reflected the truth about women. Both feminist belief systems are taking the stereotype and then weaving around it a new system of values. The reworked social belief they peddle is not just specifying what gender differences exist but which ought to exist and how they should be valued. In addition, they fall into the trap attached to the use of any stereotype: the people described are treated as homogeneous. In this case all women are deemed equivalent. Without justi-fication, women are treated as if they comprised a group rather than merely a social category, to use Tajfel's (1981) distinction.

The role of the 'expert' in creating social beliefs about psychological differences between men and women

The ability of psychologists or other social scientists to change social beliefs about gender differences has already been questioned above. When they discover facts which challenge social beliefs they are largely ignored—though no doubt their information may feed the polemic and propaganda of certain small sections of the public. Where their findings support—even partially— popular conceptions, they are accepted, popularized, and used to bolster dominant rhetorics. A nice example of this comes from the work on gender differences in intellectual ability. The dominant social belief, before the popularization of this work, was that women were less logical and creative than men but more intuitive. The experts have revamped this social belief suggesting, no matter how cautiously, that women on average are inferior in spatio-mathematical tasks and superior on verbal tasks (Hargreaves and Colley 1986). Popular conception has ignored the qualifying caveats about 'averages' and has garnered the information that women are better linguists but hopeless mathematicians, scientists, and technologists. Such an interpretation of the 'facts' fits prior social beliefs. In such a set-up the work of the expert is little more than fodder for the existing belief systems.

It is, however, possible for the expert to generate a new social belief. In the realm of gender differences there are several examples: the Cinderella complex (Dowling 1982); pre-menstrual tension syndrome; and the female fear of success (Horner 1970). Each of these have labelled, and thus made concrete, an aspect of the female psyche supposedly distinct from the male. These new representations of the female psyche have had marked effects upon the explanations of women's actions and it may be argued that they have actually changed their actions.

Dowling (1982) asserted that women fear independence; they want to be emotionally protected, cocooned from the harsh demands of the world. Yet, simultaneously they want emotional autonomy. The conflict between these two desires is the Cinderella complex; it creates ambivalence in relationships and in motivation. The Cinderella complex can be used to 'explain' indecision and self-destructive repetition in the patterns of relationships at home and at work. It provides a rationalization for the rejection of freedom. Dowling suggests that women experience 'gender panic' when faced with independence. Achieving independence challenges the woman's claims to womanliness because being a woman is so intimately tied to dependence. Women shunning independence can now be 'explained' and somehow excused, their condition has been diagnosed, labelled, and converted into a syndrome by social science.

Pre-menstrual tension is another perfect excuse clause, in this case for irritability and emotionality during the days preceding menstruation; some women report feeling deprived since they have never experienced it, they are said to doubt that their system is functioning properly. The introduction of such a notion can be seen as the seed for a whole set of social beliefs about women; particularly, for social attributions about their behaviour.

The notion of the female fear of success has worked in a similar way. Horner (1970) found that some women would rather avoid success. Reasons given for this have ranged from the intrapsychic to the cultural (Monahan et al. 1974). There is evidence that the fear of success may be restricted to success in domains defined as masculine and women do not fear to be good at feminine activities (Cherry and Deaux 1978). Weinreich-Haste (1984) reports a series of studies which do not even support the contention that women fear success in male preserves. In fact, as early as 1976, Tresemer was arguing that the proposition that women fear success was unproven. It is unproven but exceedingly popular. It has been assimilated into the battery of social beliefs about the female psyche with great alacrity. It is not difficult to see why. It fits neatly with others which argue that a patriarchal society does not prevent women from gaining equal power, rather that women handicap themselves. The implication is that women who fear success cannot expect to achieve it. Of course, this usage of the construct is not concerned with attempts to explain why women may fear success, only with the 'fact' that they do, which can then be used to explain their failure in so many arenas of competition with men.

The incorporation of the fear of success notion and the Cinderella complex into dominant social belief systems are fine examples of the way that social science findings which are suspect but which harmonize with existing social arrangements gain credibility and influence. People accept them, they fit easily into existing conceptual schemata which they then strengthen and extend (Carlsson and Jaderquist 1983). They are also good examples of the way in which social beliefs come into being and why they survive. The fear of success construct and the Cinderella complex were based on 'facts' but they gain general credence as social beliefs because they represent good explanations for the status quo. Some argue that they can be used to legitimize the disproportionately small number of women in positions of eminence. They represent psychological explanations for what alternatively would have to be acknowledged as social subordination. They act as a smoke-screen for other more telling reasons for that subordination—as long as no one is particularly concerned with why women may fear success or independence, they can operate as mediating red herrings.

The role of social 'experts' in the development of social beliefs requires considerable conceptual clarification. Their connection with the major agencies of social influence, the mass media and the education system, is fascinating. These agencies mediate the 'expert' message but the question then becomes: what distortions do they introduce and what processes determine the nature of these distortions? Attention to the development of social beliefs requires an examination of the relative power of agents of social influence which has not yet been conducted.

Social beliefs about sex roles

Gender stereotypes are differentiated from sex-role concepts. However, there is much debate about how they should be differentiated and there is no consistency in usage. Stoppard and Kalin (1981) suggested that the gender stereotype represents what people think *are* the characteristics of the sex, while the sex-role concept represents what they think *ought* to be the attributes and actions of the sex. However, more commonly, sex-roles refer to the social positions, plus their behavioural prescriptions, which are most often ascribed to each sex (Chetwynd and Hartnett 1978). Sex-role concepts specify what sorts of social situations are appropriate for each sex to become involved with, and what sorts of activities are expected from them in leisure or work settings (Condor 1986). The most obvious sex-role difference clearly lies in the sorts of work deemed appropriate for men and women (Kaplan and Sedney 1980). The sex-role system locates the woman in the home with domestic chores to do; it fixes the man at work in the world outside. Of course, the social belief that a woman's place is in the home and a man's in the labour market is undoubtedly under attack. Martin and Roberts (1984) in a Department of Employment survey of 5588 women between 16 and 59 years of age showed the pattern of change. A vast majority declared that a woman's place is not in the home even though they went on to say employment does not play a central role in a woman's life. Most felt that a woman with pre-school children should not go out to work, even when they were themselves at work with small children. The older women in the sample were more likely to comply with the traditional notions of domesticity. It is a hymn to the power of the dominant social belief system since these older women had on average spent 60 per cent of their potential working life actually in employment outside the home. Younger women are spending proportionally greater amounts of time in the labour market. In Britain in 1979, 51.3 per cent of married women were in work. By 1991, the Department of Employment predict that married women will be 28.7 per cent of the entire labour force.

The erroneous social belief about the domesticity of women is paralleled by a set of beliefs about what they do and should do when in employment outside of the home. There is a strong social belief which draws a heavy distinction between male and female jobs or occupations. This operates in terms of both horizontal and vertical segregation of the labour market. Horizontal segregation refers to the tendency for women and men to do different types of work. Women congregate in the clerical (40 per cent of total jobs held by women) and the education, caring, and health (20 per cent) sectors. In industry, women take the unskilled or semi-skilled jobs, while men dominate in the skilled areas (Chiplin and Sloane 1982). Vertical segregation concerns the distribution of the sexes across different status levels within a single type of work. Here it is found that even in those occupations where women are numerically dominant (for example, nursing and school teaching) they do not get a proportionate number of the top jobs.

Social belief systems reinforce vertical and horizontal segregation. Jobs associated with men are invested with a masculinity of their own: engineering is considered heavy, dirty, macho. Women who suggest that they might encroach upon the territory are viewed with suspicion; their femininity is questioned; their motives inspected (Breakwell 1985). There is now a whole pantheon of social beliefs which adheres to women who try to break the traditional occupational mould whether vertically or horizontally. Of course, social science has contributed to that mythology with notions such as the 'Queen Bee syndrome' which has been used to caricature successful powerful women, who, it is hypothesized, become more macho than the male and suppress women who would join them at the top. Despite its repeated disproof (Cooper and Davidson 1982), the myth of the Queen Bee persists and certainly influences how successful women are judged and how they perceive themselves.

Consideration of how social beliefs about sex roles are perpetuated leads to a question about their transmission. There has been considerable discussion about how social beliefs about sex roles are transmitted to children. Certainly, very young children are able to say what is appropriate behaviour for a boy and what for a girl; they also have a clear idea of the sexual division of labour in the adult world. Archer (1984) considers four dimensions of gender roles which change developmentally: rigidity, complexity, consistency, and continuity. He suggests that in childhood the male gender role is rigid, but less clear in adulthood where it acquires greater complexity and inconsistency. The female role in childhood is less rigid but shifts to low levels of flexibility in adolescence and across the life-span shows much more dramatic changes than that of the male. Basically, Archer argues that a little girl can do a greater range of things than a little boy and still be considered an acceptable girl. A little boy has to be more boyish to justify his gender image. At adolescence, the freedom swings to the young man; the young woman achieves gender acceptance by maintaining activities within a circumscribed limit. With childbirth and/or marriage the woman has the option of a number of accepted gender roles. The man in our society still has only one: provider. The reversal of roles at that stage is still a rarity, despite unemployment, skill shortages and equality of opportunity.

Social beliefs about gender role are clearly age-related. They equally clearly have to be transmitted to the individual whose conformity is expected. Most are tutored within the home and family but their transmission is bolstered by the major media of cultural socialization. Sex role distinctions are reinforced by the representation of the sexes in the mass media. For instance, television advertisements have been examined for the sex-role images they portray. Manstead and McCulloch (1981) showed that on British TV, women are more likely than men to be shown as product-users, in dependent roles, at home with domestic products, and in non-expert capacities where they offer no arguments in favour of the product. (These results have been replicated by Livingstone and Green 1986, and for radio adverts by Furnham and Schofield 1986.) They suggest that advertisements place people in situations consonant with prevailing cultural values but they are also selective, reinforcing certain preferred meanings and representations. It could be argued that advertisements merely reflect social beliefs rather than transmitting them. Yet this does not seem to hold true. Jennings et al. (1980) showed that advertisements where sex roles were reversed had the power to change the self-confidence and independence of women watching them. It seems that advertisements which normally act to support dominant social beliefs do have considerable power to change them. It also seems that in advertisements we have access to the structure of dominant social beliefs regarding gender differences, access which is independent of the individuals holding the social belief. Though advertisements have been the major target for analysis, it seems reasonable to suppose that most TV programmes operate in a similar manner to transmit sex-role expectations.

Where the mass media act to socialize people of all ages, the education system represents a major force in transmitting sex-role expectations to children. Most studies of sex roles emphasize the influence of the school in shaping both the behaviour and cognitions of boys and girls in a way which bolsters gender differences (Deem 1980; Weitzman 1979). The educational establishment represents a significant influence in perpetuating social beliefs about gender and perhaps in introducing the novel notions promulgated by 'experts'.

Heterogeneity in social beliefs about sex roles

The discussion of sex roles, and indeed psychological gender differences, has concentrated primarily on the dominant social beliefs. It is evident that these are not the sole social beliefs. At the beginning of this chapter it was suggested that any important social phenomenon will have a number of social belief systems attached to it; as many as there are interest groups involved with it. To some extent, social beliefs about sex roles vary by socio-economic class (Newson and Newson 1976) and by ethnic group (Romer and Cherry 1980); they certainly vary across time in one culture and across different cultures (La Fontaine 1978). Surprisingly, there is no evidence to suppose they vary by sex. But perhaps this should not be so surprising, given that all members of a particular sub-culture will be subject to the same socializing influences and similar material circumstances.

Social beliefs and identity

It seems that it may be necessary to differentiate between how social beliefs operate to characterize and provide concrete representations of a social category and how they work to shape the perception of an individual's self-concept, including one's own self. The social beliefs that the individual holds about everyman and everywoman may be very selectively applied to close associates or to oneself. For instance, a woman might accept the social belief that women are more passive, but fail to recognize either her best friend or herself as passive. Of course, this separation of social beliefs from what might be labelled personal beliefs is often given as the reason for the tenacity of stereotypes and prejudice: evidence from personal experience which might disrupt them is rarely treated as relevant; it is either reconstrued to conform or is discounted (Hartley 1981; Alper 1973). The relation of social beliefs about gender to the self-concept has been the object of some study.

Androgyny

The notion of psychological androgyny is interesting in this context. Bem (1977) argued that despite the dichotomized view of gender propagated in dominant social beliefs, many people of both sexes describe themselves as possessing both masculine and feminine characteristics. Spence and Helmreich (1978) argued that masculinity and femininity are independent dimensions of the psyche and that it is possible to score high on both, one, or neither. On this basis, they suggest that there are four sex-role identities: the androgynous (high on both masculinity and femininity); the masculine sex-typed (high on masculinity and low on femininity); the feminine sex-typed (high on femininity and low on masculinity); and the undifferentiated (low on both). It is important to understand that sex-role identity is not dependent upon biological sex. One quarter of the US college sample used by Spence and Helmreich proved to be androgynous, the figure being similar for men and women. These androgynous individuals had higher self-esteem and achievement than the other sex-types. They found that 8 per cent of their male sample were feminine sex-typed but 14 per cent of their female sample was masculine sex-typed, which probably indicated something about the relative social desirability of the two sex-role identities within the college community.

Several studies (for example, Williams 1979; Hargreaves *et al.* 1981; Keyes 1984) have now suggested that androgynous individuals have more stable mental health, greater creativity, and better personal adjustment than those with other sex-role identities. The undifferentiated and feminine seem to fare worst. Most interesting in relation to social beliefs are the findings of Wolff and Taylor (1979) that the androgynous have a greater awareness of sex-role stereotypes but are less willing to accept them and are less willing to use them as criteria for evaluation. The androgynous seek to react to both sexes similarly and seem to achieve some equality in treatment. In stark contrast, the sex-typed of both sexes focus upon the man in any situation where there is a choice. The sex-typed, whether masculine or feminine, know the stereotype of their own sex but are much more vague about the sex-role prescriptions of the other sex. The androgynous seem to have access to a broader range of social beliefs and a more diffuse range of types of relationship with members of both sexes. The parameters of their identities are more heterogeneous and there is some, not unambiguous, evidence that this is associated with greater psychological resilience and social skill.

The concept of androgyny is not without its critics (for example, Lenney 1979); it is, nevertheless, a fascinating piece in the jigsaw depicting social beliefs about gender differences. Taken at face value the evidence seems to imply that people who know the most about social beliefs about sex-role stereotypes are least influenced by them in the formation of their own identity. However, the causation could be reversed: an identity which subsumes both masculine and feminine components will acquire information about the social beliefs applicable to both. It seems likely to be a chicken-and-egg question. It will be interesting to monitor how far the current trend to label and develop a concrete social representation of the androgynous person in the social sciences will start to alter social beliefs about gender differences and modify the identity pigeon-holes open to the majority.

Instrumental self-definition

Studies of young women entering sex-inappropriate jobs (Breakwell and Weinberger 1982) have show that they are very sensitive to the social beliefs about gender differences specific to the workplace. These young women, training to be engineering technicians, could distinguish between their own beliefs about themselves, about the typical female technician, and about the ideal technician, and between these and the beliefs of their workmates and supervisors about such targets. They had a clear idea of what was expected of them as a woman in a 'man's job' and were willing to shape their self-presentation to the requirements of the social belief. The men believed, and this applied in over 20 firms, that the female technician should not be too sexy or aggressive, nor too reserved or excessively zealous; she should not emulate or compete with male counterparts. The female trainees knew what the men believed and the ones who were becoming successful defined themselves in the required manner. Whether this self-definition was simply a surface veneer or something which was permeating the self-concept is not known. It certainly represented success achieved through living up to the stereotype. It is a case where understanding the social beliefs of another group about the operation of gender differences in a specific context is an essential prerequisite for the development of social identity. The girls in the study were able, when asked, to evaluate themselves and their social identity against a range of social belief systems, shifting their frame of reference each time. It seems that individuals may have an instrumental or utilitarian relationship with belief systems other than their own.

Conclusion

It is necessary to resist the temptation to seek a theory of social beliefs *per se*. What social psychology needs to provide is a theory which exposes the relationships between constructs which have been discussed for years: identity, attitudes, attributions, beliefs, and intergroup processes. Such an integrative theory would use social beliefs as a mediating variable between social structure and process, and individual identity and action (Breakwell 1986). It would treat social beliefs not only as being determined by social structure but also as influential determinants of individual cognition and behaviour. The theory would see the genesis of social beliefs in intergroup dynamics and the consequences of social beliefs at both the group and the individual levels. Social beliefs about gender differences are a product of a history of relations between men and women, and vary according to culture, but they generate a polemical context within which individual men and women form an identity that shapes their actions (Williams and Giles 1978). This does not represent an overly deterministic stance toward the person's identity-formation: the individual purposively responds to the social belief structure, perhaps seeking to change it rather than being changed by it; either way it contextualizes identity.

References

Alper, T.G. (1973). The relationship between role orientation and achievement motivation in college women. *Journal of Personality*, **41**, 9–13.

Archer, J. (1984). Gender roles as developmental pathways. *British Journal of Social Psychology*, **23**, 245–56.

Archer, J. and Lloyd, B. (1982). *Sex and gender*. Penguin, Harmondsworth.

Ashmore, R.D., Del Boca, F.K., and Wohlers, A.T. (1986). Gender stereotypes. In *The social psychology of female–male relations* (ed. R.D. Ashmore and F.K. Del Boca). Academic Press, New York.

Bem, S.L. (1977). On the utility of alternative procedures for assessing psychological androgyny. *Journal of Consulting and Clinical Psychology*, **45**, 196–205.

Best, D.L., *et al.* (1977). Development of sex-trait stereotypes among young children in the United States, England and Ireland. *Child Development*, **48**, 1375–84.

Breakwell, G.M. (1985). *The quiet rebel*. Century, London.

Breakwell, G.M. (1986). *Coping with threatened identities*. Methuen, London.

Breakwell, G.M. and Weinberger, B. (1982). *The Right Women for the Job*. Manpower Services Commission Publication. University of Surrey Press, Guildford.

Broverman, I.K, Broverman, D.M., Clarkson, F.E., Rosenkrantz, P.S., and Vogel, S.R. (1970). Sex role stereotypes and clinical judgements of mental health. *Journal of Consulting and Clinical Psychology*, **34**, 1–7.

Broverman, I.K., Vogel, S.R., Broverman, D.M., Clarkson, F.E., and Rosenkrantz, P. S. (1972). Sex-role stereotypes: a current appraisal. *Journal of Social Issues*, **28**, 59–78.

Carlsson, M. and Jaderquist, P. (1983). Note on sex-role opinions as conceptual schemata. *British Journal of Social Psychology*, **22**, 65–8.

Cherry, J. and Deaux, K. (1978). Fear of success versus fear of gender-inappropriate behaviour. *Sex Roles*, **4**, 97–101.

Chetwynd, J. and Hartnett, O. (eds) (1978). *The sex role system: psychological and sociological perspectives*. Routledge and Kegan Paul, London.

Chiplin, B. and Sloane, P.J. (1982). *Tackling discrimination at the workplace*. Cambridge University Press.

Condor, S. (1986). Sex role beliefs and traditional women: feminist and intergroup perspectives. In *Feminist social psychology* (ed. S. Wilkinson). Open University Press, Milton Keynes.

Cooper, C. and Davidson, M. (1982). *High pressure: working lives of women managers*. Fontana, Glasgow.

Deaux, K. (1985). Sex and gender. *Annual Review of Psychology*, **36**, 49–81.

Deem, R. (1980). *Schooling for Women's Work*. Routledge and Kegan Paul, London.

Deschamps, J.-C. (1982). Social identity and relations of power between groups. In *Social identity and intergroup relations* (ed. H. Tajfel). Cambridge University Press.

Dowling, C. (1982). *The Cinderella complex: women's hidden fear of independence*. Fontana, Glasgow.

Eichenbaum, L. and Orbach, S. (1983). *What do women want?* Michael Joseph, London.

Eichler, M. (1980). *The double standard: a feminist critique of feminist social science*. Croom Helm, London.

Fransella, F. and Frost, K. (1977). *On being a woman*. Tavistock, London.

Furnham, A. and Schofield, S. (1986). Sex-role stereotyping in British radio advertisements. *British Journal of Social Psychology*, **25**, 165–71.

Glennon, L.M. (1979). *Women and dualism: a sociology of knowledge analysis*. Longman, New York.

Greenglass, E.R. (1982). *A world of difference: gender roles in perspective*. Wiley, New York.

Hargreaves, D. and Colley, A. (eds) (1986). *The psychology of sex roles*. Harper Row, London.

Hargreaves, D., Stoll, L., Farnworth, S., and Morgan, S. (1981). Psychological androgyny and ideational fluency. *British Journal of Social Psychology*, **20**, 53–5.

Hartley, D. (1981). Infant-school children's perception of same- and opposite-sex classmates. *British Journal of Social Psychology*, **20**, 141–3.

Hewstone, M., Jaspars, J., and Lalljee, M. (1982). Social representations, social attribution and social identity. *European Journal of Social Psychology*, **12**, 241–71.

Horner, M.S. (1970). Femininity and successful achievement: a basic inconsistency. In *Feminine personality and conflict* (ed. J. Bardwick *et al.*). Brooks/Cole, Belmont, CA.

Jennings, J., Geis, F.L., and Brown, V. (1980). Influence of television commercials on women's self-confidence and independent judgement. *Journal of Personality and Social Psychology*, **38**, 203–10.

Kaplan, A.G. and Sedney, M.A. (1980). *Psychology and sex roles: an androgynous perspective*. Little, Brown and Co., Boston.

Kelley, H. (1967). Attribution theory in social psychology. In *Nebraska symposium on motivation*, Vol 15 (ed. D. Levine). University of Nebraska Press, Lincoln, Nebraska.

Keyes, S. (1984). Gender stereotypes and personal adjustment: employing the PAQ, TSBI and GHQ with samples of British adolescents. *British Journal of Social Psychology*, **23**, 173–80.

La Fontaine, J.S. (ed.) (1978). *Sex and age as principles of social differentiation*. Academic Press, London.

Lenney, E. (1979). Androgyny: some audacious assertions towards its coming of age. *Sex Roles*, **5**, 703–19.

Lipshitz, S. (ed.) (1978). *Tearing the veil*. Routledge and Kegan Paul, London.

Livingstone, S. and Green, G. (1986). Television advertisements and the portrayal of gender. *British Journal of Social Psychology*, **25**, 149–54.

Maccoby, E.E. and Jacklin, C. (1974). *The psychology of sex differences*. Stanford University Press, Stanford, CA.

Manstead, A.S.R. and McCulloch, C. (1981). Sex-role stereotyping in British television advertisements. *British Journal of Social Psychology*, **20**, 171–80.

Martin, J. and Roberts, C. (1984). *Woman and employment: a lifetime perspective*. HMSO, London.

Monahan, L., Kuhn, D., and Shaver, P. (1974). Intrapsychic versus cultural explanations of the 'fear of success' motive. *Journal of Personality and Social Psychology*, **29**, 60–4.

Newson, J. and Newson, E. (1976). *Seven years old in the home environment*. Allen and Unwin, London.

Oakley, A. (1981). *Subject women*. Fontana, Glasgow.

Romer, N. and Cherry, D. (1980). Ethnic and social class differences in children's sex role conceptions. *Sex Roles*, **6**, 245–63.

Sayers, J. (1982). *Biological politics*. Tavistock, London.

Spence, J.T. and Helmreich, R.L. (1978). *Masculinity and femininity: their psychological dimensions, correlates and antecedents*. University of Texas Press, Austin.

Spender, D. (1985). *For the record: the making and meaning of feminist knowledge*. Women's Press, London.

Stoppard, J. and Kalin, R. (1981). Gender stereotype and sex-role concepts. *British Journal of Social Psychology*, **20**, 224–5.

Tajfel, H. (ed.) (1981). *Human groups and social categories*. Cambridge University Press.

Tresemer, D. (1976). Fear of success: popular but unproven. *Psychology Today*, March, 82–5.

Weinreich-Haste, H. (1984). Cynical boys, determined girls? Success and failure anxiety in British adolescents. *British Journal of Social Psychology*, **23**, 257–63.

Weitzman, L. (1979). *Sex role socialization*. Mayfield, Palo Alto, CA.

Williams, J.A. (1979). Psychological androgyny and mental health. In *Women: sex-role stereotyping* (ed. O. Hartnett, G. Boden, and M. Fuller). Tavistock Publications, London.

Williams, J.A. and Giles, H. (1978). The changing status of women in society: an intergroup perspective. In *Differentiation between social groups* (ed. H. Tajfel). Academic Press, London.

Williams, J.E., Giles, H., Edwards, J.R., Best, D.L., and Davis, J.T. (1977). Sex trait stereotypes in England, Ireland and the United States. *British Journal of Social and Clinical Psychology*, **16**, 303–9.

Wolff, L. and Taylor, S.E. (1979). Sex, sex-role identification, and awareness of sex-role stereotypes. *Sex Roles*, **5**, 177–84.

Wylie, R.C. (1979). *The self concept*. University of Nebraska Press, Nebraska.

Index